# Tragic Manhood and Democracy

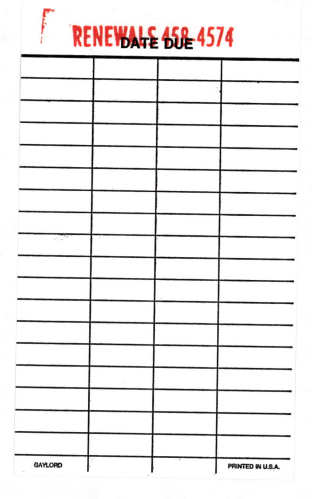

*For Carol Gilligan*

# Tragic Manhood and Democracy

*Verdi's Voice and the Powers of Musical Art*

DAVID A. J. RICHARDS

**sussex**
ACADEMIC
PRESS

*BRIGHTON • PORTLAND*

The right of David A. J. Richards to be identified as Author of this work has been asserted in accordance with the Copyright, Designs and Patents Act 1988.

2 4 6 8 10 9 7 5 3 1

*First published 2004 in Great Britain by*
SUSSEX ACADEMIC PRESS
PO Box 2950
Brighton BN2 5SP

*and in the United States of America by*
SUSSEX ACADEMIC PRESS
920 NE 58th Ave          Suite 300
Portland, Oregon 97213–3786

*British Library Cataloguing in Publication Data*
A CIP catalogue record for this book is available from the British Library.

*Library of Congress Cataloging-in-Publication Data*
Richards, David A. J.
    Tragic manhood and democracy : Verdi's voice and the power of musical art / David A. J. Richards.
        p. cm.
    Includes bibliographical references and index.
    ISBN 1-84519-041-6 (hardcover : alk. paper) —
    ISBN 1-84519-042-4 (pbk. : alk. paper)
    1. Verdi, Giuseppe, 1813–1901. Operas—Criticism and interpretation. 2. Opera—Social aspects. 3. Tragedy in music. 4. Masculinity. I. Title.
ML410.V4R49 2004
782.1′092—dc22

                                    2004010993
                                    CIP

Typeset and designed by G&G Editorial, Brighton
Printed by MPG Books, Ltd, Bodmin, Cornwall
This book is printed on acid-free paper.

# Contents

## *Part* III  **Between Patriarchal and Democratic Manhood**

# Preface

What is tragedy? This work argues that it is, at once, art and science, an absorbing art and precisely observed empirical inquiry into human psychology, whose subject matter is the dilemma of manhood under democracy. The work's appoach expands the discussion of the idea of the tragic to include music drama in general and the operas of Verdi in particular, and explores the indispensable contribution of tragedy to a truthful democratic understanding of the personal and political psychology of manhood under democracy. Its interdisciplinary method triangulates a political theory of structural injustice resting on the suppression of voice (underlying evils like racism, sexism, and homophobia), a developmental psychology of gender (drawing on the work of Carol Gilligan), and an interpretation of tragic art (including the expressive role of music in it). I investigate the enormous contemporary appeal of opera in general and Verdi's operas in particular as in the tradition of Greek tragedy, innovating forms of musical voice that speak to democratic culture about traumatic breaks in relationship (leading to loss of voice in relationship) supposedly required by democracy, namely, an armored democratic manhood defined by patriarchy. The marks of trauma are loss of voice and memory, and disassociation. Tragic art has been so important to democratic cultures because it exposes truths of our complex human psychology under democracy otherwise unspeakable, and its appeal to music is sometimes necessary to our recognizing its truths, enabling us to experience suppressed voices and memories otherwise inaccessible. The tragic art of music drama has been and remains an important inquiry into psychological truth. Psychologists ignore it at their peril.

The exploration of the tragic impact of patriarchy on democratic voice is, on my analysis, at the heart of the power and appeal of Verdi's innovations in musical voice that offer an analytics of traumatized voice (including a voice of relationship and a voice of identification) under patriarchy. At its core is a complex psychic geography of the impact of patriarchal practices on a range of personal and political relationships (parents to children, siblings to one another, and adult men and women), a geography that speaks more truthfully about the perils of conventional manhood than the patriarchal pieties about us. For Verdi, the code of honor was, in its nature, a political system – fundamental to the family, politics, and religion – that enforced its demands by forms of physical and psychological violence directed by men and women at anyone who deviated from its demands; its force is particularly ferocious against voices of men, keeping them in rigid conformity to its demands. Its psychological force derived from the way in which its demands were developmentally inscribed into the human psyche by traumatic separations that suppress the voice of relationship (leading to identification with the patriarchal gender stereotypes required of one) precisely at the points where such voice might reasonably contest the justice of the honor code's demands. Verdi's tragic musical drama speaks of an emotional loss that literally cannot under patriarchy be spoken, namely, what I call the tragedy of patriarchy, a divided psychology that lives in the tension between patriarchal practices and democratic principles.

My interest in both the subject matter and interdisciplinary method of this work arose from ongoing conversations with Carol Gilligan in a seminar on gender and democracy we have co-taught at the New York University School of Law for the past five years. Carol early in this period was working on the book subsequently published as *The Birth of Pleasure*,[3] and her thinking about tragic stories of love, rooted in patriarchy, stimulated my own thinking about my longstanding passion for the tragic music dramas of Verdi. I first proposed my argument to Carol at one of our lunch meetings in a draft outline that roughly corresponds to Part II of this work, and she urged me to begin work on the manuscript that has culminated in this work. Various drafts of it were read by Carol and by at least two classes of the gender seminar we co-teach. It was Carol's brilliant critical eye and ear which guided my research and writing, giving me a resonance for a creative voice that was, for me, otherwise inhibited by doubt. It was Carol who, after we attended together a performance of Verdi's *Luisa Miller* at the Metropolitan Opera (an opera Carol had not known), was moved to tears (and moved me to tears) by experiencing with me its vision of two tragically oppositional fathers, patriarchal and democratic, urging me to bring my work to the attention of others, who might, like her, see Verdi's art in the way she now experienced it. Throughout my work on this book, she could not have been more generous, more supportive, and more loving. I am grateful to her and to our remarkable students, and also to Zvi Triger, who rendered invaluable research assistance.

The book was researched and written during summer research leaves supported by generous research grants from the New York University School of Law Filomen D'Agostino and Max E. Greenberg Faculty Research Fund.

A work of this sort, so rooted in my Italian-American personal history, arose in conversation as well with those closest to me. My partner of some thirty years, Donald Levy, has listened patiently to my views on opera for a very long time, and his love for me nurtured the voice of this book. My sister, Diane Rita Richards, generously read earlier drafts of the manuscript for me, and her advice and support have been as indispensable to my work on it as has been her love.

Finally, comments on the manuscript of opera-loving friends have also been most helpful, including John Peschel, Oscar Chase, Paul Chevigny, and Roberto Mazzetta.

NEW YORK, N.Y.
MAY 3, 2004

"It may be a good thing to copy reality; but to invent reality is much much better.

These three words: 'to invent reality', may look like a contradiction, but ask Papa! [Shakespeare]. Falstaff he may have found as he was; but he can hardly have found a villain as villainous as Iago, and never, never such angels as Cordelia, Imogene, Desdemona, etc., etc. And yet they are so very real! It's a fine thing to imitate reality, but it is photography, not painting."

*Giuseppe Verdi, letter to Clarina Maffei, October 20, 1876*[1]

"Vivremo insiem e morremo insiem
Sara l'estreme anelito,
Sara, sara un grido, un grido:
Liberta!"

"We will live and die together!
Our last breath
Will be a cry:
Liberty!"[2]

---

[1] Franz Werfel and Paul Stefan, eds., *Verdi: The Man in His Letters*, Edward Downes, trans. (New York: Vienna House, 1942), at p. 336.
[2] Duet of Carlo and Rodrigo, Act II, scene 1, *Don Carlos*, pp. 98–9 libretto to CD, Italian version, Verdi, *Don Carlos*, conducted by Carlo Maria Giulini, EMI classics.

# Part I

## Tragedy, Musical Voice, and Democracy

## Chapter 1

# The Idea of Tragedy and the Dilemma of Democratic Manhood

## Verdi's Analytics of Traumatized Voice Under Patriarchy

Terry Eagleton's recent book, *Sweet Violence: The Idea of the Tragic*,[1] explores an ancient topic, the idea of the tragic, arguing that much traditional and contemporary discussion of the idea suffers from an overly narrow range of examples and an ideologically distorted conservatism. I agree with both charges, and want here not only to expand the range of examples discussed under the rubric of the idea of tragedy but to forge as well an approach to this topic that fundamentally connects its understanding and assessment to political liberalism. Eagleton himself observes that much of the best contemporary discussion of tragedies, both those of Attic drama and a playwright like Chekhov, frames its discussion in terms of painful transitions to democracy or from traditional ways of living to modernity.[2] My own approach is very much along these lines, but much more centered, than the approach of Eagleton and others, on the contested place of feminism within liberal democracy.

My interest in a study of a broader range of examples is, however, even more expansive than Eagleton's. His examples are mainly literary, works of the written and spoken word. But my interest here is to expand the discussion of the idea of the tragic to include music drama in general and the operas of Verdi in particular. Since Nietzsche there has been been, of course, no dearth of serious discussion of music drama, but such discussion has been largely confined to Nietzsche's own operatic obsession, the works of Richard

---

[1] See Terry Eagleton, *Sweet Violence: The Idea of the Tragic* (Oxford: Blackwell, 2003).

[2] See *id.*, pp. 143–4, 1832, 236.

Wagner.[3] My aim here is to enlarge the discussion to include the works of Giuseppe Verdi, which, in ways I argue at length, embody some of the most important modern tragedies dealing with our contemporary dilemmas of manhood (and womanhood) and democracy.

I am a constitutional law scholar, whose work has been prominently concerned with toleration and free speech, privacy, anti-racism, feminism, and gay/lesbian rights.[4] I have been increasingly troubled by contradictions between the tenets of liberal democracy and the persistence of various forms of structural injustice I have called "moral slavery" (extreme religious intolerance like anti-Semitism, racism, sexism, and homophobia).[5] Among these contradictions, I have been puzzled by the role of gender as a way of suppressing voices that would otherwise contest such injustice. The contradictions between democracy and injustice are apparently held in place by a conception of manhood whose terms required such suppression of voice. Why are patterns of unjust gender inequality still so persistent even in the United States?[6] Why is the denial of such unjust gender inequality still so popular?[7] Why are unjust patterns of political psychology still so stable and so difficult to resist? These and other questions are not normative, for they

---

[3] See, for example, Carolyn Abbate, *Unsung Voices: Opera and Musical Narrative in the Nineteenth Century* (Princeton: Princeton University Press, 1991); Lydia Goehr, *The Quest for Voice: Music, Politics, and the Limits of Philosophy* (Berkeley: University of California Press, 1998); Philippe Lacoue-Labarthe, *Musica Ficta (Figures of Wagner)*, Felicia McCarren, trans. (Stanford, CA: Stanford University Press, 1994). Cf. Catherine Clement, *Opera or the Undoing of Women*, Betsy Wing, trans. (Minneapolis: University of Minnesota Press, 1989).

[4] These books include David A. J. Richards, *A Theory of Reasons for Action* (Oxford: Clarendon Press, 1971); *The Moral Criticism of Law* (Encino, CA: Dickenson-Wadsworth, 1977); *Sex, Drugs, Death and the Law: An Essay on Decriminalization and Human Rights* (Totowa, NJ: Rowman & Littlefield, 1982); *Toleration and the Constitution* (New York: Oxford University Press, 1986); *Foundations of American Constitutionalism* (New York: Oxford University Press, 1998); *Conscience and the Constitution: History, Theory, and Law of the Reconstruction Amendments* (Princeton: Princeton University Press, 1993); *Women, Gays, and the Constitution: The Grounds for Feminism and Gay Rights in Culture and Law* (Chicago: University of Chicago Press, 1998); *Italian American: The Racializing of an Ethnic Identity* (New York: New York University Press, 1999); *Identity and the Case for Gay Rights: Race, Gender, Religion as* Analogies (Chicago: University of Chicago Press, 1999); *Free Speech and the Politics of Identity* (Oxford: Oxford University Press, 1999).

[5] For the fullest development and defense of this position, see David A. J. Richards, *Women, Gays, and the Constitution: The Grounds for Feminism and Gay Rights in Culture and Law* (Chicago: University of Chicago Press, 1998).

[6] See, in general, Deborah L. Rhode, *Justice and Gender* (Cambridge, MA: Harvard University Press, 1989).

[7] See, on this point, Deborah L. Rhode, *Speaking of Sex: The Denial of Gender Inequality* (Cambridge, MA: Harvard University Press, 1997).

arise from a recognized gap between the normative promises of constitu-tionalism and a persistent psychology of gender under democracy that evidently cannot deliver on such promises. We need a way into exploring the tension between our ethical ideals and our personal and political psychology.

I am a gay man in a loving relationship with my partner, approaching now thirty years. My private and public life also led me to the question of manhood. If the basic human right to intimate life is as much owed gays and lesbians, as persons, as it is to heterosexuals, how could a 1986 majority of the Supreme Court dismissively fail to extend its constitutional principle on fair terms to them[8] (the Court only reconsidered this ruling in 2003[9]), or the Congress of the United States by large majorities withhold federal recognition from same-sex marriage or some thirty-five states pass anti-same-sex marriage laws?[10] The degree to which our constitutional democ-racy has had, in contrast to others,[11] such notable difficulty in hearing my voice was rooted as well in a dominant conception of manhood that I increasingly questioned, both as a man and a gay man.

The writing of this book has led me to see that manhood and the estab-lishment of manhood may well be the most challenging problem for contemporary constitutional democracy, a legacy that has haunted democ-racy since its invention in ancient Athens. *Tragic Manhood and Democracy* investigates this problem through the role and appeal of tragic art in democratic culture in a trajectory I trace in the ancient world in the Attic tragedies and in the modern world in the musical tragedies of Verdi. The normative foundations of democracy (rule by the people) impose demands of egalitarian voice which are very much in tension with the requirements of patriarchy (suppressing voices that might reasonably contest the unjust political enforcement gender stereotypes both on women and men). The appeal of tragedy is that it explores the relevant matters of *voice* and *sup-pression of voice* as tensions within the personal and political psychology of democratic citizens, as men self-consciously living in the contradiction between the normative demands of democracy and patriarchy. Both the

---

[8] See *Bowers v. Hardwick*, 478 U.S. 186 (1986).

[9] See *Lawrence v. Texas*, 539 U.S. 558 (2003).

[10] For discussion, see David A. J. Richards, *Women, Gays, and the Constitution*, at p. 452. On the action by the states, see Vicki L. Armstrong, "Welcome to the 21st Century and the Legalization of Same-Sex Unions," *Thomas M. Cooley Law Reviews,* 18(1), 85–117 (2001).

[11] See, for an illuminating comparative study, Yuval Merin, *Equality for Same-Sex Couples: The Legal Recognition of Gay Partnterships in Europe and the United States* (Chicago: University of Chicago Press, 2002).

art of the Attic tragedians and that of Verdi show us how the development of democracy itself gives rise to a development of patriarchal manhood and how this contradiction is sustained through the suppression of voice, the voice both of men and women. It thus brilliantly lays bare how the personal and political psychology of manhood under democracy can and does live in such contradiction. The musical art of Verdi, in particular, enables us to hear the underworld of suppressed voices of men that sustain this contradiction.

There are, of course, many ways to explore the increasingly important study of the psychology of gender,[12] but one of the most promising such approaches, in my judgment, is Carol Gilligan's study in *The Birth of Pleasure* of the differential development of boys and girls in terms of earlier traumatic separations and disassociation in boys (at age 5–6) than girls (at age 11–12).[13] Boys endure such trauma and disassociation (centering on separation from their mothers) at an earlier period than girls when they are more vulnerable to its effects, and carry its effects deep in their psyches as men, sometimes crippling their later capacity for intimate relationships. Gilligan's findings rest, of course, on sensitive and perceptive research on boys and girls as well as adults, but her work also includes an appeal to the arts, as an equally important resource for the empirical study of human psychology. David Lodge has recently cogently argued that the art of the novel offers an invaluable road into the complexities of human consciousness, one that students of human consciousness ignore at their peril.[14] Gilligan's methodology, as a developmental psychologist of gender, has embodied Lodge's procedure for a very long time, for the same reasons that other penetrating psychologists like Sigmund Freud and Gilligan's teacher, Erik Erikson, explored psychology through the arts and history before her. The deepest students of the human psyche understand that both art and history, as interpretive disciplines, explore our complex inner psychological world, and offer an invaluable way into mapping its complexities. Gilligan's recent book, concerned with the effects of the differential developmental experience of trauma in boys and girls, powerfully uses novels and plays (including the comic and tragic plays of Shakespeare) as resources that subtly preserve the range of voice and insight before the trauma, the impact of such trauma on loss of memory and voice, and the

---

[12] See, for a range of varying perspectives, Mary M. Gergen and Sara N. Davis, *Toward a New Psychology of Gender: A Reader* (New York: Routledge, 1997).

[13] See Carol Gilligan, *The Birth of Pleasure* (New York: Knopf, 2002).

[14] See David Lodge, *Consciousness and the Novel: Connected Essays* (Cambridge, MA: Harvard University Press, 2002), at pp. 42, 45, 51–2, 56, 58–61.

struggles to recover voice in the process of undoing disassociation and empowering resistance.

The turn of this book to the investigation and interpretation of tragic art uses such art, as Gilligan's work suggests we should, as a way into the investigation of how a patriarchal culture rests on the traumatic suppression of voice (in boys, in particular, from a developmentally vulnerable early age) and the impact of such suppression on tensions within the theory and practice of democracy (in particular, on a psychology of manhood that regards such tragic loss as a requirement of democracy and is, for this reason, threatened by a feminist discourse that challenges both the necessity and justice of patriarchy). In so doing, I offer a fresh, original understanding of what tragedy is, and wherein its appeal consists. Tragedy is, I argue, as much art as science, exposing to democratic citizens psychological truths of internal contradiction not otherwise available. Because it speaks of trauma, whose marks are loss of voice and memory and disassociation, tragedy examines issues which are otherwise culturally unspeakable. As Walter Kaufman showed,[15] Greek tragedy spoke of issues its philosophy could not even acknowledge. The appeal of tragedy is thus its truthfulness. Tragic art, in its nature often unbearably painful, has such enormous interpretive appeal because it tells us the multi-layered truth about these tensions, including the truth about inner voices and underlying negative emotions that we cannot under patriarchy speak (including, for men, voices traumatically suppressed since their boyhood).

Verdi studies the impact of patriarchy through the Mediterranean honor code (chapter 2). That code, I argue, is a specific cultural crystallization of the unjust demands of patriarchy (an order that places sons and daughters under the hierarchical authority of the voices of fathers[16]). Its force rests on unjust repressive violence, directed against any voice or action that threatens its authority. Both men and women enforce the demands of such codes when they repress any voice that dissents from them, but such codes are particularly ferocious against men's voices. The propensity to violence in men, elicited by any threat of shame to their sense of honor as defined by such codes, plays the pivotal role in such forms of unjust coercion and sometimes forms of terror. Manhood under patriarchy is defined by the propensity to such violence, as the measure of one's being a man. Women are often the objects of such violence, but other men, as James Gilligan[17]

---

[15] Walter Kaufman, *Tragedy and Philosophy* (Garden City, NY: Doubleday, 1968).

[16] See, on this point, Carol Gilligan, *The Birth of Pleasure*, pp. 4–5.

[17] See James Gilligan, *Violence: Reflections on a National Epidemic* (New York: Vintage Books, 1997); James Gilligan, *Preventing Violence* (New York: Thames & Hudson, 2001).

points out, are even more often its objects. The role such patriarchal codes of honor have traditionally played in the sense of male honor has been easily manipulated into acquiescence in a broad range of unjust forms of violence, including war and terror.[18] Verdi's art maps its underlying psychology of disassociation.

The unjust demands of such codes of honor enter into the psyches of men through the developmental psychology of early boyhood trauma that Gilligan describes, and such codes in turn rationalize further traumatic breaks in relationship of both men and women in a self-perpetuating cycle (see chapters 4–7). If the psychological marks of traumatic experience are loss of voice, memory, and disassociation, this psychology is without tragedy culturally invisible. Tragedy has largely been an art by men for men because it arises from and examines this developmental history of trauma that happens earlier for boys than girls, and it studies the impact of such history on manhood under democracy and patriarchy that bears particularly heavily, even disastrously, on men. Indeed, it is endurance of such a tragic burden that defines heroic manhood under democracy. Patriarchy under democracy, as we shall see, certainly suppresses women's voices as well, but tragedy largely studies these impacts on womanhood under democracy incidental to its concern for shifts in its gender binary, manhood. Such suppression of voice requires both women and men to live in disassociation – not to know, let alone act on, the relational intelligence buried in their emotional and moral lives.

My argument carries Gilligan's procedure beyond the arts of the spoken and written word into the musical arts – in particular, music drama. This turn to music drama is integrally connected to the topic of my argument, the idea of the tragic. Nietzsche's early essay, *The Birth of Tragedy from the Spirit of Music*, explores a similar connection, arguing that the truth of tragic drama, at least before what Nietzsche preposterously takes to be its Euripidean decadence,[19] required musical expression to make its point about some dark emotional truths unacknowledged by the modes of Socratic philosophy and legal argument in the Athenian democracy.[20] I make a rather different sense of this connection than Nietzsche, but I agree

---

[18] See, on this point about religious terrorism, Mark Juergensmeyer, *Terror in the Mind of God: The Global Rise of Religious Violence* (Berkeley: University of California Press, 2000), at pp. 182–207.

[19] For a cogent defense of the greatness of the tragic art of Euripides, see Walter Kaufmann, *Tragedy and Philosophy* (Garden City, NY: Doubleday, 1968).

[20] Friedrich Nietzsche, *The Birth of Tragedy* in *The Birth of Tragedy and The Genealogy of Morals* Francis Golffing, trans. (Garden City, NY: Doubleday & Co., 1956), at pp. 3–146.

that the musical arts make possible the exploration of tragic truths that neither philosophy nor law could then acknowledge.[21] In her important recent book, *Upheavals of Thought*, Martha Nussbaum, a contemporary feminist philosopher, makes a related point. She argues that the philosophical marginalization of the emotions cuts us off from our humane intelligence, notably interprets music as a way that we maintain contact with such emotions, and prominently addresses the devastating consequences such marginalization has on understanding the place and weight of loving relationships in our lives.[22] My argument further builds on the insights of both Gilligan and Nussbaum in its turn to tragic art in general and musical tragedy in particular as a way of advancing understanding of a developmental psychology of gender that holds so much structural injustice in place.

The penetrating psychological power of Verdi's mature music dramas cannot reasonably be reduced to the stage dramas Verdi often sets, many of which, as dramas, are sometimes laughably melodramatic, for example, Victor Hugo's "Le Roi s'amuse" (the basis for *Rigoletto*), or Alexandre Dumas' "Las Dame aux camelias" (the basis for *La Traviata*). There is, however, nothing laughable in Verdi's settings, which touch unbearably moving tragic depths. Verdi's expressive tragic powers arise from his *musical* settings, both vocal and orchestral, laying bare through his musical art traumas and their consequences in breaking a wide range of relationships that we take to be central to the humane value of a human life. The experience of these works shows how music and music alone enables the human psyche not only to experience emotions otherwise unavailable, but to experience memories otherwise so painful that we cannot acknowledge, let alone speak of them. Music is the route into psychological truths otherwise unspeakable, truths that more rationalistic disciplines like philosophy and law were not able to acknowledge or explore (see discussion of Greek philosophy in chapter 8). What my argument shows is that there is a systematic psychological structure to the tragic power of Verdi's musical dramas that we can understand in terms of the tragic contradictions between democracy and patriarchy, including the impact of such contradictions on a manhood armored from love and prone to unjust violence both in their private and public lives.

A claim of this sort is, inextricably, interpretive and psychological. On

---

[21] See, for elaboration of this point, Walter Kaufman, *Tragedy and Philosophy* (Garden City, NY: Doubleday, 1968).

[22] See Martha C. Nussbaum, *Upheavals of Thought: The Intelligence of Emotions* (Cambridge: Cambridge University Press, 2001).

the one hand, it aspires to make the best sense we can of works that move and absorb us; but, on the other, it argues that what moves us in the art is its uncompromising psychological truth, enabling us better to understand and acknowledge our complex psyches as men and women living under democracy and patriarchy. Since our conception of manhood and womanhood is both democratic and patriarchal, Verdi's art takes us into the psyche that can hold such contradictions in place. It is, like all great art, revelatory of our human situation.

On the argument I make here, the power and appeal of tragedy for many men, including myself, is that it offers us a way at least of hearing the inner voices and emotions, rooted in early trauma, that we cannot under dominant patriarchal conventions acknowledge, let alone discuss. Verdi's famous letter about Shakespeare as inventing truth (the epigraph on p. x) appeals, I believe, to the artistic invention of inner voice as, though an invention, psychologically truthful to the inner complexity of our psychic lives; and I have turned to tragic art in general and Verdi's musical art in particular precisely because it offered what I found to be the most truthfully complex psychology of these issues available to me. If I am right about this, the unity of music and drama is, as Wagner suggested,[23] one of the best ways to dig into the deepest recesses of our culture, revealing tensions and contradictions that are not otherwise faced, let alone examined. The study of Verdi's musical art enables us to examine tensions between our lives and our ideals that we cannot otherwise acknowledge, let alone study. We cannot even begin to come to terms with the gaps between our principles and practices until we at least acknowledge such tensions. Verdi's art acknowledges such contradictions and links them systematically to the role forms of patriarchy play in our lives.

There is a sense in which issues of unjust sexism are very much on the surface of Verdi's work, as in the bitterly tragic irony of the Duke of Mantua's glittering "La donna e mobile" ("Woman is wayward") in the astonishing Act III of *Rigoletto*, rationalizing the Duke's wayward amours in terms of the fickleness of women when one of them, Gilda, will shortly sacrifice her life for him. My interpretive suggestion is that the tragic appeal of his art turns on a deeper and more pervasive exploration of the ways in which what I call patriarchy tragically disrupts relationships at every significant level of relationship in society, personal and political, and

---

[23] See, for his most extended exploration of this theme, Wagner's "The Artwork of the Future," in Albert Goldman and Evert Sprinchorn, eds., *Wagner on Music and Drama*, translated by H. Ashton Ellis (New York: Da Capo Press, 1964), at pp. 179–235. See, for example, *id.*, at pp. 217–26.

fundamentally shapes a personal and political psychology not only of sexism, but religious and ethnic intolerance, expressing itself in forms of unjust violence in private and public life. Verdi was not, of course, a political theorist of liberal democracy, but his art was acutely sensitive to the psychological dimensions of a longstanding problem within the theory and practice of political democracy, namely, the tension between the normative demands of liberal democracy (rooted in the Lockean criticism of patriarchy) and patriarchal practices unjustly not subject to those demands. Verdi experienced this problem in the struggles of nineteenth-century Italy from the patriarchal feudalism of its past to a form of national unity in ostensible service of political liberalism. The Italian struggles more starkly posed the tensions within political liberalism that were more easily ignored in more traditionally liberal societies (like Britain), because the patriarchal code of honor was still so conspicuously powerful in Italian society during the period of its transition to liberal constitutional institutions. Verdi's artistic attention was thus arrested by the tensions between such patriarchal practices (embodied in the demands of the honor code) and the political liberalism to which he and other Italians aspired. The enduring value of Verdi's artistic exploration of this problem is the way in which he, unlike more optimistic political liberals of his and later periods, examines the problem forthrightly in terms of a structure of patriarchal practices that are for Verdi most centrally in play in private family relationships though in public life as well, and explores the tension between such practices and liberal principles in the terms of tragedy. A problem that many political liberals cannot even acknowledge is thus, for Verdi, the central problem within liberalism, and it is a problem fraught with tragic consequences we can barely acknowledge.

My account, of course, builds on the work of other astute students of Verdi's art (notably, studies of Julian Budden[24] and Gilles De Van[25]). The

---

[24] See the magisterial three-volume study, Julian Budden, *The Operas of Verdi, Vol. 1, From Oberto to Rigoletto* (New York: Oxford University Press, 1973); *The Operas of Verdi, vol. 2, from Il Trovatore to La Forza Del Destino* (New York: Oxford University Press, 1978); *The Opera of Verdi, Vol. 3, From Don Carlos to Falstaff* (New York: Oxford University Press, 1981).

[25] See Gilles De Van, *Verdi's Theater: Creating Drama through Music*, translated by Gilda Roberts (Chicago: University of Chicago Press, 1998), which traces Verdi's artistic development from melodrama to music drama, sensitively reading the ways in which Verdi explores the impact of patriarchal practices on relationships within families. I trace a similar development, but show how it may be systematically explained in terms of Verdi's growing sense of the unjust impact of patriarchy on voice and the difficulties of resistance. In contrast to De Van, I argue, on the basis of Verdi's life (including his relationship to Giuseppina Strepponi) and works, that the best interpretive reading of his art is as a stance of resistance.

argument, however, asks and answers important new questions. For example, I draw often upon Julian Budden's study of Verdi's operas for its penetrating analyses of the increasingly subtle musical expression (both vocal and orchestral) Verdi innovates to express tragic experience and feeling. But, I ask deeper explanatory questions about these innovations, namely, both *how* and *why* Verdi's mature *musical* art (starting with *Luisa Miller*) gives such precise authentic voice to such experiences. And I offer answers in terms of Verdi's speaking to a democratic culture about the contradictory demands of democracy under patriarchy in precisely the same way as Attic drama.[26] My account thus shows how the tragic power of Verdi's mature art can be systematically explained in terms of the way his musical innovations reveal the traumatic impact of patriarchy on voice (including Verdi's ways of giving expression to what I call the voice of relationship and the voice of identification). The force of patriarchy, for Verdi, rests pervasively on the traumatic breaking of loving relationships, which leads through disassociation to identification with the gender stereotypes required by patriarchy. The psychological force of such identification rests on loss of real relationship, a confusion of voices that Ferenczi first noticed as a psychologist in victims of trauma (the victim taking on the voice of the victimizer), but artists from Euripides to Verdi studied before him (see chapter 2). Verdi's musical genius was to forge an art of musical voice that precisely captures not only the loss of voice underlying trauma, but the voice of relationship it disrupts and the distortions of voice it imposes. Such distortions include identification with the terms of gender stereotypes, which Verdi expresses through a voice of identification, as well as the underlying emotional loss and desolation of our suppressed voice and feelings, which Verdi's art also expresses. Certainly, the development of Verdi's vocal art is combined with a comparable development in his orchestral skill and subtlety, but, unlike Wagner, the center of his art is always expressive voice because, on Verdi's conception of tragedy, the tragic ravages of patriarchy show themselves through its destructive impacts on the psyche, the voice of loving relationship. Verdi's musical art offers a precise analytics of such traumatized voice under patriarchy, enabling men in particular to hear the moral cry buried in their psyches. Only the close study of Verdi's operas can make this point with the required appreciation of Verdi's creative achievement and unsparing insight into the psychology of trauma and its effects (the heart of my argument in chapters 4–7). Such effects include, for Verdi, the ways in which patriarchy distorts politics and

---

[26] De Van, for example, correctly observes the tragic character of Verdi's art, but does not explain its tragic dimensions, *id.*, at p. 343.

ethics and even religion, as Verdi shows in *Don Carlos* the ways in which the desolation of a patriarchal father and king psychologically deforms the image of God in the Christian Gospels into the terror and atrocity of the Inquisition (see chapter 5, section 2). Verdi's insight into this universal psychology is all too contemporary, showing us the roots of what Mark Juergensmeyer has described as the psychology of wounded patriarchal manhood underlying the global rise of religious violence today.[27] I use Budden's descriptions as the data that I organize and explain in terms of the framework offered here. But, I also ask and answer why Verdi's revelation of such a pervasive structure of traumatic separation (for example, of parents from children) has such arresting tragic appeal to audiences, today more than ever, as men (straight and gay), under the impact of feminism, are often painfully self-conscious of living in continuing contradiction. On the account I offer of the tragic appeal of Verdi's art, it anatomizes in exquisite psychological detail how, in the experience of men and women, inner voices longing for intimate friendship and love (the voice of relationship) are silenced by the trauma of disrupted relationships enforced by unjust, gender-defined demands of codes of honor (expressed through the voice of identification) calling for violence (physical and psychological) triggered by any deviance from gender stereotypes of patriarchal hierarchy and control. We truthfully hear in Verdi's art buried voices in ourselves, the shock of recognition that marks great art.

Verdi's *musical* art gives incomparable expression to the negative emotions of the traumatic loss of intimate relationships that the external demands of patriarchy mindlessly inflicts not only on women but on men. Verdi's art, for example, enables us to hear the voices – screaming with pain – of persons often burdened by unjust stereotypes: Rigoletto, the hunchback, as he learns he has killed his own daughter (*Rigoletto*); Azucena, the gypsy, who watched her mother burned at the stake as a witch and blindly killed her own son in vengeance and yet tenderly loves as a mother the son of her enemy (*Il Trovatore*); Violetta, the courtesan, who speaks the terrors of abandonment and death (*La Traviata*); Gustavo, the gay or bisexual man, who yearns for an inaccessible beloved (*Un Ballo in Maschera*); the aged Philip II, who mourns his lovelessness and friendlessness (*Don Carlos*); Aida, the black slave, who grieves for her homelessness, and is tangled in conflict between her lover and father and with the jealousy of another woman (*Aida*);

---

[27] See Mark Juergensmeyer, *Terror in the Mind of God: The Global Rise of Religious Violence* (Berkeley: University of California Press, 2000), especially at pp. 182–207. Cf. Walter Laqueur on the "machismo" of terrorist groups, Walter Laqueur, *The Age of Terrorism* (Boston: Little, Brown, 1987), at pp. 150, 153–4.

Othello, the Moor, who screams with grief when he realizes he has unjustly killed the woman he loved (*Otello*). The tragic expressive power of this art is reflected in its appeal to so many men in diverse cultures, like Inuttiaq in Jean Briggs's study of eskimo family life, who endlessly and loudly played on the tape recorder his "favorite music, 'Il Trovatore,' 'The music that makes one want to cry,' he called it."[28] Verdi's art bridges outer and inner worlds in an increasingly subtle study of the psychology of gender that sustains such a public and private tragedy. The main burden of my argument is to show in detail the psychological power and depth of the psychology of gender Verdi's art reveals to us, including its close study of voices suppressed and distorted by patriarchal demands.

Verdi's musical art holds, as it were, a Shakespearean mirror up to our inner emotional lives under patriarchy, enabling us to acknowledge resources of emotional intelligence and resistance that patriarchy represses and marginalizes. It offers a complex psychological, anti-essentializing picture of the ways in which both men and women are sometimes complicitous with, and sometimes resistant to, the demands of patriarchy, and the price they pay for both complicity and/or resistance. It offers us, as I hope to show, a detailed psychological geography, in Carol Gilligan's terms,[29] both of what the demands of patriarchy are and how they enter into the psyche and draw psychological support from the repression of voice associated with the disruption of a range of pivotally important relationships (personal and political) from childhood into adulthood (chapters 5–7). The interest of my account must come as it clarifies the interpretive appeal of Verdi's operas for myself and others, as we find in them a tragic statement of the price we pay for patriarchal practices that render all forms of human love and friendship (personal and political) tragically impossible, whether parent for child, siblings for one another, or adults for one another. The idealizations imposed by gender stereotypes cover lack of real relationship and loss, a psychology that Verdi's art sensitively explores through a voice of identification in religious experience, sometimes as humane consolation (*La Forza del Destino*), sometimes as demonic rationalizations of personal and political atrocity (*Don Carlos*). Such idealizations also rationalize the pedestal, often racialized, that divides good (asexual) from bad (sexual) women, a psychology that Verdi's art also sensitively explores in its tragic effects on any love that challenges such unjust barriers (*La Traviata*, *La Forza del Destino*, *Aida*, *Otello*). Such racialized gender stereotypes play a

---

[28] See Jean L. Briggs, *Never in Anger: Portrait of an Eskimo Family* (Cambridge, MA: Harvard University Press, 1970), at p. 154.
[29] See Carol Gilligan, *The Birth of Pleasure* (New York: Knopf, 2002), at p. 3.

pivotally important role in rationalizing forms of religious and ethnic intolerance, often unleashed on forms of free sexual voice that express themselves in love across the barriers of religion and ethnicity and even, I suggest, gender. Verdi's art astutely shows and studies all these connections.

There is an ambiguity in how tragic artists from Aeschylus to Verdi understand the tragedy of patriarchy they reveal to us. On the one hand, they may, like Aeschylus, regard such disruption of intimate life as the regrettable though necessary price for sustaining the demands of a democratic civilization. On the other, they may, like Euripides, more skeptically question whether such tragic losses are indeed required to sustain democracy (see, on these points, chapter 2). It does not follow from a culture's responsiveness to tragic art that it resolves the tragedy as democratic ideals would require.[30] Italians may respond tragically to Verdi's art and not, for that reason, better acknowledge the demands of feminist justice, let alone a just respect for the range of sexual orientations. Verdi himself was certainly not a feminist in the contemporary sense. He questioned, as we shall see, the impact of the honor code on free sexual voice, but he also, like Aeschylus, saw other practices that for me call for feminist resistance as in the tragic nature of things. But, his understanding of the tragedy of patriarchy is, I believe, unparalleled since the Attic tragedians in its exploration of its dimensions of tragic loss not only for women but for men.

Verdi, the greatest tragedian in the history of opera, focuses attention on what I define as 'the tragedy of patriarchy'; it works particularly on men, though, of course, on women as well. It is Verdi's very obsession with the tragic representation of male psychology that makes his work, from my perspective, so compelling today. Opera appealed to creative artists and audiences in the nineteenth century because such works sometimes engaged important political issues like liberalism and anti-Semitism.[31] But, many of these works are today mainly historical curiosities. Verdi's mature operas, which certainly had such appeal in the nineteenth century both in Italy and elsewhere, speak, if anything, more ugently to our situation than they may have to his own. I take this extraordinary fact as something I hope to explain. As men and women try collaboratively to understand and resist the culture that has made the tragedy of patriarchy so pervasively normative, we are absorbed by Verdi's art as resources of voice for understanding and for resistance more urgent today than they have ever been (chapter 7). The

---

[30] For a view of Verdi along these lines, see Gilles De Van, *Verdi's Theater*.

[31] See, for example, Diana R. Hallman, *Opera, Liberalism, and Antisemitism in Nineteenth-Century France: The Politics of Haley's La Juive* (Cambridge: Cambridge University Press, 2002).

particular interest of Verdi is what his art tells us both about the role played by voice and the representation of voice in this tragedy. Eric Bentley observed that "the root of the scream is the root of tragedy itself",[32] giving expression to "one's own individual form of radically negative feeling, whatever it may be: it can even be a lack of feeling, for what happens to many when they are upset it that they anesthetize themselves, they prevent themselves from feeling."[33] My view is that the tragedy of patriarchy remains largely invisible to many men because their very sense of masculinity has been uncritically rooted in the very denial of the feelings that would enable them to recognize their plight. The greatness of Verdi's tragic art is that it finds a voice for men to hear the silenced scream, which makes at least publicly thinkable, as great tragic art always has, a wisdom not otherwise attainable. If ancient Attic tragedy was indeed born, as Nietzsche argued,[34] from the spirit of music, it may be Verdi, not Wagner (as Nietzsche once believed),[35] whose work gives tragic voice its most authentic and adequate modern musical expression. The larger interest of my argument may be its rethinking of what tragedy is and how its psychological depth and appeal cannot be understood independent of its underlying structure, what I call the tragedy of patriarchy. If I am right, Verdi's creative importance has been inexplicably underestimated in important recent studies of opera as a quest for voice,[36] a rather gaping scholarly lacuna which suggests the depth of the continuing problem of patriarchy in suppressing discussion of what, in my view, are the central issues which motivate not only tragedy as an enterprise but the quest for voice as a central preoccupation of the arts in general and music in particular.

---

[32] Eric Bentley, *The Life of the Drama* (New York: Applause Theatre Books, 1991), p. 279.

[33] See *id.*, p. 277.

[34] Friedrich Nietzsche, *The Birth of Tragedy* in *The Birth of Tragedy and The Genealogy of Morals* Francis Golffing, trans. (Garden City, NY: Doubleday & Co., 1956), at pp. 3–146.

[35] On the relationship of Wagner and Nietzsche, see Bryan Magee, *Wagner and Philosophy* (London: Allen Lane, The Penguin Press, 2000), at pp. 286–342.

[36] See, for example, Carolyn Abbate, *Unsung Voices: Opera and Musical Narrative in the Nineteenth Century* (Princeton: Princeton University Press, 1991); Lydia Goehr, *The Quest for Voice: Music, Politics, and the Limits of Philosophy* (Berkeley: University of California Press, 1998); Philippe Lacoue-Labarthe, *Musica Ficta (Figures of Wagner)*, Felicia McCarren, trans. (Stanford, CA: Stanford University Press, 1994). Cf. Catherine Clement, *Opera or the Undoing of Women*, Betsy Wing, trans. (Minneapolis: University of Minnesota Press, 1989).

# Chapter 2

# Tragic Art

## PATRIARCHY IN ANCIENT ATHENS AND VERDI'S ITALY

The interpretive power of tragedy arises against a certain background, namely, the contradiction between the normative appeal of democracy and entrenched patterns of structural injustice. On the one hand, the normative appeal of democracy rests on equal voice over our common political lives; on the other, entrenched patterns of structural injustice (for example, patriarchy) rest on deprivations of voice to whole classes of persons. What I call the tragedy of patriarchy is the depiction of this contradiction in terms of traumatic breaks in relationship that are, as tragic losses, required to sustain the conditions of democratic order. I first explore these issues in the context of Athenian democracy, and then investigate at greater length the tensions between the patriarchal demands of the code of honor and political liberalism explored by Verdi in the context of the Italian struggle for democratic unity in the nineteenth century. I analyze the power of Verdi's musical voice as an expression of the impact of the tragedy of patriarchy on public and private life, and offer a view as well of how and why his life and relationships (in particular, his relationship to Giuseppina Strepponi) led him to develop such an extraordinary critical perspective on this tragedy, in particular, its traumatic disruption of intimate loving relationships. In chapter 3, I examine why Verdi's tragic vision makes its point through music, and argue that music has this indispensable interpretive power because it explores emotions and memories that cannot otherwise be discussed.

## Democracy and Tragedy in Ancient Greece

Structural injustice is exemplified by evils like racism, extreme forms of religious intolerance (anti-Semitism), sexism, and homophobia.[1] It involves two features. First, an entire class of persons is traditionally regarded as not having basic human rights like conscience, speech, intimate life, and work. Second, this deprivation is rationalized in terms of dehumanizing stereotypes whose uncritical appeal rests, in a vicious circle, on stereotypes of ethnicity or religion or gender or gendered sexuality that arise from the long history of deprivation. The abridgement, in particular, of the basic rights of conscience and speech of such subordinated groups debars the voices and perspectives that most reasonably contest such stereotypes, cramping discourse to the sectarian measure of the dominant orthodoxy. Often such discourse expresses uncritical mythologies that unjustly enforce stereotypical idealizations or denigrations that rationalize the dehumanizing terms of the structural injustice.

Our political institutions only allow us reasonably to question such mythologies when they open up an appropriate liberal space of public discourse and debate within which such questions may, at least, be raised. The continuing interest for us of the Athenian invention of tragedy among its other democratic institutions is that it opened up such a space of choice for citizens between the values of an archaic tribal past and the new political realities of the democratic city-state.[2] Of course, Athenian citizenship was circumscribed to men and narrowly defined in ethnic terms, and importantly rested on slavery and ethnically chauvinist imperialism.[3] Athenian tragic theatre for this reason understandably critically contrasted the archaic heroes under the politics of kingship in Homer with the democratic responsibilities of Athenian male citizens, including military service in the interdependent male-bonded phalanxes of hoplite armies.[4] But even within these constraints, Athenian tragedy sometimes remarkably revealed and even discussed "the fictive quality of otherwise unchallenged cultural accommodations."[5]

Attic tragedies were written and played by men for largely male audi-

---

[1] See, on these points, David A. J. Richards, *Women, Gays, and the Constitution: The Grounds for Feminism and Gay Rights in Culture and Law* (Chicago: University of Chicago Press, 1998).
[2] See, in general, Jean-Pierre Vernant and Pierre Vidal-Naquet. *Myth and Tragedy in Ancient Greece*, Janet Lloyd, trans. (New York: Zone Books, 1988). See also J. Peter Euben, *The Tragedy of Political Theory: the Road Not Taken* (Princeton: Princeton University Press, 1990).
[3] See, on these points, Sheila Murnaghan and Sandra R. Joshel, *Women and Slaves in Greco-Roman Culture* (London: Routledge, 1998), pp. 1–21.
[4] See Simon Goldhill, *Reading Greek Tragedy* (Cambridge: Cambridge University Press, 1986), at pp. 91–2, 120, 143–5.
[5] See Peter Euben, *The Tragedy of Political Theory*, at p. 144; see also *id.*, at pp. 154–5, 162.

ences, the audience of self-governing, exclusively male citizens of the Athenian democracy. The tragedies are clearly about the new responsibilities of manhood under the democracy (in contrast to the previous rule of kings). Manhood is, however, defined as a gender binary with reference to womanhood. The tragic points about requirements of democratic manhood are thus strikingly made in terms of womanhood, which explains why the tragedies so prominently feature the depiction of women. There is now a large, probing literature about the role women thus play in the Attic tragedies, as male playwrights, performers, and audiences define and explore their new democratic responsibilities as men by reference to a new conception of women, one that is often strikingly misogynist (democracy, as it were, requiring new forms of patriarchy).[6]

I discuss three Athenian tragedies (*The Oresteia*, *Oedipus Tyrannus*, and *Iphigenia at Aulis*) as ways of framing the tensions between the demands of democracy for egalitarian voice and the role patriarchy (abridging the voice of half the human race) was believed necessarily to play in sustaining democracy. Democracy is depicted as requiring a new psychology of manhood, one that replaces the old psychology of rule by kings or tyrants by a new psychology of democratic manhood. The tragedies depict the required psychological transition to democratic manhood in terms of traumatic breaks in relationships to women, tragic emotional losses required for the kind of gender binary that can psychologically support the demands of democracy.

*The Oresteia* of Aeschylus is an illuminating case in point. The trilogy offers a founding myth of the Athenian democracy as its institutions offer a putatively just resolution to the unending cycle of horrors of murder and revenge of the archaic men and women of kingship under the House of Atreus. Its terms crucially include, of course, a mythology that enforces misogyny. The Athenian jury is evenly divided about the guilt or innocence of Orestes, weighing his guilt in killing his mother Klytemnestra against her guilt in killing her husband Agamemnon. The decisive vote is left to Athena, the patron goddess of Athens. Apollo had set the stage in mythological terms:

---

[6] For examples of this important literature, see Froma I. Zeitlin, *Playing the Other: Gender and Society in Classical Greek Literature* (Chicago: University of Chicago Press, 1996); Helene P. Foley, *Female Acts in Greek Tragedy* (Princeton: Princeton University Press, 2001); Simon Goldhill, *Reading Greek Tragedy* (Cambridge: Cambridge University Press, 1996); Daniel Mendelsoln, *Gender and the City in Euripides' Political Plays* (New York: Oxford University Press, 2002); Ruby Blondell, Mary-Kay Gamel, Nancy Sorkin Rabinowitz, Bella Zweig, *Women on the Edge: Four Plays by Euripides* (New York: Routledge, 1999).

" . . . Conception
is not so simple a thing. Scientists tell us
a mother receives the sperm, the homunculus,
the complete new being that grows within her womb,
The mother is the nurse but nothing more!
This is not the general view, I am frank to say,
But popular opinion is often wrong,
And the proof of this counterintuitive theory is here
In the courtroom, and I call upon her as witness –
Athena, whose father was Zeus but who has no mother,
Whatsoever, in any way, shape, or form.
No goddess brings forth a child without a father,
But it happens the other way, and proves our point.
We honor you, Pallas, admire your great city,
And love and respect its people. I sent Orestes
Here, for that reason, believing he would have justice,
A fair hearing, and then the exoneration
I know he deserves."[7]

Athena rationalizes her decision in such terms:

" . . . It's a close question
but I have to favor Orestes. I had no mother,
and I am my father's daughter. The death of a wife
who killed her husband is bad, but not so bad
as the death of a father and king."[8]

Aeschylus thus frames the misogyny of Athenian political and legal practices as the necessary price for the very foundation of the democracy. The
democracy is, in these terms, the improvement that it is over the moral
chaos of the archaic period precisely because it self-consciously rejects that
period's more flexible gender arrangements (reflected in the political
powers exercised by Klytemnestra and the prophetic powers of voice of
Cassandra).

But, the very way *The Oresteia* thus makes the foundational case for
democracy in terms of gender raises for us fundamental questions both of
political justice and psychology. The case is made, as we have seen, mythologically: what Apollo deems the anti-scientific popular view (that women
play an important role in birth) is ultimately questioned in terms of the

---

[7] Aeschylus, *The Oresteia*, David R. Slavitt, trans. (Philadelphia: University of Pennsylvania
Press, 1998), pp. 139–40.
[8] *Id.*, p. 143.

mythology of Athen's birth from Zeus. The men in the Athenian audience for *The Oresteia* undoubtedly found this argument compelling, but its very terms have suggested to contemporary scholars interested in the Western construction of sexism that, on the merits, its case is self-consciously mythological and thus subject to reasonable doubt on independent grounds of justice and democratic legitimacy.[9] Indeed, the very appeal to mythology at this point suggests underlying doubts, largely suppressed, even among Athenian citizen-men. The very tragic structure of the play suggests, however, further contemporary questions about the political psychology of the Athenian men who would have found its misogyny compelling.

*The Oresteia* tragically addresses Athenian citizens in terms of the choice of two models: the men and women of the archaic past, and the contemporary responsibilities of democratic citizens. Attic tragedy thus dramatizes a double consciousness: one reflected in the archaic characters, the other in the chorus that critically reflects on their actions in light of values and concerns shared with the Athenian audience. The first chorus of *The Oresteia* reflects in these terms on Agamemnon's sacrifice of his daughter, Iphigenia, as the price allegedly required by the goddess, Artemis, to give favorable winds for the Greeks' ships to leave Aulis for Troy. The chorus conceives Agamemnon's choice as tragic because each of its alternatives inflicts humanely compelling moral losses (killing one's child versus a failure of honorable military leadership), and it accepts that his choice was dictated by "Necessity, Goddess Ananke."[10] The chorus nonetheless blames him not for his choice, but for his psychology in making the choice. "An act," Martha Nussbaum sensitively observes, "that we were prepared to view as the lesser of two hideous wrongs and impieties has now become for him pious and right . . . : if it is right to obey the god, it is right to *want* to obey him, to have an appetite . . . for the crime, even to yearn for it with exceedingly impassioned passion."[11] The Aeschylean tragic chorus here, as elsewhere, critically comments on a corrupt masculine psychology of diassociation from the humane losses required by what the chorus takes to be even justified tragic choices.[12]

*The Oresteia* extends its examination of this powerful political psychology beyond such choices. Thus, the chorus itself becomes a focus for the study

---

[9] See, on these points, Froma J. Zeitlin, *Playing the Other: Gender and Society in Classical Greek Literature* (Chicago: University of Chicago Press, 1996), pp. 87–119.

[10] Aeschylus, *The Oresteia*, at p. 17.

[11] Martha C. Nussbaum, *The Fragility of Goodness: Luck and Ethics in Greek Tragedy and Philosophy* (Cambridge: Cambridge University Press, 1986), pp. 35–6.

[12] See *id.*, pp. 39, 40, 50.

of its motives and effects. It truncates its description of the death of Iphigenia abruptly:

> "What happened then, we did not see
> The eyes, the brain,
> Turn away at such events.
> For wisdom that the gods dole out
> We pay in pain
> That we hope, at last, relents
>
> As the dawn comes with its wan light
> To offer relief
> From dreams we could scarcely bear,
> Sordid, horrid, shameful, woeful,
> And so full of grief
> That even the brave despair."[13]

When the herald informs the chorus of the Greek victory at Troy and of Agamemnon's imminent return, they refuse to answer his queries about their "desperation" under the rule of Klytemnestra:

> "Some things, we have learned, it is better
> neither to speak nor even think of. Silence,
> even that of the grave, can be anodyne."[14]

But, the most stark Aeschylean examination of this political psychology comes with the chorus's refusal to hear what Cassandra tells them about the cycle of violence of the House of Atreus which will shortly again engulf them (as Agamemnon is murdered by his wife). Cassandra responds with ever more precise descriptions and diagnoses the chorus's failure to understand as rooted in a lack of feeling:

> "I shall speak more clearly to make you understand,
> What I foretell need not, like some blushing bride,
> Peep out from behind its veil. But bold and blunt
> As the sunshine's dazzle at morning. I shall enlighten
> Even the blind, who must feel if they cannot see.
> Blood! Do you understand that? Human blood,
> And the stink of it that has fouled these silent stones!
> There is a chorus here – not you, but the Furies,
> Raging at sin and eager for retribution,
> Chanting their hatred of evil and bewailing the years
> They have had to wait for the cleansing. Blood will have blood,

---

[13] Aeschylus, *The Oresteia*, p. 18.
[14] *Id.*, p. 27.

For Thyestes' sins! For murder! Unspeakable crimes . . .
Are these expressions of psychic trauma or real,
The shameful truths you all know and fear to whisper
Along or even to think of alone, in silence?"[15]

Aeschylus dramatizes such disassociated feeling in the chorus as the mirror image of the disassociated feeling in Agamemnon and other archaic heroes as the political psychology of both victims and perpetrators of traumatic violence, which feeds on itself in a cycle of violence that only the institutions of Athenian democracy can appropriately domesticate and civilize by restoring patriarchy (as the Furies transform themselves into the Eumenides).[16] If democracy requires that men are no longer kings, masculinity must at least be defined in terms of the hierarchy of patriarchy. *The Oresteia* would thus have been understood by its Athenian audience as bringing to an end the political psychology that sustained the horrors of politics in the archaic period.

But *The Oresteia* makes its concluding case for Athenian democracy, as we earlier saw, mythologically in a way that reasonably raises questions certainly today not only of democratic legitimacy, but of its implicit perpetuation of the political psychology it claims to end. *The Oresteia* assumes that patriarchy, resting on the structural injustice of sexism, is the price that must be paid for civilization. *The Oresteia* thus naturalizes the structural injustice of sexism (an abridgement of basic rights to women, rationalized in terms of mythological stereotypes of gender that reflect the injustice, including, in particular, the loss of rights of conscience and voice) as foundational to democracy. Its injustice itself imposes a traumatic separation of men from women, a loss of relationship in public and private life that rests on the loss of moral voice of women as moral agents (as the Furies are domesticated into the Eumenides). The plausibility of this founding narrative for Athenian male citizens thus rests on idealizations that rationalize yet again the psychology of traumatic loss (the loss of the mother, as Athena has no mother) that Athenian democracy claimed to transcend.

A comparable traumatic separation is the subject of Sophocles' *Oedipus Tyrannus*. The play is a study of the personal and political psychology of an archaic hero-king, Oedipus, whose disastrous pride is contrasted by the chorus to the rule of law implicit in democratic Athens:

"I pray, may destiny permit
that honestly I live my life

---

[15] *Id.*, p. 48.
[16] See *id.*, p. 151.

in word and deed.
That I obey the laws
The heavens have begotten
And prescribed.
Those laws created by Olympus
Law pure, immortal,
Forever lasting, essence of the god
Who lives in them.
On arrogance and price
A tyrant feeds.
The goad of insolence,
Of senseless overbearing, blind conceit,
Of seeking things unseasonable,
Unreasonable,
Will prick a man to climb to heights
Where he must love his footing
And tumble to his doom.
Ambition must be used to benefit the state;
Else it is wrong, and God
Must strike it from the earth."[17]

The political psychology of Oedipus is rooted by Sophocles in his traumatic separation from his parents who, fearing the oracle's warning, intended infanticide, exposing him with rivets through his ankles.[18] Oedipus' traumatic separation and later killing of his father and marriage to his mother shape a psychology incapable of trusting or heeding the judgment of others, including Teiresias, Creon, and his wife–mother. His self-blinding at the end of the tragedy bespeaks his psychological disassociation from relationship and experience. The play imparts a patriarchal message that the fraternal bonds between men called for by democratic citizenship require exactly the opposite psychology to that of Oedipus: namely, a bond between father and son and a traumatic separation from one's mother. This traumatic separation is rationalized, like the comparable break in relationship between men and women in *The Oresteia*, as in the nature of things, required for the kind of relations between men required for Athenian democratic citizenship. But, the personal and political psychology thus forged not only supports a patriarchal hierarchy between men and women which renders personal relations between them problematic; it also naturalizes a father–son pair that is itself hierarchically ordered in terms of patriarch and

---

[17] Sophocles, *Oedipus Tyrannus*, Luci Berkowitz and Theodore F. Brunner, trans. (New York: W.W. Norton, 1970), at p. 20.

[18] See *id.*, at pp. 23–4.

subordinate that renders egalitarian relationships between men problematic as well. The new psychology of democratic man, required for democratic citizens to supplant the hierarchical rule of kings, thus psychologically reinscribes patriarchal hierarchy in relations among men. As I shall shortly put this point in the context of my discussion of *Iphigenia at Aulis*, identification with the father replaces voice in relationship to one's father, which does not psychologically support a democratic ethos of relationships expressive of the deliberative voice of free and equal citizens. Once again, as in *The Oresteia*, Attic tragedy psychologically frames patriarchy as the indispensable foundation of democratic citizenship and thus subverts its underlying values of free and equal voice.

Aeschylus and Sophocles write as Athenian patriots defending its democratic institutions, sharply separating the political psychology of the archaic period from that of citizens of Athens. But if, as I have suggested, the same political psychology supports and indeed rationalizes the injustice of the Athenian democracy, it may subject it to associated incentives to unjust political violence. Near the end of his career as a playwright Euripides writes his play *Iphigenia at Aulis* late in the history of the Athenian democracy during its decline in the wake of its defeat in the Peloponnesian War, addressing the Athenian democratic mind to the question of how and why it may have squandered its democratic promise in such disastrous imperialistic ventures.[19] The play examines the psychology of political violence in two interrelated forms: first, the unjust grounds for the Trojan War; and second, Agamemnon's choice to sacrifice his daughter to secure his leadership of that unjust venture. Euripides frames the tragedy in terms of the underlying psychology of disassociation of both father and daughter that covers over the loss of their traumatic break in relationship with a mythological idealization of gender that rationalizes political violence (both the war and the murder of his daughter). The move from relationship to idealization is marked in both cases by shifts in voice. When Agamemnon believes he can still extricate himself from the tragic choice, he refuses to accept the adulterous affair of his brother Menelaos' wife, Helen, with the racialized barbarian Paris as a wrong that could justify war or the sacrifice of his daughter.[20] As the chorus later puts the point, the affair reflects consent and mutual sexual desire.[21] It is certainly not rape. But later when

---

[19] See Euripides, *Iphigenia in Aulis*, in Ruby Blondell, Mary-Kay Gamel, Nancy Sorkin Rabinowitz, Bella Zweig, *Women on the Edge: Four Plays by Euripides* (New York: Routledge, 1999), at pp. 305–89.

[20] See *id.*, pp. 341–2.

[21] *Id.*, p. 348.

Agamemnon regards himself as having no way of extricating himself from the choice, he characterizes such affairs as "thefts of Greek wives", and rationalizes the Trojan War on grounds of protecting Greek wives from rape:

"Greece must be free, and so much as it is in you
and me for her to be free, so much we must do,
and not, since we are Greeks, have our wives
taken from us by force, by barbarians."[22]

Correspondingly, Iphigenia greets her father with a passionate expression of relational attachment:

"Mother, running ahead of you – don't be angry –
I have to throw my arms around Father.
I want to run to you, Daddy,
And throw my arms around you after such a long time.
I need to see your face. Don't be angry."[23]

She struggles to bring her father back into relationship with her:

"Be with me now. Don't focus on your responsibilities."[24]

It is in such relational terms, not in terms of her mother's coldly logical reasoning with her husband,[25] that Iphigenia initially voices her plea to her father not to kill her for political ends:

"If I had Orpheus' way with words, Father,
to persuade by singing, so that rocks would come to me,
and by words I could charm whomever I wanted,
that's what I would have done. But as things are,
as my wise saying I will offer only my tears . . .
. . . I wrap my body
around your knees, the body which this woman bore to you.
Don't kill me before my time! It's sweet to look upon the light . . .
I first called you 'Father,' who first called me 'child.'
I was the first who sat upon your knees,
Gave you sweet kisses, and got them in return.
This was what you said then: 'Will I see you, daughter,
In the house of your fortunate husband,
Living and thriving in a way that's worthy of me?'
This was my answer as I touched your beard
Which I'm grasping now with my hand:

---

[22] *Id.*, p. 375.
[23] *Id.*, p. 350.
[24] *Id.*, p. 350.
[25] *Id.*, pp. 371–2.

(26)

'What about my seeing you? Will I welcome you as an old man
with the sweet hospitality of my house, Daddy,
paying back the work of nurturing you gave while raising me?'
I still hold the memory of those conversations,
But you've forgotten them, and you want to kill me."[26]

But when Iphigenia identifies with her father's plan, she speaks in a very different voice. While in her relational plea she wondered, "What do I have to do with the marriage of Helen and Paris?",[27] her identification is expressed in radically different terms:

"All of Greece, great Greece, is looking at me now!
In me lies the setting forth of the ships, the ruin of the Trojans,
And women, in the future, even if barbarians try something,
Never again to allow them to rob those happy women from Greece,
Once they have paid for theft of Helen, whom Paris stole . . .
. . . This man must not go into battle with all the Greeks for a woman's sake, or die.
It's more important for one single man
To look upon the light than a thousand women.
If Artemis wishes to take my body,
Will I, a mortal, stand in the way of a goddess?
No! Impossible! I give my body to Greece.
Make the sacrifice! Eradicate Troy! For a long time to come
That will be my monument, my children, my marriage, my fame!
It's proper for Greeks to rule barbarians, Mother, not barbarians Greeks,
Because they are slaves, but Greeks are free!"[28]

The shift between Iphigenia's two voices, which Aristotle erroneously criticizes as inconsistent characterization,[29] in fact brilliantly dramatizes the underlying political psychology as Iphigenia, responding to her father's demands, voices a painful break in relationship by losing her relational voice, shifting to a voice of identification with her father's mythology of gender (rationalizing her murder).

Euripides here dramatizes a shift in voice (from relationship to identification) that Sandor Ferenczi, in his pathbreaking paper "Confusion of Tongues Between Adults and the Child: The Language of Tenderness and of Passion,"[30] was later to identify and discuss in the psychology of patients

---

[26] *Id.*, pp. 373–4.

[27] *Id.*, p. 374.

[28] *Id.*, pp. 380–1.

[29] Aristotle, *Poetics* 1454a31–32, in Jonathan Barnes, ed., *The Complete Works of Aristotle* , vol. 2 (Princeton: Princeton University Press, 1984), pp. 2316–2340, at p. 2327.

with a traumatic history of early sexual abuse as children. Ferenczi had been puzzled why the usual psychoanalytic procedures of free association and transference did not work with these patients, "*a child indeed* who no longer reacts to intellectual explanations, only perhaps to maternal friendliness."[31] Psychoanalytic objectivity replicated the circumstances of the trauma, which led the patient to "repeat now the symptom-formation exactly as he did at the time when the illness started."[32] Ferenczi observed:

> "It is difficult to imagine the behaviour and the emotions of children after such violence. One would expect the first impulse to be that of reaction, hatred, disgust and energetic refusal. 'No, no, I do not want it, it is much too violent for me, it hurts, leave me alone,' this or something similar would be the immediate reaction if it had not been paralysed by enormous anxiety. These children feel physically and morally helpless, their personalities are not sufficiently consolidated in order to be able to protest, even if only in thought, for the overpowering force and authority of the adult makes them dumb and can rob them of their senses. *The same anxiety, however, if it reaches a certain maximum, compels them to subordinate themselves like automata to the will of the aggressor, to divine each one of his desires and to gratify these; completely oblivious of themselves they identify themselves with the aggressor.* Through the identification, or let us say, introjection of the aggressor, he disappears as part of the external reality, and becomes intra- instead of extra-psychic . . . In any case the attack as a rigid external reality ceases to exist and in the traumatic trance the child succeeds in maintaining the previous situation of tenderness."[33]

Such children, prematurely identifying with adults, suffer "a *traumatic progression*, of a *precocious maturity*."[34] Iphigenia responds analogously to her father's traumatic project of homicide first by speaking in her own relational voice and then, after identification, speaking in his voice (thus, the confusion of tongues). It is part of the psychological power of such traumas that identification with the aggressor buries them as the victim loses memory and voice as an independent agent.[35]

---

[30] See Sandor Ferenczi, *Final Contributions to the Problems and Methods of Psycho-Analysis*, Michael Balint, ed., Eric Mosbacher et al., trans. (London: The Hogarth Press, 1955), pp. 156–67.

[31] *Id.*, p. 160.

[32] *Id.*, p. 160.

[33] *Id.*, p. 162.

[34] *Id.*, p. 165.

[35] On the complexities in Ferenczi's studies of trauma, see Ruth Leys, *Trauma: A Genealogy* (Chicago: University of Chicago Press, 2000), pp. 120–89. For more recent studies, see Judith Herman, *Trauma and Recovery* (New York: Basic Books, 1997); Bessel A. van der Kolk, Alexander C. McFarlane, and Lares Weisaeth, eds., *Traumatic Stress: The Effects of Overwhelming Experience on Mind, Body, and Society* (New York: The Guilford Press, 1996).

Euripides sensitively dramatizes this shift in voice as the political psychology that explains patterns of political violence, such as the ultimately disastrous imperialism of the Athenian democracy in the Peloponnesian War. *Iphigenia at Aulis* explores the background psychology of two such patterns: the unjust grounds for the Trojan War; and Agamemnon's choice to murder his daughter to secure his leadership of that unjust venture. In both cases, Iphigenia's shift in voice, echoing her father's comparable shift, quite clearly moves from moral clarity to ideological obfuscation under the impact of a political psychology that rests on the loss of relational voice. As we have seen, Agamemnon, the chorus, and Iphigenia quite clearly understand that Helen's adulterous affair with Paris is consensual and mutually desired, but, under the impact of the shift in voice, consensual adultery is ideologically transformed into rape in the terms of a racialized barbarian that rationalizes the Trojan War. Similarly, Agamemnon certainly sees the wrongness of killing his daughters and works to avoid it; the pleas of his daughter for her life echo his own earlier stated judgments. But the shift in voice leads both to suppress these judgments, as Iphigenia literally repeats her father's words about her necessary sacrifice for the glory of Greece.[36] Iphigenia's identification with her father ideologically transforms her into a gender stereotype, one freighted with the same mythological misogyny that we earlier saw in the speeches of Apollo and Athena at the end of *The Oresteia*, stated by Iphigenia as a moral axiom:

> "It's more important for one single man
> to look upon the light than a thousand women."[37]

The working hypothesis of this work is that the structural injustice of sexism has been traditionally supported by this political psychology, which I call the 'tragedy of patriarchy'. The structural injustice is naturalized by regarding what are, in fact, contestable cultural stereotypes of gender as compelled by the nature of things. The underlying political psychology is one that traumatically requires the loss of voice (of both women and men) that could reasonably challenge the structural injustice, and mandates in its place identification with the mythological cultural stereotypes that perpetuate the injustice. These stereotypes, themselves arising from the unjust suppression of voice, themselves pervasively rationalize unjust forms of violence in both private and public life, forms of violence specifically triggered

---

[36] See Euripides, *Iphigenia at Aulis*, at p. 375 (Agamemnon) and p. 381 (Iphigenia).
[37] *Id.*, p. 381.

by any threat to a sense of democratic manhood defined in terms of the gender binary required by these stereotypes. The resulting psychology of manhood accepts patriarchy as in the tragic nature of things – traumatic breaks in relationship along lines of gender as tragic losses that must be acknowledged or at least accepted as the tragic price for civilized order. *The Oresteia*, *Oedipus Tyrannus*, and *Iphigenia at Aulis* frame this tragedy at different stages: in the one (*Oresteia*), critically discussing the failure emotionally to feel the loss, in the other two (*Oedipus*, *Iphigenia*), showing how the loss is not even acknowledged (the shift from voice of relationship to the voice of identification). Traumatic breaks in relationship along lines required by gender stereotypes (including those of parents with children and of adults with one another) are, as it were, the psychological fuel of patriarchy, losses of voice in relationship that naturalize the unjust arrangement of authority in public and private life that ascribes hierarchical authority to fathers on inadequate grounds of gender stereotypes that fail to respect the basic human rights of persons, including rights of conscience, speech, intimate life, work, and the like. The mechanism of this political psychology is to cover over the traumatic loss with patterns of disassociation which render persons no longer psychologically present in their relationships with the other persons but rather conform their conduct to the terms of the gender stereotypes. Such dissociative absence fuels identification in terms of mythological idealization, rationalizing the loss of personal conviction and voice that might otherwise reasonably challenge the idealizing stereotypes. Such psychological loss of voice rationalizes unjust forms of violence.

It is a prominent feature of my argument that this political psychology afflicts men and women, as *The Oresteia*, *Oedipus Tyrannus*, and *Iphigenia at Aulis* show, and that great tragic drama has, since its Aeschylean innovation, absorbed us as an imaginative space for understanding and probing its layered relational dimensions in our consciousness and lives. I take it, following George Steiner, that tragic drama explores "catastrophe" as "the tragic personage is broken by forces which can neither be fully understood nor overcome by rational prudence",[38] and, following Raymond Williams, such catastrophe contextually dramatizes "the real tension between old and new: between received beliefs, embodied in institutions and responses, and newly and vividly experienced contradictions and possibilities."[39] Tragedy absorbs us because it offers us plausible hypothetical representations that take seriously that such catastrophic forces exist arising in the tension

---

[38] See George Steiner, *The Death of Tragedy* (Yale University Press, 1996), p. 8.
[39] See Raymond Williams, *Modern Tragedy* (Stanford, CA: Stanford University Press, 1966), at p. 54; see also *id.*, p. 67.

between old and new, and energizes our human capacity provisionally to entertain hypotheses about them.[40] I offer here an account of what these catastrophic forces often are, namely, the personal and political psychology that naturalizes patriarchy. I call this psychology the 'tragedy of patriarchy' because the artists who have taken it so seriously frame their narratives in terms of inward divisions of consciousness that, as in *Iphigenia at Aulis*, evince both remarkable psychological resistance to traumatic loss and catastrophic acceptance of such loss as, irresistably, in the nature of things. Such lives are lived in contradiction, and tragic art tells us the truth about such contradiction and its catastrophic consequences. Men or women, as the case my be, ultimately structure their very sense of self and of others in terms of the kinds of personalities that psychologically armor themselves to endure such losses often by not acknowledging or even feeling them. Tragic art absorbs us because it truthfully enables us to feel such loss. Its greatest artists give us no simple diagnosis or remedy, since they themselves, like us, often live in contradiction.

If I am right that the underlying structural injustice of patriarchy is a deeply entrenched cultural pattern subject to criticism and change, we can presumably eventually change the underlying political psychology, which may explain the phenomenon Steiner calls the death of tragedy in the modern period.[41] But, these patterns remain still deeply entrenched, and modern tragedy often explores their catastropic consequences in the self-defeating personal relationships at the core of tragic art stretching from Ibsen to Chekhov to Eugene O'Neill to Tennessee Williams and Arthur Miller and beyond.[42] These unjust cultural patterns are subject to growing recognition and criticism, but their continuing hold on us makes the study of tragedy even more useful in our understanding their continuing psychological depth and complexity and how far we may have yet to go in coming to terms with them.

No aspect of tragedy is more arresting, from this perspective, than the ways in which it represents voice and lack of voice in both the men and women afflicted by the underlying political psychology that often frames the tragic narrative. I have already observed that the repression of personal conviction and voice to conform to idealizing gender stereotypes is fundamental to the power of patriarchy. The tragic representation of our divided

---

[40] See A. D. Nuttall, *Why Does Tragedy Give Pleasure?* (Oxford: Clarendon Press, 1996), pp. 76–7.

[41] See, in general, George Steiner, *The Death of Tragedy*; but cf. Raymond Williams, *Modern Tragedy*.

[42] See, on this point, Raymond Williams, *Modern Tragedy*.

consciousness, whether in Aeschylus or Sophocles or Euripides or Shakespeare, absorbs us today precisely in the ways it represents such issues of voice in their complex relational geography (including relations of parents to children and of siblings, and adult men and women to one another).[43]

## Democracy and Tragedy in Verdi's Art:
## The Code of Honor as Subject Matter

It is from this perspective that I propose to discuss the operas of Verdi, which are centrally relevant to such contemporary discussion for interdependent reasons both of his subject matter and his expressively voiced musicality. To begin with his subject matter, from his very first opera (*Oberto*) to his last (*Falstaff*), Verdi focuses with the force of relentless obsession on the operatic representation of a patriarchal code of honor as a profound and destructive psychological force in the relations of both parents and children and adult men and women with one another (not only men with women, but men with men, and women with women). I focus first on an anthropological description of the demands of the honor code as a specific cultural crystallization of the unjust demands of patriarchy. Once we understand its specific cultural character and demands, we may then turn to how Verdi's musical art frames and explores the psychological impact of those demands as a contradiction within political liberalism.

The honor code, in the sense Verdi explores it, is the anthropologically familiar Mediterranean code of honor which has been well studied both in its historical and contemporary settings.[44] The code importantly centers on strict social controls of women's sexuality, in particular, virginity before marriage and monogamous fidelity after marriage. A father's or brother's or lover's or husband's sense of honor, as a man, is stereotypically defined in

---

[43] On Shakespeare from this perspective, see A. C. Bradley, *Shakespearean Tragedy* (London: Penguin, 1991).

[44] See, for example, David I. Kertzer and Richard P. Saller, *The Family in Italy from Antiquity to the Present* (New Haven: Yale University Press, 1991); J. G. Peristiany, ed., *Honour and Shame: The Values of Mediterranean Society* (Chicago: University of Chicago Press); David D. Gilmore, ed., *Honour and Shame and the Unity of the Mediterranean* (Washington, D.C.: American Anthropological Association, 1987); J. K. Campbell, *Honour, Family, and Patronage* (New York: Oxford University Press, 1964); Jane Schneider and Peter Schneider, *Culture and Political Economy in Western Sicily* (New York: Academic Press, 1976). On the impact of such codes of honor on the Arab world, see Nawal El Saadawi, *The Hidden Face of Eve: Women in the Arab World*, translated and edited by Dr. Sherif Hetata (London and New York: Zed Books Ltd., 1980).

terms of his control over the chastity or fidelity of the woman in question. Such control was, in dominantly face to face and largely illiterate Mediterranean societies, understood in terms of how matters publicly appeared, so that men were vulnerable to dishonor because women (often in fact quite innocent of sexual relations) merely appeared less strictly modest and reticent in relations to men.[45] Such masculine dishonor, arising only from gossip,[46] required violence; under its terms, "the father who, disdaining his own feelings [of love for his daughter], killed his guilty daughter was praised and put forward as an example."[47] A man's most intimate feelings and relations were, under the code of honor, subject to objectifying gender stereotypes that as much rested on his repression of his personal feeling and voice as they did, as we shall see, on those of women.

For women, the honor code rendered their very sexual feelings suspect:

> "The quality required of women in relation to honour is shame, particularly sexual shame. Subjectively, the women's sexual shame is not simply a fear of external sanctions; it is an instinctive revulsion from sexual activity, an attempt in dress, movement, and attitude, to disguise the fact that she possesses the physical attributes of her sex. Maidens must be virgins, and even married women must remain virginal in thought and expression. But honour is always something imputed by others. In these matters the individual women can never retreat within her own conscience. Her honour depends upon the reputation which the community is willing to concede, not upon the evidence of facts in any difficult to determine. Therefore she protects her honour most effectively by conforming in every outward aspect of her deportment to a code of sexual shame."[48]

From this perspective, women's very sexuality was shameful as such, from which "the individual woman can never retreat within her own conscience."[49] Such codes of honor in their very nature objectified women's sexual subjectivity in terms of idealizing gender stereotypes whose force depended on the suppression of conviction and voice in silence about personal feeling.[50] Such stereotypes ascribed to women's sexuality not only a frailty that required masculine control (rationalized as protection),[51] but a diabolic power shown in the provocation of sexual desire.[52] Such stereo-

---

[45] See J. G. Peristiany, *Honour and Shame*, at pp. 66–7.

[46] See *id.*, at pp. 253–4, 256–7.

[47] See *id.*, at p. 220.

[48] See *id.*, at p. 146.

[49] See J. K. Campbell, *Honour, Family, and Patronage* (New York: Oxford University Press, 1964), at p. 270.

[50] See J. G. Peristiany, *Honour and Shame*, at p. 225.

types objectify sexual feeling as such, so that even sexual feeling in licit relations in marriage is deemed polluting.[53] Men not only come to think of their relations to women in such stereotypical terms, but women define their own sense of self in such terms and regulate their relations to one another in such terms: maintaining the chastity code rationalizes antagonism among women.[54] Community life, in consequence, "is fed by an insatiate and hostile curiosity."[55]

Codes of honor, thus understood, are aspects of highly gendered patriarchal institutions, resting on precisely the mythological idealization of gender stereotypes that our earlier study of both structural injustice and its supporting political psychology would lead us to expect.[56] Two explanations of its origins and persistence in different circumstances have been offered: first, its support of otherwise atomistic patriarchal families, enabling them through the exchange of women in arranged marriages, to organize co-operative ventures for scarce resources with other families in the absence of effective state control;[57] and second, its role in state-enforced religious and political codes of male dominance, forging a sense of masculine solidarity by allowing men lower in the hierarchy the opportunity of marrying their daughters up in the hierarchy.[58] Certainly, such roles for codes of honor existed in Italy from antiquity to the present.[59]

There is one aspect of the resulting patriarchal culture of Verdi's nineteenth-century Italy that powerfully and dramatically illuminates the tragic losses that such objectifying gender stereotypes both inflicted and covered over, namely, the sacrifice of children born out of wedlock. The honor code condemned both sexual relations out of wedlock and the illegitimate children often born of such relations, as intrinsically shameful.[60] David I. Kertzer's important study of nineteenth-century foundling homes in Italy powerfully shows the role of the honor code, enforced by local Catholic

---

[51] See *id.*, at pp. 45–6.

[52] See *id.*, at pp. 163, 168.

[53] See *id.*, at p. 156.

[54] See David D. Gilmore, *Honour and Shame and the Unity of the Mediterranean*, at pp. 68–9.

[55] See J. K. Campbell, *Honour, Family, and Patronage*, at p. 265.

[56] See J. G. Peristiany, *Honour and Shame*, at pp. 42–53.

[57] See, for this view, Jane Schneider, "Of Vigilance and Virgins: Honor, Shame and Access to Resources in Mediterranean Societies," *Ethnology* 10:1–24 (1971). See also Jane Schneider and P. Schneider, *Culture and Political Economy in Western Sicily*.

[58] See, for this view, Sherry B. Ortner, "The Virgin and the State," in Sherry B. Ortner, *The Politics and Erotics of Culture* (Boston: Beacon Press, 1996).

[59] See, in general, David I. Kertzer and Richard F. Saller, eds., *The Family in Italy*.

[60] See David D. Gilmore, ed., *Honor and Shame and the Unity of the Mediterranean*, at p. 110.

priests and the police, in bullying unwed mothers to abandon children to these homes and sometimes effectively imprisoning them in such homes as compulsory wet nurses.[61] If a man refused or was unable to marry the woman he impregnated, "it might be considered within the women's family members' rights to kill him. Italy, in fact, has a two thousand year history of just such crimes of honor."[62] Under the Italian code of honor, so concerned with appearances, the illegitimate offspring of such unions could not exist; hiding the pregnancy of an unwed mother by placing the child anonymously in a foundling home preserved the honor of the family. The consequences for the babies were usually death. In Naples, for example,

"Of the 1,835 babies remaining in the ospizio, only 74 (4 percent) lived to see their first birthday. The babies died of starvation, intestinal disorders, respiratory ailments, and other infectious diseases."[63]

Families sometimes protested such separations in terms of their "infinite grief," robbing a mother "of the dearest object of her heart,"[64] suggesting traumatizing emotional losses that must have been widespread. But such losses, consistent with the political psychology of patriarchy, were often not acknowledged but covered over with gender-stereotypical idealizations, as of the foundlings in Naples, as "children of the Madonna,"[65] most of whom, as we have seen, in fact died. Meanwhile, their real mothers, if they were wet nurses in the foundling homes, were "treated as livestock."[66]

The atrocity of such patriarchal practices rest on such mythological idealizations in terms of gender stereotypes, denying the personal feeling and voice of the persons most afflicted by such stereotypes. The high rates of both illegitimacy and abandonment of infants during this period were common knowledge[67] yet the underlying emotional trauma and loss could be given no voice and weight. In consequence, even the few public critics of the system in the nineteenth century, like Jessie White Mario, denounced the idea that mothers should nurse their own children.[68]

The Italian system of infant abandonment, echoing the abandonment of Oedipus, illustrates a larger point about the power of idealizing gender

---

[61] See David I. Kertzer, *Sacrificed for Honor: Italian Infant Abandonment and the Politics of Reproductive Control* (Boston: Beacon Press, 1993).

[62] See *id.*, p. 26.

[63] See *id.*, p. 125.

[64] See *id.*, p. 56.

[65] See *id.*, pp. 107, 122.

[66] See *id.*, p. 148.

[67] See *id.*, p. 55.

[68] See *id.*, pp. 132–3.

stereotypes over the men and women subject to the structural injustice of patriarchy. The unjust power of such stereotypes requires a supporting political psychology that must in its nature bury the personal emotions and feelings of traumatic loss that the hegemonic power of such stereotypes requires. But the Italian code of honor imposes such losses pervasively in the relations of both parents to children and adults to one another because it preposterously imposes gender idealizations, rationalizing the hierarchy of patriarchy, which deny human subjectivity and connection, including personal feeling, desire, and voice. The men and women who conform their lives to such stereotypes, perforce accept, as in the nature of things, the traumatizing separations that patriarchy requires for its stability: parents from children, siblings from one another, men from men, women from women, and, of course, men from women.

The nerve of the issue, under the Italian code of honor, is the stereotypical control by men of women's sexuality, effectively dehumanizing them as without personal conscience, conviction, feeling, or voice of moral persons and agents. We need to examine more closely the significance for personal relations of such patterns of mythological idealization of loss, exemplified, as we have seen, by "the children of the madonna." For example, it is a familiar psychological observation about Italian families, in particular, Southern Italian families, that there is an unusually close continuing bond between mothers and sons, one that has been taken to refute the alleged universality of the Oedipus Complex (Italian heterosexual boys do not, on this view, separate from their mothers in the way that resolution of the Oedipus Complex classically requires).[69] But the Italian idealization of mothers (on the model of the madonna) may no more describe reality than calling foundlings "children of the madonna." Such idealization mythologizes mothers as not only lacking a sexual self or voice, but as engaged in a total maternal devotion to their sons that demands the sacrifice of whatever self she has. It does not bring any realism or sense of justice to women's perspectives, as persons, on their roles as mothers. Rather, it looks on mothering as romantic fantasy, not as an exercise of practical reason and intelligence, and ascribes to it, as an ideal, the crippling character (for mothers and children) of what Adrienne Rich observed and criticized in the "maternal altruism . . . universally approved and supported by women."[70] On this view, Italian women, as mothers, attain patriarchal privilege, as

---

[69] See, for this argument, Anne Parsons, "Is the Oedipus Complex Universal? A South Italian 'Nuclear Complex'," in Robert Hunt, ed., *Personalities and Cultures: Readings in Psychological Anthropology* (Garden City, NY: The Natural History Press, 1967), at pp. 352–99.

they have since Roman times, to the extent they impart to their sons their sexist privileges,[71] which includes not attending to the emotional and sexual life and voice of women, including their mothers. Southern Italian husbands and fathers thus spend little time at home with their wives, seeking friendship with other men outside the home; and boys gravitate to other groups of boys outside the home. The Southern Italian idealization of women thus covers a double loss, the breaking of personal relationships not only to their sons, but to their husbands as well.[72] Appearances to the contrary notwithstanding, the patriarchal psychology of the *Oedipus Tyrannus* operates with full force both in parent–child and husband–wife relationships.

The honor code, thus understood, is held in place by a system of physical and psychological violence triggered by deviance from its demands; such external demands enter into the psyches of men and women through their loss of protesting voice and their consequent vulnerability to shaming by any appearance of deviation from the honor code and the expression of such shaming in violence, whether physical or psychological. I call the associated conception of manhood 'patriarchal manhood'. The psychology of such shaming is in conflict with a democratic ethics of reciprocity based on the free and equal voice of all persons, an ethics that expresses itself in ideals of equal respect as the foundation of friendship and love expressive of free and equal voice. The requirements of this ethics enters into our psyches through the experience of love and respect consistent with its demands, and shows itself in guilt and remorse when one culpably violates the demands of equal respect and the forms of love it makes possible.[73] I call the associated conception of manhood 'democratic manhood'. Both the honor code and its psychology of shaming are in fundamental conflict with this ethics and its psychology because the shaming demands of honor enter into our psyches through a violent suppression of voice that is condemned by an ethics of equal respect. Indeed, the power of the political psychology of honor must in large part derive from the degree to which it succeeds in marginalizing or suppressing that part of our moral psychology that rejects its demands. Conversely, a psychology awakened to the demands of equal respect (as through the experience of a love based on free and equal voice) may funda-

---

[70] See Adrienne Rich, *Of Woman Born: Motherhood as Experience and Institution*, 10th anniversary, edn. (New York: W.W. Norton, 1986), at p. 213.

[71] On Roman women, see Judith P. Hallett, *Fathers and Daughters in Roman Society: Women and the Elite Family* (Princeton, NJ: Princeton University Press, 1984).

[72] I am indebted for this point to conversations with Carol Gilligan and Donald Levy.

[73] I explore both this ethics and its associated moral psychology in David A. J. Richards, *A Theory of Reasons for Action* (Oxford: Clarendon Press, 1971).

mentally question the codes and psychology of honor theretofore taken to be axiomatic. Verdi's development as an artist powerfully, I believe, exemplifies a man torn between patriarchal and democratic manhood.

## Verdi's Life and Psychology

It would be a category mistake to confuse the expressive powers of Verdi's art, which must be taken seriously in its own terms as the complex music drama it is, with matters of Verdi's own biography or psychology. But it is also a mistake to isolate the interpretive discussion of Verdi's art from a background and life which so powerfully illuminates the development of an artistic gift to come to terms so powerfully with a tragic personal and political psychology of traumatic breaks in relationships so rarely discussed, let along represented; in particular, why Verdi was so remarkably sensitive to the impact of the honor code on intimate life. Verdi, as we shall see, knew traumatic separations at painful first hand; he also experienced an unusually close working relationship to a creative woman and lover, a relationship that gave him a resonance for his remarkable creative experiments in traumatized voice (a point developed further in chapter 8).

Verdi's early life was marked from age ten by separation from his parents, Carlo and Luigia Verdi, living in a different town to secure a better education and develop his musical talents; "he seems to have remained close to his parents in feeling, to his mother in particular, while growing away from them in other ways."[74] By seventeen, Verdi lived at the home of his second father, Antonio Barezzi, who was financially to support Verdi's further education later in Milan.[75] Barezzi's love of music and anticlericalism attracted Verdi and further separated him from the emotional world of his parents.[76] Verdi married Barezzi's daughter, Margherita, a talented singer, when they both were 22; they had two children, a boy and a girl. Within a few years, the children died from unknown infections, to be followed shortly by the death of their mother; Verdi was inconsolable;[77] his "great sorrow was not forgotten, but buried."[78]

Verdi first met the prima donna Giuseppina Strepponi at the time of *Nabucco* in 1842, when she performed Abigaille. Streponni – then 26 –

---

[74] John Rosselli, *The Life of Verdi* (Cambridge: Cambridge University Press, 2000), p. 16.

[75] See John Rosselli, *The Life of Verdi* (Cambridge: Cambridge University Press, 2000, pp. 15–25.

[76] See *id.*, at p. 17.

[77] See *id.*, at pp. 26–7, 30.

already had behind her a tumultuous career. The daughter of a composer, herself a trained musician, Strepponi had early become the family bread-winner; as a soprano able to play both the tragic and gentler heroines of Bellini and Donizetti she was a great, immediate success. Her life as head of a family, independent woman, and opera star put her under great pressure. She mismanaged both her career and personal life disastrously. By the first performance of *Nabucco* her voice was in ruins, which compelled her early retirement from the stage. A chief cause of the wreckage of her voice was overwork as a singer during which she went through a series of pregnancies – at least three, possibly four. She had an illegitimate son, whom she had brought up in Florence by her maid, and two illegitimate daughters immediately placed with working-class foster-families, the elder after a stay in an orphanage.[79] Strepponi, after her retirement, became a voice teacher in Paris. She and Verdi began their affair during his long stay there in 1847–9, and they did not marry until 1859. During this period (after leaving Paris), Verdi lived openly with Strepponi in or near his home town, Busseto, in which their relationship scandalized the community, including his parents. Verdi "did the unthinkable, breaking off relations with his parents . . . , decid[ing] to cut himself off from his parents in January 1851, when he engaged the notary Ercolano Balestra to draw up a document of legal separation from them."[80] Verdi was later to write to his foster daughter in terms that bespeak the trauma of this period:

> "This being the case, neither your husband nor the Carraras can love and respect that family [the Verdis]; and you have an obligation to keep them as far away as possible and to avoid their disagreeable bickering and terrible sorrows. I know you will say: 'But *my Parents*', '*my blood relatives*', etc. etc. For the love of God, this is sick and stupid sentimentality, which can never produce anything good. Your husband adores you; your grandfather *loves* you. But you should never trust emotions too much."[81]

During this same period of the life together of Verdi and Strepponi, "a baby girl was born to unidentified parents who had her delivered . . . to the turn-stile for abandoned babies at the Ospedale Maggiore in Cremona";[82] "it appears possible that she was Giuseppina Strepponi's daughter."[83] The

---

[78] Frank Walker, *The Man Verdi* (London: J.M. Dent, 1962), at p. 36.

[79] See John Rosselli, *The Life of Verdi*, at pp. 65–9.

[80] Mary Jane Phillips-Matz, *Verdi: A Biography* (Oxford: Oxford University Press, 1993), at pp. 278–9.

[81] *Id.*, p. 692

earlier discussed Italian practice of the abandonment of illegitimate children, requiring heart-breaking separations to preserve the public image of family honor, may have touched Verdi as intimately during his relationship to Strepponi as it had touched her before. Verdi's tragic feeling for father–daughter relationships in his operas may arise from a bleeding psychic wound of remorse he could not otherwise acknowledge.

The relationship between Verdi and Strepponi, both before and after their marriage, suggests unusual intimacy, free voice, and equality. In a revealing letter to Verdi during one of their separations, Strepponi wrote "without you I am a body without a soul."[84] Her musical experience, as a prima donna, may have collaboratively shaped the remarkable innovations in expressive musical voice in the operas Verdi writes in the wake of their sexual and emotional relationship (*Luisa Miller, Stiffelio, Rigoletto, La Traviata, Il Trovatore*):

> "And you haven't written anything yet? You see! You haven't got your poor Nuisance in a corner of the room, curled up in an armchair, to say: 'That's beautiful' – 'That's *not*' – 'Stop' – 'Repeat that' – 'That's original.' Now, without this poor Nuisance, God punishing you, making you wait and rack your brains, before opening up all the little pigeon-holes and allowing your magnificent musical ideas to emerge."[85]

Another letter speaks further of their communicative intimacy:

> "Our youth is over; nevertheless we are still the whole world to each other and watch with high compassion all the human puppets rushing about, climbing up, slipping down, fighting, hiding, reappearing – all to try to put themselves at the head, or among the first few places, of the social masquerade."[86]

A passionate note during another of their separations concluded: "Come soon, I desire you as I desire God. A kiss on your heart."[87] Strepponi in one of her diaries spoke of Verdi as a kind of savior: "I wished to become *a new woman*, worthily to respond to the honour I received in becoming his wife, and to the benefits I receive continually from this man."[88] It speaks about the marriage and underlying intimate relationship that it survived Verdi's

---

[82] See *id.*, at p. 289.

[83] See *id.*

[84] Frank Walker, *The Man Verdi*, p. 208.

[85] *Id.*, p. 209.

[86] *Id.*, p. 213.

[87] Mary Jane Phillips-Matz, *Verdi*, p. 326.

[88] See Frank Walker, *The Man Verdi*, pp. 403–4.

affair in the 1870s with the singer, Teresa Stoltz,[89] despite Strepponi's humiliation and heart break and Verdi's threat of suicide ("This woman stays, or I blow my brains out"[90]). Remarkably, Stoltz remained a frequent presence in their household as a family friend and guest to the end of their lives.

Verdi's close friend and librettist of *I Masnadieri*, Andrea Maffei, wrote to his wife, Clara, of Verdi's "adamantine temper"[91] and Strepponi of his "iron nature",[92] his "character stern, decided and very reserved, as he is."[93] Verdi himself wrote to Clara Maffei of his psychology in dealing with the demands of audiences: "I wore armour, and, ready to be shot, cried, 'Let's fight'."[94] Verdi's armored sense of personal honor showed itself in his sensitivity to personal insult throughout his life[95] It also showed itself in reticence about his own suffering: "Maybe my way is a strange way of feeling: but I believe that silence is the only comfort for great sorrows."[96] When he did speak of these matters, his words were dark: "after all, in life all is death! What exists"; "life is sorrow"; "life is the stupidest thing, and worse still, it's pointless"; "misfortune rules the world." He came to believe in "fate", and fate was not benign.[97] When he spoke of his feelings, he observed: "my mind is black, always black."[98] His relations to other men, even those devoted to him, like the great conductor, Mariani, took the form of manipulative control, even, at times, cruelty (for example, over Stoltz, who had been engaged to Mariani) and unjust rejection.[99] In supervising his farming estate at Sant'Agata (near Bussetto), Verdi was "a natural autocrat."[100] He insisted on living a wholly private life there where his ancestors had long lived, but "there was, all the same, a price to pay; Strepponi paid most of it."[101] Strepponi herself referred ironically to Verdi as "my lord and master"[102] and complained of his rages.[103] The affair with Stoltz suggests a patriarchally motivated blindness to the feelings of Strepponi.

---

[89] See Frank Walker, *The Man Verdi*, pp. 393–446.

[90] Frank Walker, *The Man Verdi*, p. 436.

[91] *Id.*, p. 125.

[92] *Id.*, p. 272.

[93] *Id.*, p. 342.

[94] Mary Jane Phillips-Matz, *Verdi*, p. 674.

[95] See, on this point, *id.*, at pp. 255, 460–1, 488–9.

[96] *Id.*, p. 682.

[97] See John Rosselli, *The Life of Verdi*, p. 30.

[98] Frank Walker, *The Man Verdi*, p. 181.

[99] See Frank Walker, *id.*, pp. 283–392.

[100] John Rosselli, *The Life of Verdi*, p. 128.

[101] John Rosselli, *The Life of Verdi*, p. 82.

Verdi's life and psychology show resistance to some aspects of Italian patriarchal traditions, and acceptance of others; his life, as we have seen, was filled with painfully traumatic separations – from his first wife and children, from his parents early in his life and from them and his community later over Strepponi, perhaps even from an illegitimate child by Strepponi. Intellectually and politically, Verdi was very much a man in the tradition of Italian Enlightenment thought of Beccaria, whose brilliant eighteenth-century criticism of the inhumanity of criminal justice (including the death penalty) was pathbreaking.[104] Verdi, born in a part of Italy then under the rule of France, associated these humane values as well with the French Enlightenment; and he thus prophetically worried, in the aftermath of the Franco-Prussian war, about the baneful influence of German militaristic culture on Italy:

> "Our literary men and politicians praise the knowledge, the science and even (God forgive them!) the arts of these conquerors. But if they examined them less superficially they would see that there still runs in their veins the ancient Gothic blood, that they are immeasurably proud, hard and intolerant, despisers of everything that is not German, and of limitless rapacity. Men with heads, but no hearts; a strong but uncivilized race. And that king who is always talking of God and Providence, and with the help of these is destroying the best part of Europe! He thinks he is destined to reform the conduct and punish the vices of the modern world!!!! A fine sort of missionary! Attila of old (another missionary of the same sort) drew back before the majesty of the capital of the ancient world; but this one is about to bombard the capital of the modern world . . . I should have liked a more generous line of politics, and the payment of a debt of gratitude. A hundred thousand of our men could perhaps have saved France. In any case, I should have preferred to sign peace, after defeat beside the French, to this intertia that will make us despised one day. We shan't avoid a European war, and we shall be devoured. Not tomorrow – but it will come!"[105]

Verdi's love of French Enlightenment ideas and culture included its advanced views on women. Verdi had read and been influenced by Madame de Stael[106] and considered writing an opera based on a feminist play of George Sand.[107] Aristocratic women, some of them friends of Verdi, had played an important role in the Risorgimento.[108] His most important inti-

---

[102] Frank Walker, *The Man Verdi*, p. 246.

[103] *Id.*, pp. 400–1, 403–4.

[104] See Cesare Beccaria, *On Crimes and Punishments*, Henry Paolucci, trans. (New York: Library of Liberal Arts, 1963 (originally published, 1764). For commentary on this period, see Franco Venturi, *Italy and the Enlightenment* (London: Longman, 1972).

[105] Frank Walker, *The Man Verdi*,,p. 279.

mate companion was Strepponi, a remarkably independent, highly intelligent, well-read, and spirited nineteenth-century Italian woman – artistically, economically, sexually. But, feminism, as a political and legal struggle for the voice and rights of women, was relatively undeveloped in nineteenth-century Italy, certainly avoiding matters of women's rights to marriage and to sexual autonomy that were under active discussion in France and elsewhere;[109] Strepponi's gratitude to Verdi for making her "a new woman" by marrying her must be understood against this Italian background. Verdi, who had resided for long periods in Paris (his affair with Strepponi notably begins there) and always aligned himself creatively and politically with French as opposed to German culture,[110] lived in a multicultural world, challenging Italian practices that were scandalized by his open relationship with Strepponi. Verdi and Strepponi withdrew into the wonderful private estate and farm that Verdi built for them at St. Agata (near Bussetto) from his growing royalties, a dream-like arcadian world of gardens, lakes, and exotic trees and plants which nurtured their intimate artistic collaboration over the years and also enabled Verdi to play the role of gentleman-farmer.

On the other hand, Verdi was, as we have seen, very much an Italian man of the nineteenth century with his own distinctive values of armored honor and holding some rather conventional views of women's roles (in late life, he did not approve of women taking courses of study and saw no other profession for them than medicine, "But only to tend women").[111] Arrigo Boito, Verdi's most brilliant librettist, paid tribute to him after his death appropriately in laudatory patriarchal terms, remembering:

> "the Maestro's conversation, the patriarchal table with the customary dishes, strictly according to ritual, the piercing sweetness of the air and of that great Palazzo Doria, of which he was the Doge."[112]

---

[106] *Id.*, p. 43. On Madame de Stael's provocative challenge to the state of Italian opera and its impact, see Gary Tomlinson, "Italian Romanticism and Italian Opera: An Essay in Their Affinities," *19th-Century Music* X/1 (Summer 1986), at pp. 43–60, at pp. 43–4.

[107] Julian Budden, *The Operas of Verdi, Volume 2*, p. 431.

[108] See, on these points, Geneviève Fraisse and Michelle Perrot, eds., *A History of Women in the West vol IV: Emerging Feminism from Revolution to World Was* (Cambridge, MA: Belknap Press of Harvard University Press, 1993), at pp. 336, 469, 477–8, 485–9, 497; Donald Meyer, *Sex and Power: The Rise of Women in America, Russia, Sweden, and Italy* (Middletown, CT: Wesleyan University Press, 1987), at pp. 3, 121.

[109] See Donald Meyer, *Sex and Power: The Rise of Women in America, Russia, Sweden, and Italy* (Middletown, CT: Wesleyan University Press, 1987), at pp. 131, 149, 449–52.

[110] See Mary Jane Phillips-Matz, *Verdi*, at p. 578.

[111] Cited at De Van, *Verdi's Theater*, p. 187.

Verdi contained within himself both resistance to and acceptance of the tragedy of patriarchy, which means he contained within himself the full range of its emotions. Anthony Storr put the point precisely:

"When a composer does succeed in penetrating the hidden regions of the psyche, he not only encounters his deepest emotions but also ways of bringing these emotions into consciousness by converting them into those ordered structures of sound which we call music."[113]

It is against this background of a life lived in contradiction and divided consciousness that we can now turn to the closer examination of Verdi's achievement as a musical dramatist obsessed, as he was, with understanding and giving artistic expression to the tragedy of patriarchy. No event may more fruitfully have divided Verdi's consciousness than the earlier discussed response of his parents and community to his relationship to Strepponi after they move to Bussetto. In his celebrated letter to the person he came to regard as his second father, Antonio Barezzi, explaining his anger at this response, Verdi appeals to liberal values:

"It is my custom never to interfere, unless I am asked, in other people's business and I expect others not to interfere in mine. All this gossip, grumbling and disapprobation arises from that. I have the expect in my own country the liberty of action that is respected even in less civilized places. Judge for yourself, severely, if you will, but coolly and dispassionately: What harm is there if I live in isolation? . . . What harm is here in this? . . .

There I've laid bare to you my opinions, my actions, my wishes, my public life, I would almost say, and since we are by way of making revelations, I have no objection to raising the curtain that veils the mysteries contained within four walls, and telling you about my private life. I have nothing to hide. In my house there lives a lady, free, independent, a lover like myself of solitude, possessing a fortune that shelters her from all need. Neither I nor she owes to anyone an account of our actions? What affairs? What ties? What claims I have on her and she on me? Who knows whether she is or is not my wife? And if she is, who knows what the particular reasons are for not making the fact public? Who knows whether that is a good thing or a bad one? Why should it not be a good thing? And even if it is a bad thing, who has the right to ostracize us? I will say this, however: in my house she is entitled to as much respect as myself – more even; and no one is allowed to forget that on any account. And finally she has every right, both on account of her conduct and her character, to the consideration she never fails to show to others.

With this long rigmarole I mean to say no more than that I demand liberty of action for myself, because all men have a right to it, and because I am by

---

[112] Frank Walker, *The Man Verdi*, at p. 509.

[113] Anthony Storr, *Music and the Mind* (New York: Ballantine Books, 1992), at pp. 186–7.

nature averse to acting according to other people's ideas, and that you, who at heart are so good, so just and so generous, should not let yourself be influenced, and absorb the ideas of a town which – it must be said! – in time past did not consider me worthy to be its organist, and now complains, wrongly and perversely, about my actions and affairs." [114]

Verdi protests the injustice of such external demands because they censoriously impose themselves without any attention to or understanding of the underlying values of intimate relationship. His liberal indignation may have challenged him more deeply to understand and represent *both* the external demands of the patriarchal code of honor (centering on the virginity of women) *and* the internal subjective emotional desolation that it inflicts on both women and men. Two years earlier, in terms that echo Victor Hugo's *Preface to Cromwell* (calling for representation of the grotesque),[115] Verdi had angrily insisted in such external/internal terms that Rigoletto must be

"ugly and hunchbacked!! Why? . . . I think it splendid to show this character as outwardly deformed and ridiculous, and inwardly passionate and full of love. I chose the subject for these very qualities and these original strokes; if they are removed I can no longer set it to music." [116]

Verdi's very imagination, as a creative musical artist, could only be fired by its expressive powers in appropriately dramatizing the external/internal split between conventional external demands, unjustly imposed by the gender stereotypes enforced by the code of honor, and its devastating emotional desolation in the lives of persons. The development of his tragic art frames this split with the growing expressive power of his musical art over his career in ways that enter deeply into the psyche.

---

[114] Frank Walker, *The Man Verdi,*, pp. 204–5.

[115] See Victor Hugo, *The Dramas Complete and Unabridged of Victor Hugo, Volume X, Oliver Cromwell*, translated by I. G. Burnham (Philadelphia: George Barrie & Son, 1896), at p. 75. Strikingly, *Rigoletto* is based on Hugo's play, *Le Roi S'Amuse*.

[116] John Rosselli, *The Life of Verdi*, at p. 93.

# Chapter 3

# Music as the Memory of Suppressed Voice in Verdi's Mature Operas

Verdi was not, of course, a political theorist of liberal democracy, but his art was acutely sensitive to the psychological dimensions of a longstanding problem within the theory and practice of political liberalism, namely, that tension between the normative demands of liberal democracy (rooted in the Lockean criticism of patriarchy) and patriarchal practices unjustly not subject to those demands. Liberalism begins in John Locke's rights-based defense of liberal constitutionalism against Robert Filmer's defense of absolute monarchy on grounds of patriarchalism.[1] But, since Mary Wollstonecraft,[2] Lockean political liberalism has been subject to reasonable criticism for its failure to carry its rights-based criticism of patriarchy as far as it should be carried, in particular, to the unjust sexist assumptions that abridge respect for human rights of women both in private and public life. Much of the criticism centers in contemporary discussions of political theory on the failure of political liberalism to subject to appropriate criticism the ways in which unjust gender stereotypes have naturalized forms of injustice to women in their ostensibly private sexual lives.[3] Even the most

---

[1] See, for the basic texts, John Locke, *Two Treatises of Government* edited by Peter Laslett (Cambridge: Cambridge University Press, 1960); Robert Filmer, *Patriarcha and Other Writings*, edited by Johann P. Sommerville (Cambridge: Cambridge University Press, 1991). On the Lockean foundations of democratic constitutionalism, see David A. J. Richards, *Foundations of American Constitutionalism* (New York: Oxford University Press, 1989).

[2] See Mary Wollstonecraft, *A Vindication of the Rights of Women*, in *The Works of Mary Wollstonecraft*, ed. Janet Todd and Marilyn Butler (1790; New York: New York University Press, 1989), 5:65–266. For commentary, see David A. J. Richards, *Women, Gays, and the Constitution: The Grounds for Feminism and Gay Rights in Culture and Law* (Chicago: University of Chicago Press, 1998), at pp. 63–72.

[3] See, for example, Carole Pateman, *The Sexual Contract* (Cambridge: Polity Press, 1988).

normatively cogent contemporary expression of political liberalism (that of John Rawls) has been subject to reasonable criticism on such grounds for its failure to take seriously injustices to women in family life.[4] The great interest of Verdi's art is its acute sensitivity to the personal and political psychology underlying this contradiction within the theory and practice of political liberalism, in particular, its roots in the patterns of family life that had largely been unjustly excluded from liberal criticism. His art explores the contradiction within liberalism as starting psychologically where political liberalism was least inclined to look, namely, in the relations of fathers and mothers to sons and daughters and men and women to one another in intimate life, precisely the areas that political liberalism had walled off from critical attention.

Verdi experienced this problem, as a patriot (like Aeschylus and Sophocles), in the struggles of nineteenth-century Italy to move from the patriarchal feudalism of its past to a form of national unity in service of political liberalism; but he also experienced it, as we have seen, as a boy in struggles with his own father, and as a man in similar struggles to defend his right to share his intimate life with a woman (Giuseppina Strepponi) condemned by the dominant honor code as contemptible and unworthy. He finds his distinctive voice as an artist in a series of operas (*Luisa Miller*, *Stiffelio*, *Rigoletto*, *Il Trovatore*, *La Traviata*) which explore the impact of the honor code centrally in such relations in intimate life, which he later develops, as we shall see, to embrace public life as well. The Italian struggles more starkly posed such tensions within political liberalism that were more easily ignored in more traditionally liberal societies (like Britain), because the patriarchal code of honor was still so conspicuously powerful in Italian society during the period of its transition to ostensibly liberal constitutional institutions. Verdi's artistic attention was thus arrested by the tensions between such patriarchal practices in intimate life and the political liberalism to which he and other Italians ostensibly aspired. The enduring value of Verdi's artistic exploration of this problem is the way in which he, unlike more optimistic political liberals of his and later periods, examines the problem forthrightly in terms of a structure of patriarchal practices that are for Verdi most centrally in play in private family relationships though in public life as well, and explores the tension between such practices and liberal principles in the terms of tragedy. A problem that many political liberals cannot even acknowledge is thus, for Verdi, the central problem within liberalism. The power of his art is that through it we are brought to an emotional knowledge of a problem we cannot otherwise acknowledge.

---

[4] See Susan Moller Okin, *Justice, Gender, and the Family* (New York: Basic Books, 1989).

Verdi offers a psychologically penetrating study of the psychic geography of the impact of such patriarchal institutions and idealizations on the lives of men and women, as children and as adults. If, as I have suggested, such idealizations cover loss, such a psychic geography may be as difficult to map as telling any truthful history that involves unspeakable trauma,[5] a difficulty heightened by the suppression of women's voices that, when free, demand that people acknowledge trauma in personal and political life. The Greek tragedians strikingly use the free voice of women to speak of trauma (Cassandra, Klytemnestra, Iphigenia), as women do when they speak in a free voice,[6] a free sexual voice which, however, has often elicited violent repression of the kind visited, for example, in the United States on Victoria Woodhull, Margaret Sanger, Emma Goldman, and Ida Wells-Barnett.[7] The great interest of Verdi's operas, from this perspective, is that its takes this territory of trauma as its subject matter, mapping the impact of the code of honor on a "a radical geography"[8] of the psyche, its traumatic impact on a range of intimate relations – both parents with children, sibling relations, and adults with one another (see chapters 5–7).

In his famous letter to Clara Maffei, chosen as the epigraph to this book, Verdi wrote of his interest as a creative artist, inspired by Shakespeare, in the invention of truth:

> "It may be a good thing to copy reality; but to invent reality is much much better.
>
> These three words: 'to invent reality', may look like a contradiction, but ask Papa! [Shakespeare]. Falstaff he may have found as he was; but he can hardly have found a villain as villainous as Iago, and never, never such angels as Cordelia, Imogene, Desdemona, etc., etc. And yet they are so very real!
>
> It's a fine thing to imitate reality, but it is photography, not painting."[9]

The invention of truth is, for Verdi (following Shakespeare), a point about the power of great art truthfully to represent the emotional complexities of human psychology.[10] Our psyche is defined as "breath . . . ; hence, life (identified with or indicated by the breath); the animating principle . . . , the source of all vital activities, rational or irrational . . . , in distinction from

---

[5] See, on this point, Dominick LaCapra, *Writing History, Writing Trauma* (Baltimore: The Johns Hopkins University Press, 2001).

[6] See Judith Herman, *Trauma and Recovery* (New York: BasicBooks, 1997).

[7] For further discussion, see David A. J. Richards, *Women, Gays, and the Constitution*, at ch. 4.

[8] See Carol Gilligan, *The Birth of Pleasure*, at p. 3.

[9] Franz Werfel and Paul Stefan, eds., *Verdi: The Man in His Letters*, Edward Downes, trans. (New York: Vienna House, 1942), at p. 336.

its material vehicle."[11] A human psychology, thus understood, must take seriously the living of a human life from an inward sense of our emotions, consciousness and self-consciousness, bodies, and, of course, voice, including the gap between our feelings and knowledge of our feelings.[12] Anthony Damasio's *The Feeling of What Happens* importantly models our psychological complexity in terms of the metaphor of our experience of the unity in complexity of melody, harmony, and polyphony in music, "the music of behavior";[13] "you are the music while the music lasts."[14] Music, however, may not just be a metaphor for our psychological complexity. It may, as it is in Verdi's art, sometimes be our only way into feelings rooted in suppressed voice we have but are not aware we have, and indeed offer us a complex and subtle cultural form through which we are brought to self-knowledge of important emotions we hold within our psyches and how and why it is so difficult to acknowledge them. We hear in such music a voice we recognize as a voice culturally suppressed in ourselves and experience a resonance for a voice that at least questions or can question such loss as the necessary foundation of our identity as men or women living under democracy. The invention of truth, in the sense Verdi means it, is the use of art's expressive fictionality truthfully to represent this inward sense of the complexities of our psyches.

However, Verdi was, unlike Shakespeare, neither a playwright nor a poet, but a dramatic musician, who always closely collaborated with poets who usually adapted already well-known plays to Verdi's operatic purposes. Not only were the plays very carefully chosen by Verdi (often with the multilingual Strepponi's collaborative help), but he was often a relentless taskmaster in working very closely with his poets to get precisely the kind of text that made most sense to him as the basis for his music dramas.[15]

---

[10] See, for illuminating discussion of this point, Anselm Gerhard, *The Urbanization of Opera: Music Theater in Paris in the Nineteenth Century* Mary Whittall, trans. (Chicago: University of Chicago Press, 1998), at pp. 412–14.

[11] *The Compact Edition of the Oxford English Dictionary*, vol. II (Oxford: Oxford University Press, 1971), at p. 1549.

[12] For a suggestive account, see Antonio R. Damasio, *Descartes' Error: Emotion, Reason, and the Human Brain* (New York: Avon Books, 1994); *The Feeling of What Happens: Body and Emotion in the Making of Consciousness* (San Diego: A Harvest Book, 1999).

[13] *Id.*, at p. 86.

[14] *Id.*, at p. 191.

[15] On these points, see the magisterial three-volume study, Julian Budden, *The Operas of Verdi, Vol. 1, From Oberto to Rigoletto* (New York: Oxford University Press, 1973); *The Operas of Verdi, 2, from Il Trovatore to La Forza Del Destino* (New York: Oxford University Press, 1978); *The Opera of Verdi, Vol. 3, From Don Carlos to Falstaff* (New York: Oxford University Press, 1981). See also Gilles De Van, *Verdi's Theater*, at pp. 61–87.

While sometimes the plays were tragic masterpieces (Shakespeare's *Macbeth* and *Othello* and Schiller's *Don Carlos*), more often they were romantic melodramas about romantic heroes and villains. Luigi Dallapiccola has forcefully made the case about these melodramas that:

> "at the time of the Italian melodrama, the libretto developed a style which – from a literary point of view – was usually without merit: it had nothing to do with the spoken language and, confined to librettos, was brought to life only by the music with which it was associated."

From Trent, in July 1906, Busoni wrote to his wife:

> "To have company for a few hours, I have bought Verdi's *Un ballo in maschera*. It is a strong work, violent, but of great power and plastic quality. Some of its moments, it seems to me, belong to the best that Verdi has written. But the libretto! And the verses!
>
> *Sento l'orma dei passi spietati* . . . I hear the footprints of ruthless steps . . .
>
> Have you ever heard anything like this?
>
> How could one fail to agree with these words? But the fact is that Verdi endeavored, above all, to make his words a springboard for a dramatic situation."[16]

Dallapiccola is not making De Van's valid point about the transition of Verdi from melodrama to music drama, since he is exploring how a work (which De Van regards as a music drama) has been musically transformed (in ways De Van's work clarifies) into such a drama from a text which, as a theatrical text, was a melodrama.[17] Another way of putting Dallapiccola's point is that Verdi's expressive powers as a musical dramatist sometimes turn plays that are at best melodramas into tragic masterpieces; to wit, Antonio Garcia Gutierrez's *El Trovador* into *Il Trovatore*,[18] Alexandre Dumas's *La Dame aux camelias* into *La Traviata*,[19] Victor Hugo's *Le Roi s'amuse* into *Rigoletto*,[20] and Augustin Eugene Scribe's *Gustave III* into *Un Ballo in Maschera*.[21]

These expressive musical powers spanned a long career, as Julian Budden authoritatively observed, "starting with a technique cruder and

---

[16] Luigi Dallapiccola, "Words and Music in Italian Nineteenth-Century Opera," in William Weaver and Martin Chusid, eds., *The Verdi Companion* (New York: W.W. Norton, 1979), pp. 193–215, at p. 195.

[17] See Gilles De Van, *Verdi's Theater*.

[18] See, for commentary, Julian Budden, *The Operas of Verdi, Vol. 2*, at pp. 58–112.

[19] See *id.*, at pp. 114–166.

[20] See, for commenary, Julian Budden, *The Operas of Verdi, Vol. 1*, at pp. 476–510.

[21] See, for commentary, Julian Budden, *The Operas of Verdi, Vol. 2*, at pp. 360–423.

more primitive than that of any young composer of comparative stature" to "a refinement of musical craftsmanship and thought that has never been surpassed and rarely equalled."[22] My argument in this book is that the remarkable development of these musical powers, which sometimes transformed melodramas into musical tragedies, centered on Verdi's innovations in musical voice progressively to give more unsparing and subtle expression to the psychic geography of the disassociated, buried emotions, rooted in the suppression of voice in relationship, which underlie what I have called the tragedy of patriarchy. What Verdi added to the Shakespearean invention of psychological truth was his invention of musically expressive voice for the psychological truth of trauma and disassociated emotion. If our psyche indeed centers in voice, we may say that Verdi's artistic powers, as a musician of expressive voice, invent truth in the sense of giving us an inward sense of the voice, distortions of voice, and suppressions of voice of the emotions of the men and women who live under the tragedy of patriarchy. His musical innovations included both how he wrote for the human voice and the growing sophistication of his orchestral voice, both in service of his expressive purposes. What makes Verdi's art so inventive, in the sense he meant that term, is that he is thus giving remarkably perceptive expression to the effects of trauma before we had any good psychological theory of the effects of trauma that we now know crucially include emotional disassociation from traumatic memories and the inability to speak about them.[23] Verdi invents a distinctive kind of musical voice (both human and orchestral) precisely to give expression to the buried emotions arising from traumatic breaks in relationship (suppressing memory and voice) required to sustain patriarchy, including its impact on the full range of human relationships (parents to children, siblings, adults to one another). These emotions include the trauma of a woman's brutal separation both from her mother and son (Azucena in Verdi's *Il Trovatore*), a former courtesan's wrenching agony at her separations (including facing her death) from the only man who touched her life with love (Violetta in *La Traviata*), and a hunchback father's traumatic loss of the daughter he desperately loved and fatally misunderstood as a woman and person (*Rigoletto*). The melodramas, on which these operas are based, are, at best, sentimental, at worst, laughably overwrought. Verdi's musical art here, as elsewhere, confronts us with the lived emotional experience of tragic catastrophe under patriarchy. What is psychologically

---

[22] Julian Budden, *The Operas of Verdi, Vol. 3*, p. 531. See, for an illuminating study of this development, Gilles De Van, *Verdi's Theater*.

[23] See Bessel A. van der Kolk et al., *Traumatic Stress*, at pp. 279–302, 565.

astonishing in Verdi's mature art is the way he shows us this process and its consequences in the full range of such personal and political relationships, as he surgically anatomizes how the patriarchal code of honor requires that all such relationships be traumatically broken, as we shall see in depth in chapters 5–7, the heart of the argument of this book.

For Verdi, the code of honor was, in its nature, a political system – fundamental to the family, politics, and religion – that enforced its demands by forms of physical and psychological violence directed by men and women at anyone who deviated from its demands. Its psychological force derived from the way in which its demands were developmentally inscribed into the human psyche by traumatic separations that suppress voice precisely at the points where such voice might reasonably contest the justice of the honor code's demands. The revelatory power of Verdi's art for men may derive from the fact that this process of traumatic breaks in relationship and suppressed voice starts earlier in boys than girls in a developmentally vulnerable period,[24] laying the foundation for a male psychology based in the consequences of trauma: disassociated feelings, and loss of voice and memory.

In the terms I developed in chapter 2 in discussing Attic tragedy, such loss of personal voice takes the form of identification with the terms of the required gender stereotype, including the propensity to violence whenever those terms are at threat. Such codes of male honor did not always take the precise form of the Mediterranean honor code earlier discussed; under Icelandic honor codes, for example, "virginity was a non-issue," as men not women were placed on a pedestal.[25] But such codes pervasively enforce gender idealizations in the form of "the widespread presence of something recognizable as the heroic ethic from the cold North Atlantic to the Arabian desert."[26] Their force rests on trauma and disassociation, an armored psychology that, through identification, becomes prone to violence against any threat to the gender idealizations that sustain the structural injustice of patriarchy and the related injustices (religious and ethnic intolerance, etc.) to which such gender idealizations are often linked. Response to such threats includes, as in the early republican period in the United States[27] and in the American antebellum South,[28] practices of duelling triggered by insults to male honor. James Gilligan's important study of violent crimi-

---

[24] See, on these points, Carol Gilligan, *The Birth of Pleasure*.

[25] See William Ian Miller, *Bloodtaking and Peacemaking: Feud, Law, and Society in Saga Iceland* (Chicago: University of Chicago Press, 1990), at p. 305.

[26] See William Ian Miller, *Humiliation and Other Essays on Honor, Social Discomfort, and Violence* (Ithaca: Cornall University Press, 1993), at p. 196.

[27] See Joanne B. Freeman, *Affairs of Honor: National Politics in the New Republic* (New Haven: Yale University Press, 2001).

nals shows us how alive this culture of insult to manhood and violence remains today,[29] and Chris Hedges, Mark Juergensmeyer, and others show how powerful it remains as the trigger to ethnic violence and genocide in the former Yugoslavia and elsewhere, including the highly gendered feelings of patriarchal humiliation that motivate the resort to terroristic violence by Islamic fundamentalists.[30]

Iphigenia's shift in voice from loving daughter to identification with a mythology of gender (the rationale for her own murder and for the unjust war against Troy) displays this process clearly. Verdi's mature art focuses obsessively on giving increasingly precise expression to such shifts as voice, the shift always being one from intimate personal voice to the voice of armored identification with the requirements of one's gender role, the latter often marked by some form of violence (whether against one's lover or one's own child or, in the case of women, one's self), a violence portrayed in later works as linked to larger patterns of religious and racial intolerance. The power of Verdi's art for men is thus precisely that it enables them to hear suppressed emotions, voices, memories, and such shifts in voice, and gives a resonance for emotions and a voice and memory not otherwise available.

If I am right about this, operatic art can, unlike the dramas or novels on which it is based, have its own distinctive revelatory power to explore certain emotional dimensions and psychological truths.[31] It misses the expressive point of opera, as Harriet clearly does in E. M. Forster's *Where Angels Fear to Tread*, to flatten the musically expressive powers of the performance she attends in an Italian town of Donizetti's *Lucia di Lammermoor* to an angry, colonialist search for the Walter Scott plot on which it is based.[32] For Harriet, the expressive freedom of an Italian audience in responding to this great opera makes them "ridiculous babies"[33] and the art "not even

---

[28] See Bertram Wyatt-Brown, *Southern Honor: Ethics and Behavior in the Old South* (New York: Oxford University Press, 1982).

[29] See James Gilligan, *Violence: Reflections on a National Epidemic* (New York: Vintage Books, 1997).

[30] See Chris Hedges, *War Is a Force That Gives Us Meaning* (New York: Public Affairs, 2002); Mark Juergensmeyer, *Terror in the Mind of God: The Global Rise of Religious Violence* (Berkeley: University of California Press, 2000), especially at pp. 78, 154, 161–2, 182–207; Amin Maalouf, *In the Name of Identity: Violence the the Need to Belong*, Barbara Bray, trans. (New York: Arcade Publishing, 2000); Michael Ignatieff, *The Warrior's Honor: Ethnic War and the Modern Conscience* (New York: Henry Holt and Company, 1997).

[31] For a classic study of the powers of opera as music drama, see Joseph Kerman, *Opera as Drama* (New York: Vintage Books, 1956).

[32] See E. M. Forster, *Where Angels Fear to Tread* (New York: Vintage International, 1992), at pp. 118–19.

respectable."[34] For Verdi, the power of opera to plumb and explore deep feelings otherwise unspeakable was its indispensable contribution to democratic critical exploration of the personal and political psychology of patriarchy. Verdi's artistic innovations in musical voice respond to the challenge of Mazzini's call for an operatic "art of the future",[35] a term Wagner may have later borrowed from him, namely, a development of romantic opera democratically to represent the personal and political challenge of liberal nationalism in Italy and throughout the world.[36] Mazzini called for reforms in opera consistent with the reforms in theatre Victor Hugo had outlined in his *Preface to Oliver Cromwell* – identifying romanticism with populist liberalism, in particular, an art like Shakespeare's that embraced whatever subject matter (including the grotesque) and forms (not observing the Aristotelian unities) that enabled the artist not to copy nature but to invent forms accurately to express the internal personal life and feeling of "the drama of life and the drama of conscience"[37] in all its individuality and local color.[38]

Verdi's ambitions and achievement were very much in line with those we have seen in Attic tragedy, representing to and exploring for the public mind of a democracy at its birth a consciousness divided between the autocratic archaic heroes of the past and the contemporary responsibilities of democratic citizens. Verdi, like the Attic tragedians, explores Italian political psychology, integrating both its public and private life, as it faced its great nineteenth-century political struggle for democratic self-rule, the Risorgimento. Verdi was both a mirror for and agent of this struggle of the Italian people (in early works whose patriotic optimism was as foundational for Italian unification as Aeschylus's *The Oresteia* was of the Athenian democracy), but his later art explored tragic contradictions in Italian public and private life along the lines of the skepticism of Euripides, albeit in a much more conflicted spirit. If the tragedy of patriarchy frames at different stages

---

[33] See *id.*, at p. 117.

[34] See *id.*, at p. 119.

[35] See N. Gangulee, *Giuseppe Mazzini: Selected Writings* (Westport, CT: Greenwood Press, 1945), at p. 247.

[36] See, for illuminating commentary on this point, Gary Tomlinson, "Italian Romanticism and Italian Opera: An Essay in Their Affinities," *19th-Century Music* X/1 (Summer 1986), at pp. 43–60. On Mazzini's liberal nationalism, see Maurizio Viroli, *For Love of Country: An Essay on Patriotism and Nationalism* (Oxford: Clarendon Press, 1995), pp. 140–60.

[37] See Victor Hugo, *The Dramas Complete and Unabridged of Victor Hugo, Volume X, Oliver Cromwell*, translated by I. G. Burnham (Philadelphia: George Barrie & Son, 1896), at p. 75.

[38] On Mazzini's influence by Hugo, see Gary Tomlinson, "Italian Romanticism and Italian Opera: An Essay in Their Affinities," *19th-Century Music* X/1 (Summer 1986), pp. 49–50.

the works of the Attic artists, Verdi's life-long obsession with the Italian honor code brings it increasingly to stage center in his tragic operas and their exploration of the contradictions and tensions in the public and private life of the Italian people both during the Risorgimento and after unification.

But Verdi's distinctive contribution to the tragedy of patriarchy takes the form of the creation of an expressive musical voice for the buried emotions and voices that sustain patriarchy. Attic tragedy, of course, used both music and dance, though we know little about actual performance practice.[39] But Nietzsche, building on Schopenhauer, sought to reclaim for the modern world the tragic power of Attic drama by insisting that its roots in Dionysian rituals of music and dance captured its deeper emotions, "an undertone of terror, or else a wistful lament over an irrecoverable loss."[40] In contrast to Hegel, for whom the perfection of Attic tragedy was its philosophical dramatization of opposing moral principles in Sophocles' *Antigone*,[41] Nietzsche and Schopenhauer use the musical form of Attic tragedy as the key to its inward emotional desolation, which could no more be philosophically articulated than a complex philosophical argument in late Plato could be musically represented. We should take seriously the suggestion of both Nietzsche and Schopenhauer that music may uniquely tap tragic emotions without agreeing as well that these emotions are ultimate metaphysical truths (Schopenhauer) or that Wagner's music dramas, based on mytholological idealization, best gave nineteenth century expression to these ancient Attic truths (Nietzsche's view at the time of *Birth of Tragedy*). Schopenhauer's and Nietzsche's misogyny was extreme,[42] and Wagner's little better.[43] All three sense the powerful role of music in giving expression to tragic feeling, but, in view of their reactionary ideological sexism, they

---

[39] For what we do know, see David Wiles, *Tragedy in Athens: Performance Space and Theatrical Meaning* (Cambridge: Cambridge University Press, 1997).

[40] See Nietzsche, *The Birth of Tragedy*, p. 27. For Schopenhauer, see Arthur Schopenhauer, *The World as Will and Representation*, 2 vols. E. F. J. Payne, trans. (Indian Hills, Colorado: The Falcon's Wing Press, 1958).

[41] See Hegel, *On Tragedy* Anne and Henry Paolucci edition (New York: Harper & Row, 1962), at pp. 73–4.

[42] See Arthur Schopenhauer, "On Women," *Essays and Aphorisms*, trans. R. J. Hollindale (Harmondsworth: Penguin, 1970), at pp. 80–8; for Nietzsche's critique of feminist movements from the point of view of "the military and aristocratic spirit", see Friedrich Nietzsche, *Beyond Good and Evil: Prelude to a Philosophy of the Future*, Helen Zimmern, trans. (Edinburgh: T.N. Foulis, 1907), at p. 188.

[43] See Jean-Jacques Nattiez, *Wagner Androgyne: A Study in Interpretation* (Princeton: Princeton University Press, 1993), at pp. 168–9, 290–91; Thomas S. Grey, *Wagner's Musical Prose: Texts and Contexts* (Cambridge: Cambridge University Press, 1995), at pp. 130–80.

make into metaphysical truths of nature psychological trauma that European patriarchal institutions, as we have seen, psychologically buried. Wagner's *Ring* certainly touches patriarchally tragic chords in Wotan's broken relationships to his children, but its emotional world is so narcissistically self-absorbed in Wotan's consciousness (in which his children appear as projected fragments) that it metaphysically reenacts patriarchy (only the consciousness of the father is taken seriously) rather than confronting its tragic impacts on all persons.[44] Verdi's musical art, in contrast, directly touches the chords sounded by Attic tragedy because it took as its subject matter the suppressed emotions and voices of the full range of persons required traditionally to render patriarchy seem so much in the nature of things.

The relationship of music to our emotions has been a subject of continuing interest to philosophers since Plato.[45] In particular, how could absolute music (music not sung in words, or not accompanying a narrative) move us? The nineteenth-century Viennese music critic, Eduard Hanslick, argued that, precisely because absolute music could not be rooted in a text or narrative, it expressed no emotions, for emotions require thoughts or beliefs (fear thus requires the belief or thought of imminent harm), and absolute music, expressing no such beliefs or thoughts, cannot express emotion.[46] The position is, of course, deeply counterintuitive about the experience of even absolute music, which we value often to the degree that we, as responsive subjects, experience in it, as music, a fuller expressiveness of our emotional lives as self-conscious beings and agents.[47] Anthony Storr has thus observed:

"the divergence between song and speech, and the development of language as the vehicle of rational thinking as distinct from emotional expression. Human beings require this division if they are to function efficiently as objective thinkers; but they also need to bridge the Cartesian gulf between

---

[44] On Wagner's solipsistic art, see Bryan Magee, *Aspects of Wagner* (Oxford: Oxford University Press, 1988); Michael Tanner, *Wagner* (London: Flamingo, 1997).

[45] See, in general, Malcolm Budd, *Music and the Emotions: The Philosophical Theories* (London: Routledge & Kegan Paul, 1992); Roger Scruton, *The Aesthetics of Music* (Oxford: Oxford University Press, 1999).

[46] See Eduard Hanslick, *On the Musically Beautiful*, translated by Geoffrey Payzant (Indianapolis, Indiana: Hackett Publishing Company, 1986). For illuminating commentary, see Malcolm Budd, *Music and the Emotions*, pp. 16–36.

[47] See, for extensive defense of this view, Roger Scruton, *The Aesthetics of Music*; Aaron Ridley, *Music, Value, and the Passions* (Ithaca: Cornell University Press, 1995). For the view that this expressiveness has standard forms analogous to language, see Deryck Cooke, *The Language of Music* (London: Oxford University Press, 1959).

mind and body if they are to live life as creatures enjoying a full complement of human feelings. A great deal of what is generally considered to be 'real life' is woefully one-sided. But listening to or participating in music can restore a person to himself."[48]

The experience of music, Storr suggested, is rooted in our bodies[49] and, as such, "is often a means of recovering personal feelings from which we have become alienated,"[50] in particular, for people:

"who are somewhat alienated from the body, because playing an instrument, singing, or simply listening to music put them in touch with their physical being in ways unmatched by reading poetry or by looking at beautiful objects."[51]

Indeed, the distinctive power of music may be to enable us to experience a range of negative emotions expressed through music that we cannot otherwise acknowledge,[52] sometimes enabling us to experience and explore as well, as Martha Nussbaum has recently observed, painful but important emotional memories and vulnerabilities to which we would not otherwise have access.[53]

The relationship of music to our alienated, negative emotions gives it extraordinary expressive power for subordinated peoples whose protesting political voices are otherwise subject to repression, censorship, and unjust stereotypical caricatures.[54] The power of music in African-American culture, both under slavery and after, spoke of a range of emotions (a sense of justice, resentment, indignation, anger, depression, sexual feeling, etc.) that were and are a powerful resource of cultural resistance to injustice,[55] a musical appeal that, in the form of jazz, rapidly extended to all Americans and to the world.[56] Similarly, during the long period of Italian subordination to foreign colonial powers, music was "the only free and

---

[48] Anthony Storr, *Music and the Mind* (New York: Ballantine Books, 1992), at p. 122.

[49] See *id.*, at pp. 24, 26.

[50] See *id.*, at p. 122.

[51] See *id.*, at p. 149.

[52] See, on this point, Jerrold Levinson, "Music and Negative Emotion," *Pacific Philosophical Quarterly* 63 (1982) 327–346, reprinted in Jerrold Levinson, *Metaphysics, Art, and Metaphysics: Essays in Philosophical Aesthetics* (Ithaca: Cornell University Press, 1990), at pp. 306–35.

[53] See Martha C. Nussbaum, *Upheavals of Thought*, at pp. 249–94.

[54] See, for discussion of the music of the Venda of the Transvaal from this perspective, John Blacking, *How Musical Is Man?* (Seattle: University of Washington Press, 1974).

[55] See, in general, Lawrence W. Levine, *Black Culture and Black Consciousness: Afro-American Folk Thought from Slavery to Freedom* (Oxford: Oxford University Press, 1977).

autonomous sign of the artistic life of the Italian people."[57] Theatrical forms like *commedia dell'arte* were rooted in Neopolitan popular satire,[58] and the Italian invention of opera, combining innovations in music and theatre and spectacle,[59] had deep popular roots and appeal in Italian culture. During a period of ongoing censorship by occupying powers, Italian opera composers in general,[60] and Verdi in particular, found ways musically to speak to the underlying emotional life of the Italian people that were, as we shall see, also a powerful resource of resistance to injustice. The very ambiguity of music gives it a power to circumvent the crude hand of the censor. Verdi dramatizes this subversive power in the opening scene of *Les Vêpres Siciliennes* where Helene, bullied by French soldiers to entertain them with a song, sings about a resistance to a violent storm that the drunk French hear as merely entertaining while the Sicilians interpret it, correctly, as a call to armed resistance against the French. Verdi, however, carries this subversive power of music into a new dimension by extending its powers of emotional appeal under and around the conventional bounds of patriarchal censorship to the negative emotions and memories of the traumatic disruption of loving relationships that patriarchy cannot acknowledge.

Music "both as practice and sonority momentarily enacts unity of mind and body, man and woman; its consumption is simultaneously a production of utopian desire for wholeness"[61] against the background of patriarchal stereotypes that deny the possibility of such equality in voice in general and sexual voice in particular; indeed, "music's ultimate pleasure lies in its greatest threat", its "'realignment' of body and mind".[62] The very idea of women performing music is, from this perspective, erotically radical,[63] a misogynist interpretation brilliantly illustrated by Tolstoy's short story, "The Kreutzer Sonata".[64] Eighteenth-century British concern with limiting

---

[56] "[J]azz remains much the most serious musical contribution of the United States to world culture," Eric Hobsbawm, *Uncommon People: Resistance, Rebellion, and Jazz* (New York: The New Press, 1998), at p. 247.

[57] See Fernand Braudel, *Out of Italy: 1450–1650*, Sian Reynolds, trans. (Tours: Flamarion, 1991), at p. 130; for discussion, see *id.*, 130–6.

[58] See *id.*, 139–46.

[59] See *id.*, 149–57.

[60] See, for illuminating general commentary, Philip Gossett et al., *The New Grove Masters of Italian Opera* (New York: W.W. Norton, 1983).

[61] See Richard Leppert, *The Sight of Sound: Music, Representation, and the History of the Body* (Berkeley: University of California Press, 1993), at p. 84.

[62] See *id.*, p. 87.

[63] See *id.*, pp. 214–15.

claims for the equality of women conspicuously expressed itself in the cen-
sorious:

> "lament of xenophobes as different in period and concern as John Dennis
> and Lord Chesterfield, neither of whom could apparently conceive of Italian
> music or musicians separately from foppishness and sodomy and the degen-
> erating effects of both on anyone who came within sound and sight of the
> practitioners, whether on the English stage (Dennis) or on the Grand Tour
> (Chesterfield)."[65]

The musics of subordinated people, including women, "serve as agents
against the silence being imposed on them."[66] In Verdi's hands, operatic
voice served these ends in a remarkably innovative way that drew upon the
power of music that ethnomusicologists have observed in tribal music: "its
performance generates the highest degree of individuality in the largest
possible community; a combination of opposites rarely achieved."[67] Verdi's
mature musical tragedies are always, consistent with the aims of Mazzini
and Victor Hugo, the tragedies of individuals in local contexts, but the
musical expression of such emotional individuality explores such universal
experiences inflicted by the tragedy of patriarchy that it has the broadest
appeal, resonating in both our private and public lives. Verdi's operas
indeed combine opposites as only music can: music expressive of the most
painfully intimate negative emotions and memories, but through a medium
(opera) resonating with an enormous audience in rapt attendance (as at the
huge Metropolitan Opera House in New York City).

Opera, which weds music to words and narrative, is not subject to
Hanslick's objection about the relationships of absolute music to specific
emotions. We experience voice in opera – whether sung by a Verdi baritone
or unsung in a Wagnerian symphonic development[68] – as remarkably
expressive of often quite intimate features of our emotional lives. When
Isaiah Berlin used Schiller's distinction between naïve and sentimental
artists to distinguish, among others, Verdi and Wagner, he contrasted the
directness with which Verdi gave expression to the emotions of his charac-

---

[64] A jealous husband construes his wife's playing the piano accompaniment to this violin
and piano sonata with another man as adultery, and kills her. See, for illuminating commentary on the story's sexism and homophobia, *id.*, at pp. 153–87.

[65] See *id.*, p. 66.

[66] See *id.*, p. 222.

[67] See Anthony Storr, *Music and the Mind*, at p. 18.

[68] See, on this point, Carolyn Abbate, *Unsung Voices: Opera and Musical Narrative in the
Nineteenth Century* (Princeton: Princeton University Press, 1991). See also Lydia Goehr, *The
Quest for Voice*.

ters from the alienated, narcissistically wounded, redemptive emotions of Wagner's mythological art.[69] The specifically tragic force of Verdi's art was its powers in giving expression to the submerged emotions of traumatic loss on which the mythological idealizations of patriarchy depended. With the force of obsession, Verdi's art with growing power and subtlety over his career forged musical voice that confronted his generation and later generations with these suppressed emotions and voices. Musical voice, in Verdi's art, gave expression to the disassociated emotions of trauma and loss, confronting the public mind of his age with the tragedy of patriarchy.

No aspect of Verdi's art was more important in this respect than the ways in which, from his earliest popularly successful opera, *Nabucco*, he insisted on representing not only the tragic effects of patriarchy on women, but on men as well, in particular, on patriarchal fathers. It is in such terms that Nabucco voices his divided consciousness as a patriarchal father:

"Debole sono, e vero, ma guai se alcun se alcun il sa!
Vo' che mi creda sempre forte ciascun . . . "

"I am weak, it is true, but woe if anyone knows!
I want people to think me still strong . . . "[70]

The most musically moving moment in the opera comes, later in the scene, when Verdi expresses his vulnerability to grief as he pleads for his daughter's life:

"Deh, perdona, deh, perdona
ah un padre che delibra!
Deh, la figlia mi ridona,
Non orbarne il genitor!"

"Oh, forgive, oh, pardon
a father who is raving!
I beg you, give me back my daughter,
Do not bereave a father!"[71]

Verdi insists that we hear the emotional loss under the patriarchal armor. The expressive powers of his art thus expose the desolation that the patriarchal code of honor inflicts both on men and women, separating them from one another, including a lived sense of their free sexual bodies and voices.

---

[69] See Isaiah Berlin, "The Naivete of Verdi," in William Weaver and Martin Chusid, eds., *The Verdi Companion*, at pp. 1–12.

[70] Verdi, *Nabucco*, libretto to recording of Riccardo Muti, Ambrosian Opera Chorus, pp. 90–1.

[71] See *id.*, at pp. 100–1.

His musical art not only enables us to hear these emotions but to understand how patriarchy tragically inflicts them. The indispensable contribution of the musicality of his art is thus, as the appeal of music often is, "both intellectual and emotional, restoring the links between mind and body."[72]

It is this emotional range of his tragic art that, I believe, explains the universal appeal of his art across the usual boundaries of gender or ethnicity or religion or sexual orientation, as "The music that makes one want to cry."[73] Indeed, its deep appeal today, as much as ever, may be its character as an expressive medium for emotional memory of traumas that cannot under patriarchy be acknowledged, enabling us to hear otherwise suppressed voices in ourselves and others that reveal contradictions in ourselves and our culture, and thus help us recover a sense of empowering memory of who we are and how we might best proceed in the light of truth. Carol Gilligan's recent work on the relationships of mothers to their young sons speaks of a world of emotional openness and perceptiveness in boys later covered over or even buried as this voice is discouraged or even suppressed earlier for boys than girls.[74] It is difficult for any man to remember this world perhaps because traumatic breaks intervene; the consequence of trauma is loss of memory and voice.[75] It is part of the appeal of Verdi's musical art, as it is of music in general, that it speaks to parts of the psyche otherwise buried and inaccessible. It spoke to me as a boy throughout the period Gilligan describes, keeping me in touch with a sense of psychological truth that kept my eyes unusually open to what was happening about me, both in my family and the larger culture. My story, briefly told, is illustrative of the point I am making, the appeal of Verdi's voice to the psyche of men craving truth against the patriarchal lies that surround them.

I would find it difficult, as a man, to think or speak truthfully about my boyhood without drawing on Verdi's art as the resonance it was for my inner voice throughout my childhood. Verdi's art is for me what the madeleine was for Proust, a way through the sensuous beauty of Verdi's art into remembering the lived sense of my boyhood's passionate attachments to my father and mother and sister and my growing anxieties about the larger

---

[72] Anthony Storr, *Music and the Mind*, at p. 183.

[73] See Jean L. Briggs, *Never in Anger: Portrait of an Eskimo Family*, at p. 154.

[74] See Carol Gilligan, *The Birth of Pleasure*, pp. 36, 38, 42–3, 44–5, 70–3.

[75] See, on this point, Bessel A. van der Kolk, Alexander C. McFarlane, and Lars Weisaeth, eds., *Traumatic Stress: The Effects of Overwhelming Experience on Mind, Body, and Society* (New York: The Guilford Press, 1996), at pp. 279–302, 565.

world. My boyhood was no more traumatic than any boy's life is, traumatic certainly (in the way the lives of boys usually are) but perhaps less so than the lives of many boys because I remained in closer relationship to my parents than may be typical.[76] I say this even though my gay sexual orientation was more obvious to some of my peers than it was to myself during this period and occasioned some bullying and contempt which was sometimes quite brutal and wounding. But I had the love of my parents (living in a remarkably egalitarian marriage) and my sister (who shared my interest in the arts), and I had Verdi's art in a constellation that may be fairly unusual in the developmental histories of other gay men absorbed by opera.[77]

I would find it difficult to write truthfully about my boyhood without Verdi's artistic voice because, without his voice, I find it much easier to tell a falsifying story more in tune with dominant gender stereotypes. My problem is, I believe, one shared by men generally, but particularly inflected by my Italian-American ethnic background, an identity subject in the America of my parents to significant racialized stigma.[78] The cultural force of unjust ethnic stereotypes is, when uncontested, that subordinated groups define themselves and their aims in terms of them. For Italian Americans, no aspect of such life has been more subject to such obfuscating stereotypes that the area of their lives on which they have traditionally placed such ultimate value – intimate family life. There is accordingly no story more difficult to tell truthfully, for such stories, subverting stereotypes, will not be popular. Such ethnic stereotypes depend, I believe, on underlying gender stereotypes.

Mario Puzo's career, as a novelist, illustrates this point. His remarkable interpretive study of an Italian-American family, the novel *The Fortunate Pilgrim*,[79] captures the dense web of Italian-American family life, including

---

[76] On traumatic breaks as endemic in American boyhood, see Carol Gilligan, *The Birth of Pleasure*; and William Pollack, *Real Boys: Rescuing Our Sons from the Myths of Boyhood* (New York: Henry Holt, 1998).

[77] The appeal of opera for gay men has been posed largely in terms of its place in the closet, in contrast to my own experience which has been that it has guided me, for reasons I discuss at length in this book, out of the closet. For some sense of the range of views by gay men on opera and on gay life, see pertinent works of Paul Robinson, *Opera and Ideas from Mozart to Strauss* (New York: Harper & Row, 1985); *Gay Lives: Homosexual Autobiography from John Addington Symonds to Paul Monette* (Chicago: University of Chicago Press, 1999); *Opera, Sex, and Other Vital Matters* (Chicago: University of Chicago Press, 2002); see also Wayne Koestenbaum, *The Queen's Throat: Opera, Homosexuality, and the Mystery of Desire* (New York: Da Capo Press, 2001), reviewed by Paul Robinson, *ibid.*, at 157–69.

[78] See David A. J. Richards, *Italian American: The Racializing of an Ethnic Identity* (New York: New York University Press, 1999).

[79] See Mario Puzo, *The Fortunate Pilgrim* (London: Heinemann, 1964).

the pivotal moral character, devotion and practical intelligence of an Italian-American mother in trying to sustain and support her children to become responsible adults. The mother, the novel's heroine, is described sometimes in terms of a divine watchfulness, more usually in heroically Napoleonic terms:

> "Luca Santa Angeluzzi-Corbo, a beleaguered general, pondered the fate and travails of her family, planned tactics, mulled strategy, counted resources, measured the loyalties of her allies." [80]

Puzo's novel, as good as it is, however, cuts against stereotype. His great popularity and success rest on a later novel, in contrast, that plays to stereotype, in which the dominant figure of the godfather rules a mafia family in which women barely exist as personalities; the character of the godfather, in fact, was a portrayal based on Puzo's mother, which gives some sense of the distortions that the force of dominant stereotypes required as the price to be paid for novelistic popularity.[81] The considerable popular success of Italian-American artists (including, most recently, the HBO series, the Sopranos) has thus largely required accommodation, certainly not challenge, to dominant stereotypes.[82] It is surely paradoxical that Italian-Americans, whose life has so centered on devotion to the family, should feel compelled, in public discourse, to so misrepresent it, finding it necessary, as in the case of Puzo's popular novel, even to change the genders of important characters in order to appeal to an American audience. That sense of compulsion rests on the continuing force of a largely uncontested form of American racism directed against Italian-Americans. The malign force of such mafia stereotypes is that, uncontested, they remake reality in their own image. Perversely, both a mafia leader like John Gotti,[83] and his

---

[80] See *id.*, 177.

[81] See Mario Puzo, *The Godfather* (New York: Signet, 1978); on Puzo's basing Don Corleone on his mother, see Camille Paglia, "At Home With: Mario Puzo; It all Comes Back to Family," *New York Times*, May 8, 1997, section C, p. 1, col. 1; "Questions for : Mario Puzo", *New York Times Magazine*, Sunday, March 30, 1997, section 6, p. 15. For illuminating commentary on this and other Italian-American narratives, see Fred L. Gardaphe, *Italian Signs, American Streets: The Evolution of Italian American Narrative* (Durham: Duke University Press, 1996).

[82] See, on this point, Carlos E. Cortés, "The Hollywood Curriculum on Italian Americans: Evolution of an Icon of Ethnicity," Lydia F. Tomasi, Piero Gastoldo and Thomas Row, *The Columbus People: Perspectives in Italian Immigration to the Americas and Australia* (New York: Center for Migration Studies, 1994), at 89–108.

[83] See Maria Laurino, *Were You Always an Italian?: Ancestors and Other Icons of Italian America* (New York: W.W. Norton, 2000), at p. 139; for their impact on violence by the young, see *id.*, pp. 141–2.

most effective Italian-American opponent, Rudolf Giuliani,[84] glamorize themselves in such terms. Such self-deceiving distortions bespeak the ways in which unjust ethnic stereotypes draw their power and appeal from intersecting stereotypes of gender and sexuality. To the extent Italian Americans (like Puzo) acquiesce in such stereotypes, they refuse to know in public what they know in private, which is to say they refuse to know what they know.

In understanding the motives to such complicity, it is surely important that such a public/private distinction is, as is often the case, highly gendered, and shaped by the same kinds of unjust gender stereotypes that have rationalized now much better understood patterns of injustice to women and gays and lesbians that have importantly rested on the uncritical privatization of injustice. We cannot know in public what we know in private because breaking the silence, which would contest mafia stereotypes, would contest as well unjust stereotypes of gender and sexuality. The mafia stereotype is in its nature a glamorization of male violence triggered by putative insults to honor, a mythology of gender that normatively legitimates what psychiatry increasingly understands as the psychopathology of male violence, triggered by the "overwhelming shame in the absence of feelings of either love or guilt; the shame stimulates rage, and violent impulses, toward the person in whose eyes one feels shamed, and the feelings that would normally inhibit the expression of those feelings and the acting out of those impulses, such as love and/or guilt, are absent."[85] The unjust gender ideology that dehumanizes women by reducing them to sex objects dehumanizes men by making them "violence objects."[86] The mafia stereotype draws its force and appeal from this underlying gender stereotype. Our acquiescence in it rests on the close linkages between our racism and sexism: we are bullied into silence by linked ethnic and gender stereotypes because breaking the silence, by speaking in our own voice about what we know, threatens our very masculinity or femininity. Violence becomes our only voice, which is, of course, no voice at all.

Both the force and character of such linked ethnic and gender stereotypes reflect a long European history, which is, of course, at least as racist and sexist as that of America. Italy, much of which was occupied by foreign powers after the fall of Rome, suffered a kind of colonial experience as a subject people. Occupying powers not only knew about but envied and imitated

---

[84] See, on this point, James B. Jacobs, *Gotham Unbound: How New York City was Liberated from the Grip of Organized Crime* (New York: New York University Press, 1999).

[85] James Gilligan, *Violence: Reflections on a National Epidemic* (New York: Vintage Books, 1997), pp. 113–4.

[86] *Id.*, p. 232.

the imperial greatness they admired in the Roman Empire, but their very status as colonial masters over the Italian people with this cultural history led them to dehumanize them in the racist terms that traditionally rationalized European colonialism both in Europe and elsewhere.[87] We can see the force of such colonializing assumptions in the contrasting depictions of human passions in France and Italy in, respectively, Stendhal's *The Red and the Black*[88] and *The Charterhouse of Parma,*[89] including, as we shall see, reflections on the role therein played by Italian opera. In *The Red and the Black*, both Julien Sorel's sexual passions for a bourgeois married matron and for a titled aristocrat are complex and nuanced psychological portraits of the conflicting imperatives of Napoleonic ambition and passionate sexual love in a corrupt post-Napolenic political culture of restored monarchy to which Julien must hypocritically accommodate himself as the condition for the success of his ambitions. In *The Charterhouse of Parma*, Fabrizio's many sexual relations to women are, until he meets Clelia, barely personal; and even then, the center of the stage is occupied by the passion for him of his aunt, the Duchessa, who, by the end of the novel, has, in service of her passion for her nephew, assassinated the king of Parma and prostituted herself with his son. Stendhal, who had served Napoleon, brings a colonialist attitude to bear on his study of Italian as opposed to French passion. The attitude is, as colonialist attitudes often are, mixed with self-consciously proclaimed admiration of the ease and availability of passionate love in Italy (as opposed to France).[90] Stendhal adored the expressive powers of Italian opera in general and of the operas of Rossini in particular,[91] associating these expressive powers with the ease and availability of Italian passion. Indeed, his self-alienated French lovers in *The Red and the Black* sometimes only feel their passions in response to their expression in Italian opera.[92] But such admiration, however real in the subtlety of Stendhal's art and life, expresses itself in a colonialist stereotype of Italian amoral familism, the Duchessa's morally uninhibited passion for her nephew.

---

[87] On this point, see, for example, Maura O'Connor, *The Romance of Italy and the English Political Imagination* (New York: St. Martin's Press, 1998).

[88] See Stendhal, *The Red and the Black*, Catherine Slater, trans. (New York: Oxford University Press, 1998).

[89] See Stendhal, *The Charterhouse of Parma*, Margaret R. B. Shaw, trans. (London: Penguin, 1958).

[90] See Marie-Henri Beyle (De Stendhal), *On Love*, H.B.V., trans. (New York: Liveright, 1947), at p. 153.

[91] See, for example, Stendhal, *The Life of Rossini*, Richard N. Coe, trans. (London: John Calder, 1985).

[92] See Stendhal, *The Red and the Black*, at pp. 338, 369, 439.

We can see the pervasive force of such stereotypical depictions of Italian family life in a long British and American tradition stretching from Shakespeare's subtle Italian villains Iago[93] to Iachimo[94] and Webster's much less subtle depictions of monstrous Italian families[95] to the Italian male villain preying on American feminine innocence in Henry James's *Portrait of a Lady*.[96] Even when a popular American movie of the 1960s, *The Light in the Piazza*,[97] quite clearly portrays an American mother in quite manipulative terms as she successfully tries to get her brain-damaged daughter married to an unsuspecting Florentine family, she is, as portrayed by Olivia de Havilland, no villain, as Italian men and women are portrayed as, effectively, so brain damaged in their intimate lives that no one could reasonably notice or be expected to notice.

Such stereotypes have power not only over the colonizers but over the colonized, which is shown by the way in which an artist like Mario Puzo only finds a mass audience when he writes in terms of a mafia stereotype that belies his actual experience as a boy in an Italian-American family. The mafia stereotype imposes a mythology of gender, an armored strutting peacock acutely vulnerable to shame that unleashes itself in violence not voice. The price Italian Americans pay for this stereotype is not merely its falsity to what we know, but its stark denial of what we do know. Mario Puzo's success derived precisely from such denial, in this case creating an image of a putative masculine heroic ideal in fact based on his mother. Such armored heroes have a long history in Western culture from the Roman warrior-hero idealized in Virgil's *Aeneid*[98] to the religious priest-hero idealized in

[93] See William Shakespeare, *Othello*, in G. Blakemore Evans et al., *The Riverside Shakespeare*, Second Edition (Boston: Houghton Mifflin Co., 1997), at pp. 1246–96.

[94] See William Shakespeare, *Cymbeline, Id.*, at pp. 1565–1611. On Shakespeare's use of Italy and Italian sources in his plays, see Murray J. Levith, *Shakespeare's Italian Settings and Plays* (New York: St. Martin's Press, 1989); Michele Marrapodi, A. J. Hoenselaars, Marcello Cappuzzo and L. Falzon Santucci, *Shakespeare's Italy: Functions of Italian Locations in Renaissance Drama* (Manchester: Manchester University Press, 1993). On the influence of Italy on the British political imagination, see Maura O'Connor, *The Romance of Italy and the English Political Imagination* (New York: St. Martin's Press, 1998).

[95] See John Webster, *The Duchess of Malfi*, Elizabeth M. Brennan, ed. (New York: W.W. Norton, 1993); *The White Devil*, J. R. Mulryne, ed. (Lincoln: University of Nebraska Press, 1969).

[96] See Henry James, *The Portrait of a Lady*, Robert D. Bamberg, ed. (New York: W.W. Norton, 1995). See, in general, Leonardo Buonomo, *Backward glances: Exploring Italy, Reinterpreting America (1831–1866)* (Madison: Fairleigh Dickinson University Press, 1996).

[97] See Leslie Halliwell, *Halliwell's Film Guide*, 4th edition (New York: Charles Scribner's Sons, 1985), at p. 825.

[98] See Virgil, *The Aeneid*, Robert Fitzgerald, trans. (New York: Vintage, 1990).

Augustine's *Confessions*[99] to the armored knights of Ariosto[100] and Tasso;[101] in all these cases, the heroic armor was forged on the basis of the repudiation of personal love, as if the price required to be an ideal man was to deny personal relationships. Puzo's idealized mythology rests on the same denial, in his case, of his intense personal relationship as an Italian-American man, to his beloved and admired mother. A falsifying image of stereotypical masculine violence, which tragically feeds on itself, rests on the denial and repudiation of personal relationships between sons and mothers.

Puzo's case exemplifies the power of patriarchy over men, including Italian-American men. He could not do truthful justice to the humane complexity of his family relationships because, to do so, would suggest what American manliness forbade, namely, that his relationship to his mother's loving voice and life had, as mine certainly did, framed his sense of a life lived with practical intelligence and moral authority. In contrast, from my earliest years, Verdi's art (although written for a different time and place) moved me more than any art I know because it spoke to me so much more truthfully about my Italian-American family and the world about us than the falsifying Italian-American art I saw about me. Verdi's musical voice spoke to me about an invisible, dark emotional underworld that I knew underlay that web of relationships, a world that we could not speak about but that was more important in a humane life than much we could speak out. His art not only enabled me to hear the underworld, but to map its structure (see chapters 5–7).

My boyhood was lived in close family relationships and in the larger network of relationships to extended family, friends, peers, teachers, and the like. I can only securely hold onto my memory of what it was like to live as a boy in such relationships by hearing how Verdi's voice gave me a sense, in Carol Gilligan's terms, of psychological "true north"[102] in tuning myself to the value of good relationships and to the emotional desolation of the disruption of such relationships. I saw through Verdi's art how remarkable the relationships in my family of origin were and how my parents (both of whom, unusually for that period, worked outside the home, my father as a civil engineer, my mother as a hospital pharmacist) struggled to hold onto

---

[99] See Saint Augustine, Confessions, Henry Chadwick, trans. (Oxford: Oxford University Press, 1991).

[100] See Ludovico Ariosto, *Orlando Furioso*, Part One, Barbara Reynolds, trans. (London: Penguin, 1975); *Orlando Furioso*, Part Two, Barbara Reynolds, trans. (London: Penguin, 1977).

[101] Torquato Tasso, *Jerusalem Delivered*, Anthony M. Esolen, trans. (Baltimore: The Johns Hopkins University Press, 2000).

[102] See Carol Gilligan, *The Birth of Pleasure*, at pp. 37, 159.

the truth of their unusually egalitarian, loving relationship, based on free voice, against considerable odds, including the dominance of patriarchal relations both within our extended family and the wider culture of family and work that were sustained by a massive suppression of resisting voices. It is very much part of my story that Verdi's voice spoke to me in the remarkable operatic voice of my father, a gift he chose not professionally to pursue but which always spoke to me of an emotional and intellectual complexity in manhood and womanhood more truthful than the then dominant cultural views. It made sense to me of a relationship, based on feminist equality, that flourished under the radar of the dominant patriarchal pieties of that period.

Verdi's musical art offered me nothing less than a complex psychic geography of disrupted relationships under patriarchy in terms of which I could take my bearings in what I increasingly saw as a dangerous, perilous emotional terrain otherwise uncharted for men, let alone gay men, by the disassociated culture of denial that was the America of my youth. His music now speaks to me as the terms of that boy's inner voice and intelligence, and I turn to examine Verdi's art as a way of explaining the complexity and terrors of the terrain he charted for me as a boy growing into adulthood. His map of this terrain of intimate life has, if anything, absorbed me even more in my adulthood, showing, as it does, tragic perils to all forms of intimate life (including my own) from forms of patriarchy that are as much destructively alive in gay as in straight relationships.

It is only the very greatest artists, like Verdi, who have anatomized the price people pay for their long acquiescence in the colonial stereotypes of ethnicity and gender imposed on them, exemplified, as I shall argue in later chapters, in the price Verdi's fathers, sons, brothers, and lovers pay for their patriarchal conventionality, the irreparable loss of love. Verdi defines our tragedy in terms of the conflicting imperatives of our public and private lives, and compels us to see feelingly the loss that we know and do not know. Verdi, in contrast to his contemporary Wagner, refuses all simplifying nationalistic mythology. Nationality (including Italian nationality) is, Verdi insists that we see, often tragically conflicted. He gives us no simple answers, but makes us see what price we pay for a sense of nationality so corrupted by unjust ethnic and gender stereotypes. Only in his last opera, *Falstaff*, does Verdi explore a feminist world where mothers and daughters unite to protect themselves and their men from the ravages of a jealous code of honor that corrupts love. The greatest tragedian in the history of opera writes, in service of this gender-bending hope, a scintillating comedy.

# Chapter 4

# Verdi and Italian Nationalism

The framework of my analysis of Verdi's art, as an investigation of the tragedy of patriarchy, is its exploration of the linkages between the political and personal psychology that support this tragedy. Patriarchy, thus understood, arranges power and authority in both public and private life in a hierarchy dominated by fathers on the basis of mythological stereotypes of gender whose force requires the repression of voice and conviction. Indeed, patriarchal men's very sense of self is defined in terms of such control, so that any diminution of it becomes an aggressive attack on the self, rationalizing violence against those who usurp such control, both women and men. The associated gender stereotypes are mythological idealizations, whose force crucially requires that both women and men lack the voice and conviction to challenge them. In effect, violence replaces voice, terrorizing both women and men into compliance. The psychology that supports patriarchy must accordingly make the underlying stereotypical idealizations seem to be in the nature of things. Patriarchy, thus understood, forges a gender binary in which the honor of men is defined in terms of the readiness to use violence against any challenge to one's control over women's sexuality, and the honor of women is defined in terms of the strict control of their sexuality for patriarchal purposes. The psychology underlying this gender binary is one that naturalizes absence of relationships based on reciprocal, mutual voice. Thus, as we saw in our earlier discussion of *Iphigenia at Aulis*, under patriarchy identification with the idealized stereotype crucially replaces voice.

But the very psychological structure, required to naturalize patriarchy, requires men not only to be absent from their relationships to women, but to one another. Patriarchy imposes hierarchy not only over women but between and among men, rationalizing violence not only against women but against other men to the extent they should challenge one's exclusive control over the sexual availability of women. Violence replaces voice in men, mirroring the absence of voice in women. Patriarchy must for this reason be in psychological tension with the aspirations to democratic constitutionalism, in which the values of voice and deliberative debate are the legitimate means to resolve disagreement among persons regarded as free and equal citizens.[1] It is also for the same reason in tension with a love based on free and equal sexual voice.[2]

The power and appeal of Verdi's tragic art are its exploration, with increasing musical subtlety and sophistication over his long career, of this psychological tension. The analogy to the Attic tragedians is, I believe, exact. Tragedy was forged in democratic Athens as a way of exposing the democracy to a double consciousness of archaic heroes and contemporary democratic responsibilities. Aeschylus, as we have seen, thus contrasts the cycle of personal and political violence of the House of Atreus with the collective responsibilities of Athenian citizens and their democratic institutions. Verdi's forging of his musical art was framed by a comparable double consciousness of, on the one hand, the cycle of faction and violence that had rendered Italians a divided, colonized people since the fall of Rome and, on the other, the responsibilities of democratic citizens in a reunified Italy. Verdi, like Aeschylus, was very much an agent of and participant in the founding of democratic institutions, including active participation in the struggles for Italian reunification (the Risorgimento) and in the Italy finally completely united under Piedmont's constitutional monarchy in 1870.[3] He knew and admired the liberal nationalist Mazzini and, in light of his successes, the constitutional monarchist of Piedmont, Cavour, who successfully got Verdi to run for and serve in the first Italian parliament.[4] Verdi's nationalism was always expressed as in service of universalistic values of liberal humanism. When he composed his "Inno delle Nazioni" ("Hymn of the Nations") for the 1862 International Exhibition in London (the year after the first Italian parliament, just mentioned[5]), both the text of Boito and Verdi's music conceive the relevant nations

---

[1] See, on this point, David A. J. Richards, *Toleration and the Constitution* (New York: Oxford University Press, 1986); and *Free Speech and the Politics of Identity* (Oxford: Oxford University Press, 1999).

[2] See, on this point, Carol Gilligan, *The Birth of Pleasure*,

[3] See George Martin, "Verdi and the Risorgimento," in William Weaven and Martin Chusid, eds., *The Verdi Companion*, at pp. 13–41.

[4] See Frank Walker, *The Man Verdi*, at pp. 188, 193, 224, 236–7.

[5] The work was not performed at the International Exhibition, but later that year in London. See Julian Budden, *Verdi*, at pp. 87–8.

(Britain, France, and Italy) as in search of common values of liberal fraternity:

| | |
|---|---|
| "In questo di giocondo | Let the world lead with joy |
| balzi di gioja il mondo, | on this happy day, |
| perche vicino agl'uomini | for humanity is nearing |
| e il regno dell'Amor! | The reign of Love!" [6] |

The "Hymn" thus praises Britain and France to the degree that either their example (Britain) or help (France) had advanced the realization of such values in Italy (the united constitutional monarchy of Italy realized the previous year). Verdi pays tribute to the multicultural variations on the common liberal theme by displaying the national anthems of each nation, followed by "a bizarre attempt to combine all three melodies."[7] Verdi's multiculturalist interpretation of nationalism marks the chasm that separates his musical nationalism from that of Wagner.

Italians experienced many of Verdi's early operas as patriotic calls for resistance to foreign colonizing tyrants, including, notably, *Nabucco*, *I Lombardi alla Prima Crociata*, *Giovanna d'Arco*, *Alzira*, *Attila*, *Macbeth*, and *La Battaglia di Legnano*. In particular, the great and moving chorus of nostalgia in *Nabucco*, "Va, Pensiero, sull'ali dorate" ("Go my thought, on golden wings"), sung by the Jewish exiles by the waters of Babylon, was experienced as an expression of the yearning of the Italian people for liberty and independence. *I Lombardi* inevitably reminded the people in Lombardy (including the Milanese) occupied by Austria of their own warlike past of resistance to German oppressors. In *Attila*, which for a time had great popular success throughout Italy, the line of Ezio, the Roman envoy, to Attila, the invader of Italy, "Avrai tu l'universo, resti l'Italia a me!" ("You may have the universe, but let Italy remain mine") aroused a frenzy of enthusiasm in Italian audiences of that period. Sometimes the words of a finale, as of *Ernani*, might be changed ("Carlo" to "Pio") to express the enthusiasm of the audience for a recent papal amnesty that ostensibly advanced the aims of the Risorgimento.[8] Even Verdi's name became a popular slogan for unification:

"By January 1859 it was evident that Cavour had reached some sort of understanding with Napoleon, and that war with Austria was imminent. Verdi,

---

[6] See Verdi, "Hymn of the Nation," in libretto to recording, *Pavarotti plus*, Tibor Rudas production, conducted by James Levine, Philharmonia Orchestra and Philharmonia Chorus, at p. 15.

[7] Julian Budden, *Verdi*, at p. 315.

[8] See Frank Walker, *The Man Verdi*, p. 151.

in Rome in February for the premiere of *Un ballo in maschera*, once again became the symbol of patriotic aspiration. Excited Italians in all cities suddenly realized that his name was an acronym of "Vittorio Emanuele Re d'Italia" (Vittorio Emanuele King of Italy), and *Viva Verdi!* was scratched on walls and shouted in the streets. Wherever his operas were performed, the audiences called endlessly for the composer, particularly if Austrians were present. And whever Verdi himself was discovered, crowds often gathered spontaneously and broke into cheers."[9]

Verdi's art, even in his early period, frames a double consciousness that counterpoints the aspirations of the Italian people to democratic unification (reflected in choruses like "Va, Pensiero") to the forces that have impeded resistance to longstanding patterns of tyranny and colonization. For Verdi, these forces obsessionally include the impact of the code of honor on both personal and political psychology even in works not ostensibly about the Risorgimento. Verdi's first opera, *Oberto*, and fifth opera, *Ernani*, bleakly, even ludicrously portray in such terms the murderous impact of the code of honor on both public and private life. Oberto, a count who led one family, has been defeated by another family; Riccardo, a young count of the other family, had seduced Oberto's daughter, Leonora, and abandoned her in order to marry Cuniza; the opera portrays Oberto's obsession with revenging himself on Riccardo though Riccardo agrees to marry Leonora; Oberto is killed, and Leonora enters a convent. All the honor-obsessed protagonists in *Ernani* – the three men and the one woman they all love – evince "an obsessive pride which turns all the characters into giant egoists, swearing mutual vengeance for the most trivial causes, doing each other monstrous kindnesses, destroying themselves and each other to satisfy some whim of punctilio."[10]

In the more explicitly political Risorgimento operas during this period, Verdi strikingly makes his musically expressive point either about the patriarchal forces to be resisted or about the voice required for resistance in terms of a new kind of voice for women. Verdi innovates a forceful, angrily ambitious voice of women struggling to either be the new patriarch in Abigaille in *Nabucco* and or to assist the patriarch in Lady Macbeth in *Macbeth*. As Verdi observed of the kind of singer he wanted for Lady Macbeth:

"I would prefer that Lady's voice were rough, hollow, stifled. Tadolini's voice has something angelic in it. Lady's should have something devilish."[11]

---

[9] See George Martin, "Verdi and the Risorgimento," in William Weaven and Martin Chusid, eds., *The Verdi Companion*, at p. 31.

[10] Julian Budden, *The Operas of Verdi, Volume1*, p. 142.

[11] Julian Budden, *id.*, p. 275.

Verdi also calls for a similar kind of forceful and indignant musical expressiveness in the women who become the agents of resistance to political tyranny (for example, Giselda's resistance to the political violence of the Crusades in *I Lombardi*, Lucrezia Contarini's rage about the injustice inflicted on her husband by the Venetian state in *I Due Foscari*, Joan of Arc's leadership as warrior-maid of the French against the British invaders in *Giovanna d'Arco*, and Odabella's murderous leadership of Italians against the invasion of barbarians in *Attila*). Verdi's musical art insists in these works that we hear women as having forceful, angry, indignant, even murderous voices, and sometimes offers those voices as the agents of the kind of resistance to tyranny that the Risorgimento requires.

It is surely of interest that these more gender-subversive representations of the voices of women yield, as in Aeschylus the Furies become the Eumenides, to more conventionally patriarchal representations as Verdi's art is addressed to Italians during a later, more hopeful period for reunification. When national unity is politically remote, more radical gender-subversive images are used to voice resistance; when such unity is closer at hand, more conventional patriarchal images are used to forge a sense of national unity. As in Aeschylus, democracy itself is portrayed by Verdi as requiring a new conception of manhood, uncritically defined in more patriarchal terms than he had previously found appealing. Verdi's most musically sophisticated Risorgimento opera, *La Battaglia di Legnano*, illustrates this latter point. *La Battaglia* was expressly written for Rome in 1849 during the brief, hopeful period of the abortive Roman republic led by Mazzini, the most consistently idealistic liberal republican of the Italian political leaders of the period.[12] The political plot (that the old friendship of Rolando and Arrigo mobilizes armed resistance to the German occupation of Italy) is in tension with the subplot of personal honor (Rolando's honor is stung by discovery that Lida, his wife, had loved Arrigo, but, believing him dead, had married, at her father's instructions, Rolando, having a child, a boy). The plots are harmonized by the heroic death of Arrigo in battle, who at his death makes clear that no sexual intimacy ever occurred between him and Lida. Arrigo observes before his death:: "Chi muore per la patria alma si rea no ha" ("He who dies for his country cannot be so guilty in his heart"). The musical representation of Lida, as obedient daughter and faithful wife and devoted mother (though still in love with Arrigo), is, of course, much the most patriarchal of all the representations of women's voice in the Risorgimento operas. The conception of nation-

---

[12] See Julian Budden, *id.*, pp. 388–415.

alism and patriotism in *La Battaglia* – the required fraternity between citizen-soldiers – is the closest of all Verdi's operas to the conception of democracy as patriarchy in Aeschylean tragedy.

In a later period when national unity appears again more remote, Verdi's art revives gender-subversive representations of women's active role in political resistance, as in Helene's politically expressive resisting voice and agency (albeit in service of the memory of her dead brother) in *Les Vêpres Siciliennes*, further discussed below. However, both Helene and the Sicilian revolutionary leader, Procida, are depicted as cynically encouraging the French oppressors sexually to exploit Sicilian women in order to arouse the injured sense of honor of Sicilian men to acts of violent political resistance, including acts of terror. Gender in this late Risorgimento work once again aligns itself with the conventional demands of the code of honor, here explicitly used by the Sicilian nationalists to forge a sense of manhood on the basis of patriarchy. Gender in later works is, however, no longer easily mapped along such conventional patriarchal lines.

Verdi's most remarkable innovations in musically expressive voice come after *La Battaglia* as both the setbacks in reunification (including the politically reactionary role in these setbacks of the Catholic Church[13]) and his relationship to Strepponi frame a deepening of his understanding and representation of the tragedy of patriarchy both in personal and political life. The quality of the musical development is illustrated by the new music Verdi wrote in 1865 for his revised *Macbeth*, in particular the harrowing musical "masterpiece of originality"[14] that he composed to the words:

| | |
|---|---|
| "Patria oppressa! Il dolce nome | Down-trodden country, lost love |
| No, di madre aver non puoi, | oh, remain for ever in our hearts, |
| Or che tutta a'figli tuoi | now that for all they children |
| Sei conversa in un avel. | Thou art converted to a tomb. |
| D'orfannelli e di piangenti | The cry of orphans and bereaved – |
| Chi lo sposo e chi la prole | this one lamenting the loss of a husband, |
| | |
| Al venire del nuovo sole | that one the loss of a child – |
| S'alza un grido e fere il Ciel. | Each new morn flies up |
| | And wounds the heavens."[15] |

Italy was now well on its way to complete reunification, but Verdi had

---

[13] See, on this point, Richards, *Italian American*, at pp. 91–2.

[14] See Julian Budden, *id.*, p. 306.

[15] Guiseppe Verdi, *Macbeth*, libretto to CD recording conducted by Claudio Abbado, conductor, Coro e Orchestra del Teatro all Scala, libretto by Francesco Maria Piave, trasnlated into English by Peggie Cochrane, Deutsche Grammophon GmbH, Hamburg, 1996.

become absorbed by the musical representation of traumatic psychological loss underlying patriarchal institutions as such, including the role of sectarian religion in supporting such unjust institutions. What had earlier musically been a Risorgimento patriotic hymn becomes now "arresting: the opening brass chorale with timpani rolls, the sustained hollow fifths of the second violins, the line of pizzicato cellos and basses with its modal inflections, the combination of 'lamenting' figures that results in ambiguities of chromatic harmony worthy of Liszt and Wagner."[16]

Verdi's art first turns to operas in which personal tragedy dominates though linked always to larger political themes – *Lisa Miller, Stiffelio, Rigoletto, Il Trovatore, La Traviata*. But he then integrates this new personal style with larger political themes in, among others, *Les Vepres Siciliennes, Simon Boccanegra, Un Ballo in Maschera, La Forza del Destino, Don Carlos, Aida, Othello,* and *Falstaff.* The chorus no longer speaks in Risorgimento anthems, but is now internally divided, sometimes along lines of competing political factions (*Simon Boccanegra, Un Ballo in Maschera*), or warring nations (*Les Vepres Siciliennes, La Forza del destino*) or people versus priests (*Don Carlos, Aida*), or of race (*Aida*), or of gender (*Falstaff*).[17] These choruses, like those in his earlier operas, include the fierce, often rhythmically propulsive expression of a people's desire for liberty and humanity against the various obstacles factions put in their way. Verdi thus represents in the chorus not just a consciousness divided between archaic heros and the responsibilities of democratic citizens, but democratic citizens fiercely divided among themselves.

Verdi's mature art thus gives salience to worries about the corruption of liberal nationalism by religious sectarianism (*Don Carlos, Aida*), as well as by the force of racism in personal and political life (*La Forza del Destino, Othello*) and as the motor of imperialistic wars (*Aida*) of the sort that Verdi condemned when Italy went to war in Africa.[18] Verdi was always, in the spirit of Mazzini, a liberal nationalist, construing the just claims of a people not in term of cultural purity or ethnic superiority, but in terms of universalistic values of liberal humanism, liberty and equality.[19] But, even this conception of nationalism is often defended, as it was by Benedetto Croce in 1943 after the fall of Mussolini, in terms of *"patria* and *amore della*

---

[16] See *id.*, p. 306.

[17] This pattern begins in Verdi's *Jerusalem*, an opera premiered two years before *La Battaglia di Legnano*, in the Act III, scene 2 in which the chorus divides into those that condemn and those that urge pity for Gaston.

[18] See John Rosselli, *The Life of Verdi*, at pp. 149–50.

[19] See, for a recent defense of a position of this sort, Maurizio Viroli, *For Love of Country*.

*patria*,"[20] a patriotism framed by the very constitutive language of patriarchy. Verdi's art, increasingly profound in its examination of the ravages of patriarchy in both public and private life, now represents nationalism as itself problematic, and he does so because he now can bring to bear on its musical representation the approach to the tragedy of patriarchy that he began to forge with *Luisa Miller* and subsequent works.. Even Verdi early operas show liberal concern with matters of religious intolerance (*I Lombardi*) and ethnic hatred (*Alzira*), but in his mature work he grounds these liberal concerns in politics with similar concerns in personal life, in particular, the relational psychology of parents and children and adults to one another under patriarchy. To be clear about these points, we must explore the psychic geography of such relationships that Verdi's mature operas musically lay bare and explore.

[20] See *id.*, at p. 168.

# Part II

## Hearing the Underworld

*Chapter 5*

# Parents and Children

Patriarchy in its nature begins in relations between parents and children with the father as such accorded hierarchical powers over his wife and children as dictated by gender stereotypes that mythologize women's sexuality in ways that require exclusive patriarchal control of access to them. The development of Verdi's art of expressive musical voice offers a psychic geography of the personal and political psychology that patriarchy imposes on intimate relations, including those of parents with children, siblings within families, and adults with one another. Verdi's art of inventing truth uses musically expressive voice to explore the traumatic break in relationship that patriarchy imposes on personal and public life; we both hear the underworld of suppressed voices and discern its psychic structure.

Verdi's history of separations had clearly fostered a remarkably independent, outsider's eye for the burdens patriarchy placed on intimate relations in the family, in particular, on the relationships of patriarchal fathers to daughters and sons. So much of Verdi's greatest tragic art centers on these relationships because, under patriarchy, the gender binary (male–female) is culturally polarized on the basis of the unjust hierarchical authority of fathers. Verdi obsessionally studies these relationships because the tragedy of patriarchy divides people from one another (men from men, women from women, and men from women) in terms of the putative exigencies of patriarchal authority.

## (1) Fathers and Daughters

No parent–child relationship was, for Verdi, more emotionally fraught with dimensions of traumatic loss than father–daughter. From the very beginning of his career, Verdi was preoccupied with this relationship, starting in *Oberto* (father seeks revenge on man who seduced daughter) and continuing in *Nabucco* (king–father's relationship to two daughters, a natural loving daughter and false adopted daughter), *I Lombardi* (father conflicts with daughter over her love for Saracen principle ), *Giovanna D'Arco* (father conflicts with daughter over her mission to save France), *Alzira* (Inca father conflicts with daughter who refuses father's desire for her marriage to Spanish leader), *Attila* (warrior–daughter seeks revenge for murder of her father), and *Jerusalem* (father conflicts with daughter over man she loves). The patriarchal code of honor subjected the father–daughter relationship to particularly close regulation and control by her father, imposing a stereo-typical mythology on his daughters's sexuality that effectively deprived her of voice and conviction. Verdi focused on such an impact not only on daughters but on fathers. As we earlier saw, *Nabucco*, his first popularly successful opera, innovatively explores the musical representation of the inner emotional desolation under the armor of the patriarchal father, as Nabucco's musical voice reveals the ways in which patriarchy deprives men as well of a voice and conviction about their emotional vulnerabilities. The patriarchal code of honor opened up a gap between the external demands of the honor code in a face-to-face society both for fathers and daughters and their internal emotions, feelings, and lives. Verdi's musical art with growing expressive power innovates voices for both fathers and daughters that explore the psychic losses underlying this gap, speaking of the desolating breaks in personal relationship that the honor code mindlessly requires.

Verdi obsessionally investigates the father–daughter relationship because patriarchy, with its unjust insistence on the hierarchical power of the father, crucially determines the terms of the gender binary (male–female) on the model of the hierarchical authority it requires fathers to exercise over daughters. The two operas that immediately follow *La Battaglia* – *Luisa Miller* and *Stiffelio* – are major steps in Verdi's life-long musical exploration of this psychic territory. But, it is only with his two later unqualified masterpieces, *Rigoletto* and *La Traviata*, that Verdi gives full musical voice to the tragic isolation the gender binary imposes on men and women, a theme he further investigates in *Simon Boccanegra*, *La Forza del Destino*, and *Aida*. These works collectively offer a piercing psychological portrait of the ways in which the patriarchally enforced gender binary, by the way in which it demands hierarchical control and submission in place of voice and dialogue, traumatically breaks relationship. Their particular unifying focus is on different aspects of the underlying psychology of father and daughter under a patriarchal system that unjustly accords fathers control over a daughter's sexuality. I begin my discussion of these works with those (*Luisa*

*Miller* and *Simon Boccanegra*) that focus on fathers who resist exercising such patriarchical authority, and then turn to the remaining works that study fathers who mindlessly exercise such authority. Of these latter works, three of them (*Stiffelio*, *Rigoletto*, and *La Traviata*) study the psychology of the gender-binary of such patriarchal fathers and the daughters that, in consequence, they either refuse to understand or to take seriously and the effects of such isolation on the daughters. The remaining two works (*La Forza del Destino* and *Aida*) focus more centrally on the tragic effects of such paternal patriarchal authority on the psychology of daughters.

Verdi does not regard it as inevitable that all fathers necessarily claim the power over their daughter's sexuality that patriarchy accords them, as both *Luisa Miller* and *Simon Boccanegra* make quite clear. The narrative of *Luisa Miller*, based on Schiller's *Kabale and Liebe* (*Love and Intrigue*), tells the tragic story of two lovers, Luisa and Rodolfo, caught between the demands of two very different fathers, Miller (who resists the patriarchal demand that he should control his daughter's choice of lover and husband) and Count Walter (who demands such control of his son's choices in the interest of Walter's dynastic ambitions). The ethical contrast of the two fathers is sharply drawn in the first act of the opera as Wurm (a servant of Walter), who has long wanted to marry Luisa, demands of Miller, "Non hai dritto dovr'essa tu?" ("Have you no control over her?"), to which Miller responds in ethical horror with one of Verdi's more warmly beautiful musical settings for baritone:

| | |
|---|---|
| "Che dici mai? | What ever are you saying? |
| Sacra la scelta e d'un consorte, | The choice of a husband is sacred, |
| Errer appieno libera deve; | she must be completely free: |
| Nodo che sciorre sol puo la morte | a knot that only death can untie |
| Mal dalla forza legge riceve. | is badly buled by force. |
| Non son tiranno, padre son io, | I am not a tyrant, I'm a father |
| Non si commanda d'figli al cor. | One does not command children's hearts, |
| In terra un padre somiglia Iddio | On earth a father resembles God |
| Per la bontade, non pel rigor. | By his kindness, not his severity."[1] |

Walter (the patriarchal father) coerces Luisa, by threatening murder of her father, to break her engagement to Rodolfo, which leads him to poison both himself and Luisa. Setting this narrative inspired Verdi to forge a more inward musical voice for the desolation not only of Luisa and Rodolfo, but for her father who faces the terrors of loss and loneliness. Miller's courageous

---

[1] See Verdi, *Luisa Miller* libretto to recording conducted by Peter Maag, National Philharmonic Orchestra, at pp. 46–7.

resistance and goodness cannot save him from the loss that Walter's rigidly inflexible patriarchal authority inflicts both on him and Miller. In particular, "the third act is undoubtedly the best of the three and Verdi's greatest achievement so far in combining large-scale structure with depth and intimacy of feeling."[2] It features a duet between Luisa and Miller (in which she agrees not to commit suicide so as to leave her father alone), another between Luisa and Rodolfo (in which they confess their love after Rodolfo makes clear they are both dying of poison), and a concluding terzetto of both with the inconsolable Miller before their deaths. By comparison Verdi's earlier works are:

"bold, exhilarating, maybe, yet lacking depth. . . . In *Luisa Miller* buds of poetry [previously] hinted at . . . burst into full flower. There is a new refinement of musical thought, a new concentration of lyrical elements within the dramatic scheme, in sum a more thorough resolution of the drama into terms of pure music."[3]

The patriarchially inflicted separations of both father from daughter and lovers from one another are voiced in exquisitely lyrical, desolating musically expressive terms. Verdi demands that we hear the emotional price patriarchy inflicts.

Verdi's most musically and dramatically mature exploration of the father who resists patriarchy is *Simon Boccanegra* in which he explores not only the effects of this gender-binary on father and daughter but its larger effects on the possibility of a republican politics. Simon Boccanegra, a corsair in service of the Genose republic, had a love affair with Maria, the daughter of Jacopo Fiesco, an aristocratic Genoese noble, leading to the birth of a daughter. The opera opens with Maria's death, and the tragic tension of the opera is framed in terms of the rage of the patriarchal father (Fiesco) against her lover (Boccanegra), who is about to be declared doge of Genoa, a position Boccanegra was prepared to accept in order to make him more acceptable to Fiesco. Fiesco enters as a lost soul, singing of his sorrow, anger, and bitterness at the death of his beloved daughter ("Il lacerato spirito"). Fiesco finds himself face-to-face with Simon, and bursts out in fury and scorn. Simon pleads for forgiveness, offering to let Fiesco kill him on the spot for his breach of the honor code. Fiesco does not wish, however, to be a murderer. He will forgive Simon if he hands over his daughter by Maria, but Simon explains that, upon the unexpected death of his daughter's custodian on a distant shore, the daughter wandered off and has been lost; Fiesco responds

---

2 See Julian Budden, *The Operas of Verdi, Volume 1*, p. 439.
3 See *id.*, p. 446.

that there can be no peace between them. In this remarkable duet between baritone (Simon) and bass (Fiesco), they "are sculpted as individuals, each within his own vocal archetype: Fiesco hard and inflexible; Simone infinitely mobile."[4] Subsequently, Simon learns he has been chosen doge at the same time he discovers the death of Maria.

The scene shifts to many years later. Simon's daughter, Amelia – her true identity unknown to anybody – had been adopted by a noble Genoese family, and is now in love with a young noble, Gabriele, an opponent of the doge, Boccanegra. Since one of Boccanegra's associates, Paolo, wants to marry the young heiress, he has come to meet her, soon discovering upon questioning about her background that she is his daughter. They are rapturously reunited, as "prolonged cries of 'Figlia' and 'Padre' . . . swell . . . to a huge climax, then melt . . . away  . . . on harp, clarinet, and basoon with horns and pizzicato strings to underpin the final chords."[5] They agree to keep their relationship secret. Boccanegra makes clear to Paolo that Amelia will not be compelled to marry a man she does not love; Paolo vows revenge. Boccanegra, now united to his daughter, brings to his role as doge a humane largeness of spirit. When two groups of counsellors are about to fight with one another,

> "the Doge steps between the contending parties with a cry of 'Fratricidi!'
>     The appeal which follows ('Plebe! Patrizi! Popolo!') is Verdi's finest monument to the baritone voice, a hymn to the ideal of universal brotherhood as uplifting as Beethoven's 'Ode to Joy' and very nearly as simple – two double periods of sixteen bars, each with a one-bar extension."[6]

Boccanegra's resistance to patriarchy exacts a painful personal price when he accepts his daughter's love for his enemy, Gabriele. In contrast to Rigoletto, Simon overcomes his blinding desire to control his daughter's sexuality to his own patriarchal ends. Rather, overcoming his patriarchal anger at the political enemy who loves his daughter and whom she loves, he experiences and accepts the loss of his daughter as an expression of love for her, as a person, that motivationally links this personal psychology of loving father–daughter relationship to a political psychology of republican fraternity that transcends the factionalized terms of Genoese republican politics. The consequence of Simon's generosity is both personal and political: the opera offers us one of the only depictions in Verdi's tragedies of a love between a man and woman (Gabriele and Amelia) that is not destroyed

---

[4] See *id.*, p. 286.
[5] See *id.*, p. 301.
[6] See *id.*, p. 312.

by patriarchal demands, and that love also unites opposing factions in a sense of civic fraternity. However, Simon, himself resisting patriarchy, lives in a patriarchal world, and falls victim to its demands. Poisoned by Paolo, Boccanegra, as he is dying, meets Fiesco for the last time:

> "Simone reveals Amelia's identity. Fiesco's astonishment is marked by a sudden key change and a pattern of parallel sixths in the orchestra. These coalesce into a series of lamenting figures which persist . . . as Fiesco weeps silently, afraid to look Simone in the face . . . Fiesco, bitterly remorseful, is won over."[7]

In *Simon Boccanegra*, Verdi portrayed a man, Boccanegra, whose love resisted the demands of patriarchy. His loneliness is portrayed by the "quite unheard of" fact that he was "without a single extended lyrical solo to himself. (Don Giovanni is the nearest to a precedent)" reflecting the fact that "Simone's life has remained shattered into fragments since the death of his beloved Maria."[8] He is musically voiced as having a warmth, flexibility, and generosity (a voice of relationship) lacking in his counterpart, the patriarchal father, Fiesco. Once united with his daughter, he is portrayed as a political leader capable of a humane largeness of spirit that transcends faction. Resistance to patriarchy, Verdi suggests, makes psychologically possible a more inclusive democratic politics.

Verdi studies the gender-binary of the rigidly controlling patriarchal father and daughter in *Stiffelio*, *Rigoletto*, and *La Traviata*. *Stiffelio* examines the linkages under patriarchy of the role of a husband (Stiffelio) and father (Stankar) in enforcing the honor code against a straying wife, Lina, who had been seduced by Raffaele. The ethical complication is that Stiffelio is an inspired and popular Protestant minister, who has, on grounds of the gospel of forgiveness in the Christian Bible, repeatedly urged others to forgive such adultery, but is psychologically unable to bring himself to such forgiveness himself, breaking out into violence against both his wife and Raffaele. To do justice to Stiffelio's struggles, Verdi creates a musical voice not to be heard again until *Otello*, namely, one that

> "is unlike any tenor role that Verdi has written so far . . . Stiffelio is a mature man, happily married (or so he thinks), who has more on his mind than the roses and raptures of passion. His line is sustained, weighty, baritonic almost, with an unusual emphasis on middle and lower registers and a tendency to move by step in wide spanning phrases buttressed by strong harmonies."[9]

Stankar, Lina's father, had suspected his daughter's infidelity, and bullies her into not confessing to her husband as she wishes to do:

---

[7] See *id.*, p. 327.

[8] See *id.*, p. 329.

"Must he himself, Stankar asks, undergo the dishonour of having to acknowledge as his daughter a self-confessed adulteress? Lina's . . . reply anticipates Gilda's part in the quartet in *Rigoletto* with a chain of broken semiquavers that suggest twisting and turning in an effort to escape." [10]

Consistent with the code of honor, Stankar has no interest is his daughter's protest that she was an unwilling partner to the intrigue; the important point is to keep the whole affair quiet. Verdi gives musical expression to the gap between external demand and personal loss:

"In Stankar's verse the crisp, almost military, orchestral pattern gives it a suitable air of inexorability. With Lina it assumes a throbbing agitation." [11]

Stankar, standing on his patriarchal honor, later challenges Raffaele to a duel; Raffaele initially demurs on the ground of his youth and Stankar's age, but is stung into violence by Stankar's:

"tu non sei che un trovatello."        "you are nothing but a foundling!"

The opera thus frames the impact of the code of honor on men's sudden explosions of violence, whether fathers, husbands, or lovers (see earlier discussion of foundlings in nineteenth-century Italy in chapter 2), all keyed to breaches of the honor code, whether one's wife or daughter or, in the accusation against Raffaele, one's mother. Verdi, however, writes some of the most personally expressive voice in the opera for the scene of personal confrontation between Stiffelio and Lina. Stiffelio calls for separation with "a restrained bitterness . . . canalized into a melody whose poignancy is all the greater for being confined within extremely formal bounds." [12] After an expression of grief, Lina signs the divorce papers;

"but no sooner has she done so than she takes on a new and unexpected dignity. Having appealed in vain to him as his wife, she will now appeal to him as her minister. Her melody is notable for its idiomatic use of hollow harmonies. The austerity is there as before yet warmth is slowly breaking in . . . The movement culminates in the sweeping phrase 'Ministro confessatemi'; then to an andante . . . embellished by a cor anglais obligato she declares that she never loved Raffaele; she was betrayed by him; that her heart is true to the husband who wishes to cast her off . . . All the restrained pathos in the scene is concentrated in the cor anglais melody." [13]

---

[9] See *id.*, p. 460.

[10] See *id.*, p. 463.

[11] See *id.*, p. 463.

[12] See *id.*, p. 470.

[13] See *id.*, pp. 470–1.

Lina speaks in the expressive musical voice of relationship to her husband for the first time in the opera, a voice of loving relationship made possible only by the dissolution of their patriarchal marriage (an irony that may have touched a resonant chord of psychological truth with Verdi – as it does for some gay/lesbian couples today – during the ten-year period when he and Strepponi, as long-term lovers and companions, were not married). Stiffelio is incredulous. The last scene of the opera frames his incredulity as in stark contradiction to his religious and ethical beliefs, as he opens the Christian Bible and reads the passage about forgiveness for the woman condemned for adultery. Such incredulity bespeaks a larger and deeper psychological problem: the mythologizing stereotypes of gender, violently enforced by the patriarchal code of honor as the terms of marriage as an institution, in their nature break relationship (including the possibility of relationship within marriage), because their terms rest on the objectifying refusal to hear personal voice and conviction.

Verdi's first unqualified masterpiece, *Rigoletto*, makes us hear the double consciousness of the hunchback Rigoletto who, on the hand, slavishly ministers to the Duke of Mantua's frivolous affairs with every pretty woman in sight and, on the other, keeps his beloved daughter Gilda under the closest possible patriarchal control so that she will not be sexually accessible to men like the Duke. Rigoletto thus maliciously undermines the patriarchy whenever it serves his interests as the Duke's minion, but, when cursed by a father whose daughter he encouraged the Duke to seduce, he reflects in his famous soliloquy, "Pari siamo", on how much he is like an assassin who has offered Rigoletto his services: "We are alike, I kill with my tongue, he with his sword":

> "Then Rigoletto laments his fate as jester – to make his master laugh at all times no matter what his own feelings. He inveighs against the heartless courtiers; then a tender phrase on the flute brings back thoughts of his daughter, and the change which comes over him when he enters his own house." [14]

Verdi anatomizes in Rigoletto the corruption of voice of persons who accommodate themselves to longstanding patterns of colonial subordination, as Italians largely had since the fall of Rome. Rigoletto has lost in public his personal voice, rather himself taking on the voice of the courtier, bitterly sardonic, jesting at injustice, heartless. He rages against the courtiers, but, as he is the worst of them, he in effect rages against himself.

---

[14] See *id.*, pp. 492–3.

In contrast, he comes to his home as a kind of sanctuary where he can feel personal voice in relationship to his beloved daughter, or so he thinks.

But, while Rigoletto's double consciousness can encompass his hypocrisy in flouting yet obeying the honor code, it cannot understand his own daughter whose feelings and voice operate outside the demands of the code. Indeed, Gilda is portrayed as not even knowing her father's name, let alone his occupation. Only when pressed by Gilda does Rigoletto describe her dead mother in musically expressive voice that aches with loss:

| | |
|---|---|
| "Ah, deh, no parlare al misero | Ah, do not speak of her |
| Del suo perduto bene | whose loss I still mourn . . . |
| Ella sentia, quell'angelo, | That angel felt pity |
| Pieta delle mie pene . . . | for my sorrows . . . |
| Solo, difforme, povero | Alone, poor, misshapen, |
| Per compassion mi amo. | From compassion she loved me. |
| Ah! Moria . . . le zolle coprano | She died . . . the unfeeling earth |
| Lievi quel capo amato. | Covers that beloved head. |
| Sola or tu resti al misero . . . | Now you alone are left to this unhappy man.. |
| Dio sii ringraziato! . . . | O God, I thank Thee . . . "[15] |

Verdi had been absorbed at this time with the possibility of setting *King Lear*. "Is it too fanciful to suppose that his new-found enthusiasm for Hugo's play proceeded from the same creative mood that has inspired him to try his hand at Shakespeare's?"[16] The tragedy of Rigoletto, like that of King Lear, arises from a father's inability to read the love of his daughter. It also arises, as does *King Lear*, from the aching psychological sense of an absent mother, to whom, at the very end of the opera, Gilda unites herself imaginatively as she dies. Rigoletto, as much a regal patriarch in his domain as Lear was in his, had psychologically regarded Gilda as giving him what her dead mother had. The absent mother marks not only Gilda's isolation, but Rigoletto's, in the same way that, as Coppelia Kahn has cogently noted of *King Lear*,[17] the absent mother marks Lear's underlying highly gendered patriarchal psychology of external masculine command and control, and inward and denied lonely, grasping neediness for feminine care. For Gilda, the absent mother represents her lack of relationship to anything remotely

---

[15] See Giuseppe Verdi, *Rigoletto*, recording, Riccardo Muti, conductor, Orchestra del Teatro alla Scala, libretto, at p. 84

[16] See Julian Budden, *The Operas of Verdi, Volume 1*, p. 484.

[17] Coppelia Kahn, "The Absent Mother in *King Lear*," in Margaret W. Ferguson, Maureen Quilligan, and Nancy J. Vickers, *Rewriting the Renaissance: The Discourses of Sexual Difference in Early Modern Europe* (Chicago: University of Chicago Press, 1986), at pp. 33–49.

resembling a loving parent, with whom she could have safely voiced her feelings and vulnerabilities, including her sexual and emotional needs. She certainly has no voice in relationship to her rigidly controlling patriarchal father, who has effectively imposed a regime of strict control on her emotions, thoughts, and movements. Gilda's lack of voice in relationship to either her father or mother leads to a voice of identification with an idealized image of her absent mother, which psychologically prepares her (like Iphigenia, see chapter 2) for the suicidal sacrifice of herself at the end of the opera, a theme of the patriarchal psychology of feminine self-sacrifice Verdi explores as well in the deaths of Violetta and Desdemona.

The tragedy arises when Gilda breaks the bonds of her father's strict patriarchal control and meets and falls in love with a young man whom she believes to be a poor student but is, in fact, the Duke in disguise. Strikingly, even the Duke, whose patriarchal wishes Rigoletto serves so slavishly, is moved by the love of Gilda (a love Rigoletto cannot understand) at least to consider a different path. We hear, but Rigoletto does not, Gilda's ecstatic adoration of this young man ("Caro nome"), "one of the most striking instances of vocal figuration used, so to speak, introspectively."[18] The code of honor exacts its revenge on Rigoletto: the courtiers, the honor of whose wives and daughters have been compromised (with Rigoletto's active complicity) by the Duke, exact their due when they kidnap Gilda, whom they suppose to be Rigoletto's mistress. Gilda is delivered to the Duke, who, after a brief though real romantic hesitation, seduces her offstage. Rigoletto's honor as a father is thus compromised. Rigoletto furiously confronts the courtiers with their infamy ("Cortigiani, vil razza dannata", "You courtiers, vile accursed race"), and then breaks down into poignant pleading with an "underlying nobility all expressed in terms of the purest Italian lyricism"[19] concluding with "the glorious, purely vocal climax at the words 'Ridate a ma la figlia' – a Verdian speciality deriving from his unique feeling for the expressive powers of the baritone voice."[20] When Gilda rushes in from the ducal apartment, Rigoletto with unexpected dignity orders the courtiers to leave them ("Ite di qui voi tutti", "Out with you all"). When Rigoletto learns from Gilda what happened, the music turns to "the most deeply felt movement of all ('Piangi piangi fanciulla') 'Weep, child, weep'."[21] But, Rigoletto's grief for his daughter soon turns, consistent with the honor code, to vengeance.

---

[18] See Julian Budden, *The Operas of Verdi, Volume 1*, p. 497.
[19] See *id.*, p. 501.
[20] See *id.*, 501.
[21] See *id.*, 502.

In the musically glorious last act of *Rigoletto,* Rigoletto confronts his daughter (who is still in love with the Duke) with his philandering with the sister of the assassin Rigoletto has hired to kill the Duke. Verdi presents musically the very different emotions of these four characters in the quartet "Bella figlia dell'amore" ("Lovely daughter of pleasure"), "expressed simultaneously within the most pellucid lyrical writing imaginable."[22] Rigoletto orders Gilda to return home, as he makes his agreement with the assassin to have the Duke killed; when asked the name of the victim, Rigoletto replies in a voice of identification: "Egli e 'Delitto', 'Punizion' son io" ("He is 'Crime'; I am 'Punishment'"). Rigoletto is to return at midnight to retrieve the body. Gilda, living outside her father's honor code, returns to hear the assassin's sister persuade her brother, as an alternative to killing the Duke, to kill the first person who should come that night during an approaching storm and substitute the victim's body for the Duke's. Gilda decides to sacrifice herself, entering during the musically terrifying storm, and is stabbed. When Rigoletto returns, he is given a sack containing a body he believes to be the Duke's. He is left alone, and hears the Duke's voice singing, with tragic irony (in light of Gilda's sacrifice), his earlier aria about women's flightiness: "La donna e mobile" ("Woman is wayward"). He is paralyzed, and then opens the sack to find his dying daughter. The opera concludes with Gilda's death after a heart-rending last duet (in which Rigoletto harrowingly pleads with Gilda not to leave him alone). Rigoletto whose obsession with the code of honor locked him into stereotypes that denied the voice and experience of his daughter, has blindly killed her, leaving him alone and desolate.

Verdi's *La Traviata* examines from yet another musically expressive angle the gap between the external demands of the code of honor and its underlying psychological loss and desolation. Violetta, a Parisian courtesan, has met and, for the first time in her life, fallen in love with a young man, Alfredo Germont. She gives up her former life to live, largely on her own money, with Alfredo in the country. Violetta is apparently fatherless. But the stereotypical demands of the patriarchal father–daughter relationship are psychologically brought to bear on her by Alfredo's father, Giorgio Germont, who appears suddenly to persuade her to break with his son. In the extraordinary, long duet that follows, "Germont maintains the same position throughout. His is the voice of identification with morality, sympathetic but inexorable, while Violetta's voice of relationship moves through the entire spectrum of tragic emotions."[23] Germont talks

---

[22] See *id.*, 505.

[23] See Julian Budden, *The Operas of Verdi, Volume 2*, at p. 140.

of his young daughter, "pure as an angel", whose marriage to the man she loves is threatened by Alfredo's notorious liaison with Violetta, and demands that Violetta separate from Alfredo forever. Violetta speaks in the voice of relationship: she would rather die than leave Alfredo; she is mortally ill; she has no friends, family; Alfredo is everything to her, and she to him. Germont responds with an inexorable voice of identification with patriarchal authority that, their relationship being illegitimate, she has nothing to bind her to Alfredo, and therefore nothing to hold him to her when she is no longer young and Alfredo, with male fickeless, allows his affections to wander. Violetta despairs, and Germont begs her to do what he asks. Violetta, resigned, asks Germont to tell Alfredo's sister of her sacrifice and, after her death (which she foresees with poignant terror), to tell Alfredo as well. "Nowhere in Italian opera is grief more poignantly transfigured than here."[24] After Germont leaves and Violetta is writing a note that will be delivered to Alfredo breaking off their liaison, Alfredo abruptly returns. Violetta hides the note, but she cannot hide her agitation:

> "There follows one of the most remarkable 'false crescendi' ever written – false because for most of the time the dynamics do not increase at all; but the sense of growing tension is maintained for forty bars. The real crescendo takes place only in the last two. Violetta babbles about throwing herself at the feet of Alfredo's father, appealing for his blessing – so that they can be happy . . . No she is not weeping, she is calm, smiling . . . she only wants to be beside him for every and ever; then the tension dissolves in a tremendous lyrical outburst, 'Amami Alfredo – 'Love me, Alfredo, as I love you'."[25]

Violetta tears herself from Alfredo's embrace and rushes out of the room. When her note is shortly delivered to Alfredo, Giorgio Germont returns to comfort his son and urge him to return home in the warm, nostalgic baritone aria, "Di Provenza il mar, il suol." Verdi wants us to hear the deep, sincere feeling of the patriarchal father, but he also demands that we hear as well his extraordinarily insular patriarchal egotism as he demands (after the conspicuous agony he has just inflicted on Violetta) that Alfredo think how much he has hurt his father, recalling his son to a sense of honor:

| "Ah, il tuo vecchio genitor | You do not know |
|---|---|
| Tu non sai quanto soffri! | What pain your old father has suffered! |

---

[24] See *id.*, p. 144.
[25] See *id.*, p. 147.

| | |
|---|---|
| Te lontano, di squallor | With you away |
| All suo tetto si copri . . . | His home has been desolate indeed. |
| Ma se alfin ti trovo ancor, | But if in finding you again |
| Se in speme non falli, | His hopes are not in vain, |
| Se la voce dell'onor | If the voice of honour |
| In te appien non ammuti, | Is not silent for you |
| Dio m'esaudi. | God has heard me!" [26] |

"The voice of honour" is, for Germont, callously armored against the kind of display of feeling he has just seen and not seen in his previous scene with Violetta. Alfredo will have none of his father's provincial sentimentality. But he is very much his father's honor-obsessed son as he showed earlier in the act when, upon learning that Violetta has been supporting him in the country, he angrily expresses "O grido dell'onore" ("Oh, cry of honour") before he rushes off to raise money; and he shows the same honor-based violence when he later humiliates Violetta in public in a way that horrifies not only her friends but his father as well. The last act discloses Violetta's bedroom as she lay dying. Giorgio Germont has written her that Alfredo has been told of her sacrifice, and he and Giorgio will return shortly. She *speaks* "in a sepulchral voice" the words "It is late" ("E tardi"). Her aria ("Addio del passato") is "a farewell to past dreams of happiness with a pathetic oboe to open and close the two strophes and to link their respective major and minor sections";[27] "the string writing is remarkable."[28] When Alfredo enters and flies into her arms, they rapturously greet other, exchanging words of love and forgiveness. Verdi with remarkable psychology acuity portrays Violetta as blaming herself, "La rea son io" ("I'm the one to blame"), suggesting she may accept at least some of the terms of her honor-based plea to Alfredo in the previous act to forget her, "Scorda un nome ch'e infamato!" ("Forget a name that's without honour!"). Their mutual forgiveness leads to the andante of the duet ("Parigi, o cara, noi lasceremo", "We'll leave Paris, my dearest"). Violetta's first thought is to go to church to thank God for Alfredo's return, but she falls back fainting, and her maid goes for the doctor. "Tell him," Violetta adds, "that I want to live now that Alfredo has come back":

"The agitated motion of the music is arrested by a powerful brass unison; and in a phrase quite chilling in its restraint she tells Alfredo that if his return cannot restore her to health nothing can prevent her from dying . . . Then

---

[26] See Giuseppe Verdi, *La Traviata*, recording, James Levine, conductor, The Metropolitan Opera Orchestra, libretto, at pp. 63–4.

[27] See Julian Budden, *The Operas of Verdi, Volume 2*, p. 157.

[28] See *id.*, p. 157.

despair rises to the surface in the cabaletta ('Ah! Gran Dio! Morir si giovine'), a melody whose pathos resides neither in the harmonies nor in the tonality but rather in the accents, phrasing, and melodic intervals." [29]

The finale brings in Germont, now ready to claim Violetta as his daughter.

"She greets him weakly; and, as he looks at her, for the first time and only time in the opera he betrays strong emotion . . . Only now does he realize the wrong he has done her." [30]

Before her death, Violetta gives Alfredo a medallion; "and if he should meet some pure-hearted girl who loves him, he must marry her and give her the portrait, telling her that it is of one who prays for them both." [31] Violetta by this point has, by virtue of her passion for self-sacrifice, psychologically moved, in the terms of the pedestal underlying the code of honor, from bad woman to good woman, albeit soon (as good women for Verdi usually are) doomed to be dead and absent:

"Di chi nel ciel fra gli angeli          Who from heaven, amongst the angels,
Prega per lei, per te.                    Prays always for her and for you." [32]

The power of the honor code takes over Violetta's psychology as she faces death, as it was later to take over Desdemona's in Verdi's *Otello*. Violetta feels a sudden resurgence of life:

"The orchestra reflects her growing excitement while her voice remains almost expressionless, low in her register, quasi parlando, then rises with the orchestra to a fortissimo climax at which she falls back senseless. The others exclaim in horror . . ." [33]

*La Traviata* "is Verdi's most intimate music drama; and the feelings it portrays are those of individual humanity down the ages." [34] Its feelings are, to a remarkable extent for the place and period, those of a free sexual woman (Violetta) – generous, intelligent, her emotions portrayed as moving through the full range of human feeling – whom the code of honor could barely acknowledge as human. It is Verdi's most astonishing confrontation

---

[29] See *id.*, p. 160.

[30] See *id.*, p. 162.

[31] See *id.*, p. 162.

[32] See Giuseppe Verdi, *La Traviata*, recording, James Levine, conductor, The Metropolitan Opera Orchestra, libretto, at p. 94.

[33] See Julian Budden, *The Operas of Verdi, Volume 2*, p. 163.

[34] See *id.*, p. 165.

of the external demands of the code of honor with the emotional truth of the desolating loss of personal relationship that it mindlessly inflicts on women and men.

The effects of the demands of a patriarchal father on a daughter, rather than the father–daughter relationship itself, is the focus of two of Verdi's mature music dramas, *La Forza del Destino* and *Aida*. Verdi attends in these works to the effects of the demands of a patriarchal father on the psychology of a daughter whose personal love conflicts with the demands of patriarchy.

*La Forza* frames on the broadest possible political and human scale the devastating consequences for politics of the supine acceptance of patriarchy. The tragic tension of the opera arises from the "obsessive pride and vengefulness,"[35] rooted in the code of honor, of the men of a Spanish noble family, the Calatravas, against the love of Alvaro, the son of a noble Inca family, and Leonora, a daughter of the Calatrava family. Taking up again themes of racial conflict, imperialism, and miscegenation introduced in his early opera *Alzira*, Verdi re-examines the issue in his now mature musically expressive style from the perspective of the code of honor as it bears ferociously on the psychology of a woman and man who have tried to resist patriarchy, musically isolated from everyone else in the opera by "nobility and idealism."[36] As we saw in our earlier discussion of *Iphigenia at Aulis* (chapter 2), Iphigenia's shift in voice from resistance to acceptance of her father's homicidal will is expressed in her shift from a realistic view of the affair of Helen and Paris (a Greek woman with a racialized barbarian) as based on consent and desire to a mythology of rape rationalizing the political violence of the Trojan War. The code of honor mythologizes its control of women in terms of a racialized pedestal that sharply distinguishes the virtues of one's own women from the vices of women of the racialized other, and reacts with special ideological violence to consensual relationships between women and men that challenge this mythology, a historical pattern prominently exemplified in the highly gendered propensity to violence in the American South in the defense of slavery and, later, racism, rationalized in terms of protecting the honor of white women.[37] Alvaro and Leonora, whose love transcends ethnic difference, challenge patriarchy at one of its most vulnerable points.

The opera opens with a melancholy scene of the Marquis of Calatrava saying a tender good night to his daughter, Leonora; he is convinced that she has been cured of her unacceptable love for the Amerindian stranger, so why sad? She is, in fact, on the verge of eloping with Alvaro, but is

---

[35] See *id.*, p. 430.
[36] See *id.*, p. 446.

tormented by the conflict of her feeling for Alvaro with her feeling for her father:

"E si amoroso padre,       Can so loving a father
avverso fia tanto ai voti miei?   Oppose my wishes so strongly?"[38]

After he leaves, Leonora expresses agonized indecision about her elopement in her first aria, "Me pellegrina ed orfana" ("An orphan and a wanderer"), "a heartbroken farewell to hearth and home," [39] whose words were taken by Verdi from Somma's libretto for *King Lear* that Verdi kept in his possession for many years, but never set to music (the text was an aria for Cordelia after she had been disinherited and driven out by her father).[40] Leonora, loving both her father and Alvaro, is emotionally conflicted about her choice, hoping against hope that Alvaro will arrive too late. Verdi's music for Leonara (like that for Don Carlos in his next opera) suggests more than just indecision, but some more psychologically complex neurotic conflict rooted in unresolved tensions between passion, idealism, and family attachments. When Alvaro arrives, she confronts him with her doubts, and he offers her the choice that they should part now. But she is swept up in their mutual love, and agrees to elope with him. When interrupted by her irate and armed father and servants, Alvaro begs the Marquis to strike him dead, but the Marquis refuses to soil his hands with the blood of anyone so vile and baseborn. Alvaro in an act of surrender throws down his pistol, which accidentally goes off killing the Marquis. Dying, the Marquis curses Leonora, as she and Alvaro flee.

The traumatic breaking of relationship between Leonora and her father is compounded by that of Leonora and Alvaro, as they are separated in the scuffle that follows the death of the Marquis, and are united, and then only by fortuitous circumstances, at the end of the opera, at which time Leonara is vengefully killed by her own brother, Carlo. The opera musically explores

---

[37] See, for discussion of the diagnosis of this racist pathology by Ida Wells-Barnett in response to the lynchings of black men after the Civil War, Richards, *Women, Gays, and the Constitution*, at pp. 185–90. For general discussion of the underlying cultural pattern, see Bertram Wyatt-Brown, *Southern Honor: Ethics and Behavior in the Old South* (Oxford: Oxford University Press, 1983); Kenneth S. Greenberg, *Honor and Slavery* (Princeton: Princeton University Press, 1996); Richard E. Nisbett and Dov Cohen, *Culture of Honor: The Psychology of Violence in the South* (Boulder, Colo: Westview Press, 1996); Peter Spierenburg, *Men and Violence: Gender, Honor, and Rituals in Modern Europe and America* (Columbus, Ohio: Ohio State University Press, 1998).

[38] Verdi, *La Forza del Destino*, libretto to recording conducted by Riccardo Muti, Orchestra e Coro del Teatro Alla Scala, at pp. 54–5.

[39] See Julian Budden, *The Operas of Verdi, Volume 2*, p. 450.

[40] See *id.*, p. 450.

the ways in which the psychology of traumatic separation impacts those who have tried to resist patriarchy, and certainly does not downplay the difficulties of resistance. In persons with flint-like integrity like Leonara and Alvaro, there is, of course, their sense of ethics after the death of the Marquis:

> "Consumed with feelings of guilt and remorse, they make no attempt to find one another. Eleonara believes Alvaro to have sailed for South America; Alvaro imagines Eleonara to be dead."[41]

Both Leonora and Alvaro, deeply alone and isolated, solace their remorseful broken hearts with forms of fatalistic idealism which call for self-sacrifice, not for a resistance based on moral agency. Leonora finds psychological solace in the humane religion of the Franciscan monks who give her refuge – Verdi, the religious sceptic's, tribute to the appeal of the humane Catholicism of Manzoni, whom he had long admired and recently met.[42] Both of Leonora's two great arias, "Madre, pietosa Vergine" ("Mother, merciful Virgin") and "Pace, pace, mio Dio!" ("Peace, peace, O my God!") – the first as she enters her monastic refuge, the second at the moment her refuge is threatened – are prayers speaking from a sense of absent relationship, the absence of a loving father or mother or sibling or husband or friend, that cover over an anxiety and terror that the music insistently expresses. Indeed, we musically hear one of the few moments of Leonara's relief from her remorse-ridden anxiety when Father Guardino, the abbot of the order, extends to her a paternal sympathy and understanding she never knew from her patriarchal father or brother, as her accompanying words make clear:

| | |
|---|---|
| "Piu tranquilla l'alma sento | My soul is now more at peace, |
| Dacche premo questa terra; | Since coming to this refuge. |
| De'fantasmi lo spavento | The fearful ghouls |
| Piu non provo farmi guerra. | Have ceased to war upon me. |
| Piu non sorge sanguinante | No longer does the bloodstained ghost |
| Di mio padre l'ombre innante, | Of my father haunt my sight; |
| Ne terribile l'ascolto | No longer does the frightful curse |
| La sua figlia maledir. | Of a father torture his daughter's mind."[43] |

Verdi portrays a similar psychology of traumatic despair sublimated into idealism, first, in Alvaro's turn to heroic military service in Italy in the War of the Austrian Succession, and, second, his own later turn to the monastic

---

[41] See *id.*, p. 429.
[42] See *id.*, p. 440.

brotherhood of Franciscan friars. The psychological alternatives, Verdi suggests, of patriarchal manhood, once it traumatically breaks loving relationships, are thus either militaristic heroism or monastic discipline.

Following Victor Hugo's suggestion that romantic theater (following Shakespeare) not observe the classical unities, Verdi paints in *La Forza* with a broad historical brush, incorporating into the Spanish play on which it is based scenes from his friend Maffei's recent Italian translation of Schiller's *Wallensteins Lager*[44] (*Wallenstein's Camp*), dealing with soldiers of diverse backgrounds and nationalities who nonetheless serve together under an admired commander. Alvaro serves in *La Forza* as such a commander – a psychological strength that arises, Verdi suggests, directly out of his resistance to patriarchy. Carlo, the supine executor of the demands of the honor code, appears, in contrast, petty, small, and egotistical, incapable of any political largeness of spirit.

These larger political implications of the resistance to patriarchy are studied further in *Aida* in the contrasting father–daughter relationships of the pharaoh and Amneris, and Amonasro and Aida. Amneris, the daughter of pharaoh, ruler of Egypt, is in patriarchal lock step with her father for much of the opera; she identifies with his militaristic ambitions against racialized Ethiopia, and is happy to marry Radames, the victorious general against the Ethiopians, whom she has long loved, as her father proposes after his victory, rewarding Radames by making him his successor. Only after Radames had frustrated her plans and is facing death at Egypt's hands for treason does she turn against the patriarchy, and then not so much against her father, but the priests who inexorably refuse any extenuation.

Aida, the daughter of the Ethiopian king, Amonasro, is, in contrast, portrayed as in fundamental conflict not only with Egypt's but with her father's patriarchal will. She and Radames have fallen in love in resistance to patriarchy (Egyptian and Ethiopian), which is to say as an expression of mutual personal sexual need not the external demands of the patriarchal code of honor. Aida is a slave in Egypt and racially other as well. The love of Aida and Radames must be clandestine, for it flouts the terms of patriarchal idealization of women of one's ethnic group and degradation of women outside one's group. Aida is musically introduced as in psychological conflict, first, with Amneris, who loves and wants Radames, and, second, over her conflicting love with her father and country and for Radames, who is appointed to lead the Egyptian armies against the

---

[43] Verdi, *La Forza del Destino*, libretto to recording conducted by Riccardo Muti, Orchestra e Coro del Teatro Alla Scala, at pp. 100–1.

[44] See Julian Budden, *The Operas of Verdi, Volume 2*, pp. 431–2.

Ethiopians. Her joining with the public's cries to her lover, "Ritorna vincitor!," is musically followed by remorse and internal conflict:

| | |
|---|---|
| "I sacri nomi di padre, d'amante | The sacred names of father, of lover, |
| Ne prfferir poss'io, ne ricordar; | I cannot utter, nor yet recall, |
| Per l'un . . . per l'altro . . . confusa, tremante | For the one . . . for the other . . . confused, trembling, |
| Io piangere vorrei, vorrei pregar. | I would weep, I would pray."[45] |

When Amonasro, after defeat by Egypt, is brought to Egypt and sees that he can use his daughter's clandestine love to serve his patriarchal purposes, Aida even then resists him. She yields only when convinced in her own conscience that the very political fate of her nation turns on agreement.

Importantly, her great scene of resistance comes after her extraordinarily beautiful, exquisitely scored, desolate aria of longing for her native land, "O patria mia," in which she comes back obsessively to the thought and feeling that she will never see again her beloved home land, "O patria mia, mai piu ti revedro." Her resistance to Amonasro is all the more remarkable because it comes at such devastating emotional cost, her country as opposed to her love. Amonasro tells his daughter that he has a plan to enable her to get the better of her mistress, and evokes the fair land of Ethiopia to which he and his daughter might soon return. Ethiopian victory is certain if they know which route the Egyptians will take. When Aida realizes what is being asked of her, she refuses in horror. Amonasro bursts into a fiery denunciation:

> "'A murdered nation,' Amonasro cries, 'will point the accusing finger at you.' Finally he evokes the vision of Aida's dead mother rising from her grave to denounce the daughter who has betrayed their people ('Una larva orribile, fra l'ombre a noi s'affaccia . . . '). Here a formal sequence embedded in the free-ranging melody provides the launching-pad for Amonasro's ultimate taunt: 'You are not my daughter; you are the slave of the Pharaohs!' Again the metre changes to the quinario as Amonasro's words are hurled with devastating effect between orchestral explosions ('Non sei mia figlia. De'Faraoni tu sei la schiava!') – one of the most remarkable instances of that 'parola scenica' so dear to the composer's heart."[46]

Aida falls to the ground, begging for her father's pity; she will not be unworthy of her country. Amonasro reminds her that only with her aid can an oppressed people rise again ("Pensa che un popolo, vinto, straziato", "Remember that a people, conquered, tormented"):

---

[45] Verdi, *Aida*, libretto for recording conducted by Claudio Abbado, Coro e Orchestra del Teatro alla Scala, at pp. 72–3.

[46] See Julian Budden, *The Operas of Verdi, Volume 3*, p. 238.

"Once again the emotions of the moment appear transcended. There is more here than Amonasro's satisfaction at having got his way. Compassion, irony – who can tell? But it brings no comfort to Aida. While throbbing violins begin a slow twelve-bar climb she winds up the movement with that phrase to which Verdi attached to much importance ("O Patria, quanto mi costi!" . . . ), sounding all the more desolate for the ray of light which preceded it." [47]

Aida's strength in resisting patriarchy gives her the ability even to sacrifice her love when it serves the national aims of justice of an oppressed people, an issue that had been close to Verdi's heart throughout his life. That Verdi gives musical expression to these ambitions through and in the voice of a black woman struggling, against conflicting romantic impulses, for integrity in resisting the enslavement of her people by a theocratically ruled white people surely shows, as Paul Robinson has decisively demonstrated against Edward Said,[48] that he aligns resistance to theocratic patriarchy with resistance to racist imperialism, an imperialism which, in fact, he deplored in the Italy of the late nineteenth-century.[49] What is even more remarkable in Verdi's own stance of resistance is that, contrary to the dominant patriarchal gendering of nationalism of his period, we musically hear the voice of resistance as a woman's voice and not the militaristic women's voice of the early Risorgimento operas (Joan of Arc, Odabella), but a heart-broken women's voice, whose struggle to justice is portrayed in all its aching psychological complexity of loss and desolation.

## (2) Fathers and Sons

No relationship is structurally more important psychologically to maintaining and transmitting patriarchal hierarchy than the father–son relationship both in terms of the kind of authority exercised by fathers and the obedience expected of sons. Verdi's growth as a person and artist may have been acutely sensitive to the unjust demands such patriarchy may impose on sons, caught, as he was early on in life, in a psychological force field of growing distance from his natural father, Carlo Verdi, and attrac-

---

[47] See *id.*, at p. 240.

[48] See Paul Robinson, "Is *Aida* an Orientalist Opera?," in Beverly Allen and Mary Russo, eds., *Revisioning Italy: National Identity and Global Culture* (Minneapolis: University of Minnesota Press, 1997), at pp. 156–68; cf. Edward W. Said, *Culture and Imperialism* (New York: Alfred A. Knopf, 1993), at pp. 111–31.

[49] See John Rosselli, *The Life of Verdi*, at pp. 149–50.

tion to the person he regarded as his second father, Antonio Barezzi, and later on (at a crucial stage in his artistic development), the triangular tensions among his two fathers and his attachment to Giuseppina Strepponi (see chapter 3). On Verdi's reading of such patriarchal authority, the very hierarchical character of such authority may lock fathers and sons into rigid patterns of mutually uncomprehending command and submission, which require the repression of the personal voice and conviction in both fathers and sons that might reasonably challenge such authority. Verdi's three earliest treatments of the relationship – *I Due Foscari*, *Alzira*, and *I Masnadieri* – portray a psychology of heart-breaking loss, in which fathers and sons can barely read, let alone understand and act on, their love. In *Foscari*, the father, the doge of Venice, regards himself as compelled, in his role as doge, to condemn his own son to exile, though he knows his son to be innocent. In *Alzira*, the son, who succeeds his father as governor of Peru, conflicts with his father's pleas for more humane treatment of the Inca, and is eventually assassinated. In *Masnadieri* (based on Schiller's *The Robbers*) a father is misled by one son to reject another, who, in consequence, becomes a violent bandit. The bandit son, who loves his father, saves his nearly blind father from atrocious mistreatment by his brother and, after admitting his life of crime and accepting prison as his penalty, defiantly proves his mettle to his fellow bandits by killing the woman he loves. Patriarchal manhood is locked into a cycle of isolation and competitive violence, triggered by insults to honor.

Verdi's most mature treatments of the psychology of the patriarchal father–son relationship are *Luisa Miller*, *Les Vêpres Siciliennes*, and the astonishing *Don Carlos*. In these works Verdi portrays father–son relationships so structured in terms of the rigidly controlling aims and purposes of the father that father and son are as much in incommensurable emotional and intellectual worlds as Rigoletto and Gilda. The consequences for both fathers and sons are psychologically crippling not only for them in their personal relations to one another and to others, but crippling as well for ethical and political psychology as such. Some of Verdi's most psychologically probing explorations of the desolation and loss underlying masculine psychology under patriarchy come in these works, pivotally framed in terms of the impact of the father–son relation on personal and political psychology.

In *Luisa Miller*, Verdi begins to explore the larger implications of a rigidly patriarchal father not only for his family but for larger issues of politics and ethics. Count Walter, as a rigidly controlling patriarchal father bent on using his own son for dynastic purposes, can barely understand, let alone give weight to his son's passion for Luisa. He rationalizes his destruction of his son's happiness and his injustice to Luisa and her father in terms of his patriarchal ambitions and authority:

| | |
|---|---|
| "Egli delira: sul mattin degli anni | He is raving mad: during the morn of our |
| vinta da cieco affeto spesso e ragion! | Years reason is often thwarted by blind |
| Del senno empia il difetto affection! | The father must compensate |
| Per figlio il padre! | For his son's lack of wisdom!"[50] |

Walter, locked into the self-rationalizing stereotypes of patriarchy, justifies his ambitions in terms of the legacy for his son, which, if they can include murder, can certainly include force and fraud in breaking his son's relationship to Luisa so he will marry someone more dynastically suitable. There is no political or moral evil that may not be rationalized in such patriarchal terms. At the end of the musically extraordinary last act of the opera, Rodolfo learns too late the truth: Luisa was forced by his father to give Rodolfo up to save her own father, and he has now poisoned himself and Luisa as his own contribution to patriarchal stupidity (killing Luisa for her alleged infidelity to him). In their concluding duet, Rodolfo and Luisa debate the power of patriarchy in larger theological terms.

| | |
|---|---|
| "RODOLFO | |
| Ah! maledetto, il di che nacqui | Ah, cursed be the day I was born, |
| Il mio sangue, il padre mio! | My blood, my father, |
| Fui creato, avverso Iddio, | I was created, hostile God, |
| Nel tremendo tuo furor. | In your terrible fury! |
| LUISA | |
| Per l'istante in cui ti piacqui, | For the moment when I was your beloved, |
| Per la morte che s'appressa, | For the death which is approaching, |
| D'oltraggiar l'Eterno, ah! cessa. | Ah, cease, cease, abusing the Eternal Father, |
| Mi pisparmia un tano orror . . . | Spare me such horror."[51] |

His father's obsessional patriarchy has, for Rodolfo, made God in his own evil image, and made his son into His instrument. Verdi will powerfully return to this theme, as we shall see in *Don Carlos* and in Iago's "Credo" in *Othello*.

---

[50] See Verdi, *Luisa Miller*, libretto, Peter Maag conductor, National Philharmonic Orchestra, London: Decca Record Co., 1988, pp. 94–5 (Gwyn Morris, trans.).

[51] See Verdi, *Luisa Miller*, libretto, London: Decca Record Co., 1988, pp. 148–9 (Gwyn Morris, trans.).

The personal and political implications of the patriarchal father–son relationship are at the center of Verdi's late Risorgimento opera, *Les Vêpres Siciliennes*,[52] in which father and son remain throughout in emotionally and politically different worlds. Henri, a young Sicilian patriot, opposes the French occupation of Sicily under their brutal commander Montfort, and joins the duchess Helene (whose brother was killed by Montfort and whom Henri loves) and Procida in their struggle against the French. Montfort, however, has learned from a letter from a Sicilian woman whom he forced to become his mistress years before that Henri is his son, and now aches to establish a relationship with his son, albeit that he is his sworn political enemy. Montfort takes pride in the haughty defiance of his son, and offers him the prospect of honor in serving in the French forces, which Henri rejects because it rests on honor as an end in itself, not in service of any just end. The opera thus pits the impact of the psychology of patriarchy (on both fathers and sons) against the justice of Sicilian resistance to oppression, albeit, as Montfort points out to Henri, guerilla resistance that does not observe the rules of war (the opera ends grimly with Sicilian slaughter of the unarmed French at a wedding party). Verdi focuses his musically expressive powers on our hearing the emotions of Montfort:

> "Montfort sings his only aria ('Au sein de la puissance') in which he laments the loneliness of power and the sense of emptiness it brings; yet at the thought of his son he feels his spirit reborn . . . Montfort is perhaps the most fully realized character in the opera; a King Philip who has not yet become old and bitter."[53]

When Montfort tells Henri of his parentage, Henri's "chief sorrow is that he has now lost Helene for ever" and points to his absent dead mother as permanently separating father from son, as the music portrays "father and son united in private misery,"[54] and "unfulfilled longing felt successively by father and son on either side of the barrier that separates them."[55] Henri rushes from the room, but when the Sicilian patriots (including Helene and Procida) try to kill Montfort at a party, Henri protects his father, leading to their arrest. When he later tries to explain himself to Helene, she stops her expression of indignation when she learns Montfort is Henri's father. Henri ends his self-defense with: "You gave your life to avenge your brother. I have done more: I have given away my honour for my father's sake."[56] The

---

[52] See Julian Budden, *The Operas of Verdi, Volume 2*, at pp. 169–242.

[53] See *id.*, p. 209.

[54] See *id.*, p. 212.

[55] See *id.*, p. 213.

[56] See *id.*, p. 225.

plotters are about to be executed, but Montfort tells Henri he will stay the executions if Henri will acknowledge him as his father which, at the last moment, Henri does. Montfort knows he does not have his son's love but has at best compelled a public confession of their link; whatever the appearances, their emotional alienation remains. It is Montfort's patriarchal tragedy that he cannot read, let alone take seriously either his son's moral world or the world of the people with whom his son identifies, and thus fails to understands the risks to which his blinding desire for love exposes both his son and himnself. Montfort generously declares Henri and Helene will be married; Helene initially resists, until Procida mysteriously tells her that she must do so for the good of Sicily. Helene happily agrees, not realizing that Procida plans to use the wedding as the occasion for a mass killing of the unsuspecting, unarmed French. The opera ends in a blood bath. Montfort's patriarchal illusions, arising from his stark isolation from his son, lead to the death of him and his son.

If *Les Vepres* portrays a patriarchal father's futile longing for the love of his son, *Don Carlos* (based on the Schiller play) examines the psychology of the patriarchal father–son relationship from an altogether darker and deeper perspective on its corruption not only of personal life but of politics, ethics, and religion itself. Verdi, after visiting the Escurial in 1863, wrote: "It is severe and terrible, like the savage monarch who built it."[57] Within four years "the savage monarch" was to be accorded unforgettable musical expression. Verdi's interest in Philip II is in how patriarchy corrupts not only politics but religion, a corruption that the long Spanish colonization of Italy had extended there as well, including the aggressively sectarian political role of the Catholic Church in obstructing support for Italian democratic unification throughout Verdi's life.[58]

Don Carlos, son of Philip II, king of Spain, had come to France to meet, without revealing his identity, Elizabeth, daughter of the king of France, whose marriage to Carlos was (he then believed) to be the peace treaty that would end war between France and Spain. As the opera opens,

"To a clarinet figure coiling up from the chalumeau register Carlos steps out of hiding. His opening utterance ('Fontainebleau, foret immense et solitaire') establishes him at once as a tenor of sensibility, of a dreamy inwardness quite foreign to the Rodolfos and Manricos of Verdi's Italian operas..Every phrase reflects the prince's mood, half rapt, half melancholy. But as soon as Carlos tells us that he has left the court of Madrid, risking his father's anger, an abrupt figure quietly raises its head in the orchestra as if to warn us from

---

[57] See Julian Budden, *The Operas of Verdi, Volume 3*, p. 5.
[58] See, on this point, Richards, *Italian American*, at pp. 91–2.

which quarter the tragedy will arrive. The lower register of the clarinet is enough to suggest that faint chilling of the spine that puts the listener on his guard."[59]

When they meet, Elizabeth and Carlos fall in love and thus do not need or require patriarchy to legitimate their relationship. Their relationship is, however, abruptly broken by the patriarchy, as they learn that Philip and the king of France have agreed that Elizabeth will marry Philip, not his son.

"The lovers' frozen horror finds expression in a typically murky orchestral gesture, based in a diminished seventh with prominent use of a low clarinet; it is repeated three times, leading to the first of the two themes from which the main structure of the finale is built ('L'heure fatale est sonnee') . . . In the march-like tramp of the rhythm we seem to hear the remorseless approach of the 'cruelle destinee' of which the lines speak . . . "[60]

The opera thus takes as its framing premise the traumatic loss inflicted when patriarchy breaks relationship, including, as we shall see, the deeper loss in the breaking in relationship between father and son required by the unjust demands of patriarchy.

We see the consequences of this loss for Carlos and Elizabeth when, at the insistence of Rodrigue, Marquis of Posa, an idealist and close friend of Carlos, Elizabeth, now queen, agrees to meet him. Posa has sought to inspire in Carlos a political idealism like that of Alvaro in *La Forza del Destino*, an idealism that will replace the emotional loss of Elizabeth with a liberal defense of Flanders from Spanish tyranny. Posa hoped Elizabeth might act as an intermediary between Carlos and his father on this matter. The scene between Carlos and Elizabeth is "not only satisfying as musical structure but one of the most impressive fusions of music and drama to be found in all opera."[61] Carlos begs Elizabeth to get his father to send him as an envoy to Flanders, but when she exclaims "Mon fils!" tenderly, his voice breaks out in despair. Summoning her self-control, Elizabeth replies that if the king will listen to her, Carlos can leave for Flanders the next day. Carlos is wounded by her lack of feeling about his going away, exclaiming:

| " . . . Insense! | . . . Fool! |
|---|---|
| J'ai supplie dans mon delire | In my madness I made supplication |
| Un marbre insensible et glace. | To a marble statue, insensible and frozen!"[62] |

---

[59] See Julian Budden, *The Operas of Verdi, Volume 3*, p. 45.

[60] See *id.*, p. 53.

[61] See *id.*, p. 78.

Now Elizabeth is hurt. She is not indifferent, but has a sense of pride and duty. But Carlos is lost in a nostalgic dream, concluding with the words "Je meurs . . . je meurs," whereupon he loses consciousness, causing Elizabeth to fear he has died. She prays heaven to restore peace of mind to "him who was my fiance," who responds as if Elizabeth has just appeared to him in France. The emotional barriers are down between them in a revealing musical sequence "of extraordinary intensity";[63] because the couple speaks to one another in a voice of relationship: "for though the tenor's ardour is feverish and the soprano merely compassionate their feelings for one another can no longer be in doubt."[64] Carlos impulsively takes Elizabeth in his arms, exclaiming "I love you Elizabeth! The world is forgotten!" Carlos's outburst evokes in Elizabeth an equally fierce determination to resist, hurling at Carlos the taunt:

| | |
|---|---|
| "Eh bien! Donc, frazzez votre pere! | So be it! Then smite your father! |
| Venez, de son meurtre souille, | Come, stained with his murder, |
| Trainer a l'autel votre mere! | To lead your mother to the altar!"[65] |

He rushes from her presence, as Elizabeth falls to her knees to thank God: "God watched over us!" Like Leonora and Alvaro in *La Forza del Destino*, Elizabeth and Carlos will in the last scene of the opera paper over their desolating loss in relationship with idealism. Elizabeth's great aria, "Toi qui sus le neant" ("You who knew the emptiness"), apostrophizes Charles V as one who knew the vanity of all earthly things, and then begs him to carry her tears to heaven "if tears are still shed in heaven." As she puts it in her aria, "I have promised Posa to watch over [Carlos's] life. May he go on his way, glorious and blessed. As for me, my task is done and my life at an end."[66] Carlos embraces political idealism in Flanders in similar resigned terms. The entrance of Charles V, as a deus ex machina to save Carlos from his father at the end of the opera, underscores the opera's mood of an idealism covering over yet another traumatic break in relationship.

*Don Carlos* embodies Verdi's most psychologically astute and unsparing portrait of the devastating consequences of patriarchy not only for a son and

---

[62] See Giuseppe Verdi, *Don Carlos*, Claudio Abbado, conductor, Coro e Orchestra del Teatro alla Scala, libretto, at pp. 154–5.

[63] See Julian Budden, *The Operas of Verdi*, Volume 3, p. 76.

[64] See *id.*, pp. 76–7.

[65] See Giuseppe Verdi, *Don Carlos*, Claudio Abbado, conductor, Coro e Orchestra del Teatro alla Scala, libretto, at pp. 156–7.

[66] See Julian Budden, *The Operas of Verdi*, Volume 3, p. 145.

the lover from whom he has been divided, but for his father and society at large, for, in *Don Carlos*, the regime of patriarchy includes the tyranny of the Spanish Empire over Flanders and of the Spanish Inquisition over the mind of man. At the center of this patriarchal heart of darkness lies Verdi's musically complex representation of the emotional voice of the autocratic Philip II at three stages of his descent into hell: his desperate need for the friendship of Posa, his loveless marriage, and his homicidal hatred of his son.

Like his son, Philip hungers for the friendship of Rodrigue, Marquis of Posa, precisely because Posa, a person of flinty integrity, will not kowtow to Philip as a patriarchal subordinate, as all other men do. He relationally shares with Posa his most personal fears about the relationship of Carlos and his queen, Elizabeth, and makes himself vulnerable to hearing and giving weight to Posa's attack on his political tyranny:

"RODRIGUE

| | |
|---|---|
| Quoi! Vous croyez, semant la mort | What! You believe that, sowing death, |
| Semer pour l'avenir? | You sow for the future? |
| KING | |
| Regardez mes Espagnes! | Look at my Spanish dominions! |
| L'artisan des cites, le peuples des | The workman in the cities, the people |
| campagnes, | in the country, |
| Il vit a Dieu fidele, et soumis | a son they live faithful to God, and |
| sumissive | |
| Sort! | To their lot! |
| J'offre la meme paix a mes Flandres. | I offer the same peace to my Flanders . . . |
| RODRIGUE | |
| Arriere | Away with such peace! |
| Cette paix! La paix du cimetiere! | The peace of a gravgraveyard"[67] |

Budden observes:

"Philip's praise of his own peaceful government is blown to atoms by Posa's 'La paix du cimitiere' with one of those orchestral thunderbolts with which the late Verdi seems to anticipate the 'Veristi' but with far greater force; an almost atonal tremolo (all in their lowest register) and rolling timpani; the initial major second gradually widens to a bare fifth in E minor fading away on the two clarinets as Posa warns the King not to go down to history as a second Nero . . . The long solo that follows ('Est-ce la paix que vous donner

---

[67] See Giuseppe Verdi, *Don Carlos*, Claudio Abbado, conductor, Coro e Orchestra del Teatro alla Scala, libertto, at pp. 166–7.

au monde?') clothes Posa's plea for freedom with a new and far more compelling eloquence."[68]

Both Philip's and his son's extraordinary emotional need for the friendship of Posa was harrowingly expressed in an 1866 duet for father and son over Posa's body after he has, with Philip's permission, been killed by the Inquisition. The duet, now usually removed from performances (but available on a recording by Claudio Abbado[69]), did not, however, go to waste; Verdi used its music, suitably reworked, in the Lachrymosa of the *Requiem*,[70] which gives some sense of the extraordinary emotional desolation, terror and dread, and longing musically expressed in the original duet between a father and son who, locked in hatred for one another, unite in love for an inaccessible love object, Posa. Indeed, one plausible interpretation of the psychological perspective from which the *Requiem* is written is that it expresses the plea for forgiveness of a damned soul like Philip II. Certainly, its most operatically conceived and emotionally charged section, "Libera me", composed separately in the wake of *Don Carlos*, is written from the perspective of an anxious soul in despair having recognized the enormity of one's sins, a damned soul Verdi had just studied in psychological depth in the divided consciousness of Philip II.[71]

Philip's mistress, Eboli, incensed when she learns that Carlos loves the queen not her, has given the king Elizabeth's private box of papers and mementos, which make clear her love for Carlos. Verdi creatively gives musical voice to his desolating sense of lovelessness:

"'Elle ne m'aime pas', under its Italian title of 'Ella giammai m'amo' is one of the most famous arias in the Italian repertoire . . . The heavy acciaccatura sobs on horns, bassoons and strings convey that iron grief which lies at the heart not only of Philip but of the opera as a whole . . . Muted violins begin an obsessive, circling motif . . . All this is a preparation for the melodic idea which . . . forms the emotional kernel of the scene . . . 'She does not love me; her heart is closed to me; she has never loved me' . . . All of Philip is in this scene – his dignity, his pathos, his obsessive suspicions, his gloomy fanaticism. If Verdi had ever succeeded in writing the *King Lear* that tempted him for so long, could he ever have achieved a more moving portrayal of desolate old age than this?"[72]

---

[68] See Julian Budden, *The Operas of Verdi, Volume 3*, p. 93.

[69] See Giuseppe Verdi, *Don Carlos*, Claudio Abbado, conductor, Coro e Orchestra del Teatro alla Scala, libertto, at pp. 274–5.

[70] See Julian Budden, *The Operas of Verdi, Volume 3*, p. 141.

[71] On the composition of this section, see Julian Budden, *Verdi* (London: J.M. Dent, 1985), p. 101; on its later incorporation into the *Requiem*, see *id.*, at pp. 316–35.

[72] See Julian Budden, *The Operas of Verdi, Volume 3*, pp. 120–2.

The Count of Lerma then announces "Le Grand Inquisiteur", a blind man of ninety supported by two Dominican friars. Verdi has only once before written a duet for two basses – that of the two partners in crime in *Luisa Miller*. Here it serves a precise dramatic purpose: "to embody the conflict of two superhuman, patriarchal forces, Church and State, nothing less than two basses will suffice."[73] Philip seeks from the Inquisitor legitimation for killing his son. As we know from the aria that opens the scene, he has learned of the love of Carlos and Elizabeth, and turns his Oedipal fury on his son; he now seeks a religious warrant to kill him. The Inquisitor responds with casuistical argument as to why Philip should not scruple to sacrifice his son (as God sacrificed His son on the cross). Then the Inquisitor takes the initiative, demanding that Posa be handed over to the Inquisition as a heretic far more dangerous than Carlos. Philip refuses "in his present mood" seeing "his life as a vast desert stretching out before him with nobody in whom to confide but Posa."[74] How, the Inquisitor asks, can Philip consider himself a king if he requires another equal to himself? But when Philip opposes an abrupt "non, jamais" to the Inquisitor's wheeling, the claws come out:

| | |
|---|---|
| "THE INQUISITOR | |
| O Roi, si je n'etais ici, dans ce palais | O King, if I were not here, in this |
| Aujourd'hui: par le Dieu vivant, demain | palace today, by the living God, |
| Vous vous-meme, seriez devant nous | you yourself would be before us at |
| au tribunal supreme! | us at the upreme tribunal!"[75] |

When Philip angrily rejects the priest's "criminal pride,"

> "the Inquisitor retorts, 'Why have you called up the shade of Samuel?' – a key phrase in Schiller, reminding us that the paradigm of Saul, David and Jonathan underlies the relationship of Philip, Posa and Carlos."[76]

The Inquisitor concludes:

| | |
|---|---|
| "J'avais donne deux rois a ce puissant | I have given two kings to this mighty |
| empire, l'oeuvre de tous mes jours, | empire; the work of my days, |
| vous voulez la detruire . . . | you wish to destroy it . . . "[77] |

---

[73] See *id.*, p. 123.

[74] See *id.*, p. 124.

[75] See Giuseppe Verdi *Don Carlos*, recording, Claudio Abbado, conductor, Deutsche Grammophon, libretto, at pp. 206–7.

[76] See Julian Budden, *The Operas of Verdi, Volume 3*, p. 124.

Philip, defeated, begs the Inquisitor to be reconciled with him: Posa may also be killed. The central section of this remarkable duet emotionally expresses "the gradual ascendancy of the Inquisitor, spiritually armour-plated, over the vulnerable Philip."[78] Whatever emotional doubts Philip may have entertained about his patriarchal authority are now resolved by the patriarchal authority of the Inquisitor. Verdi has laid bare the emotional desolation of patriarchy that may impose its unjust demands not only on personal and political life, but on ethics and religion. He offers us a way of understanding the roots in a patriarchal psychology under threat of how and why religious fundamentalisms today turn to terror in the name of God.[79]

The personal tragedies of Philip, Carlos, Posa, and Elizabeth are structurally part of a larger political and religious tragedy, which Verdi dramatizes in the great auto-de-fé scene in which the inquisitorial burning of heretics and the pleas of the delegates from Flanders are met by Philip's implacable intolerance. The chorus divides, as it also does in the similar scene in *Aida* about the fate of the Ethiopian captives, into the voice of the people who plea for liberal tolerance and forgiveness and the voice of the priests who call for sectarian retribution. The inner psychological divisions in and among characters are thus structurally represented in divisions within the chorus, dramatizing, as the chorus in Attic tragedy did for the Athenian democracy, divisions among Italians about the meaning of their recently won nationalism.

Verdi's reading of the psychology of patriarchy in *Don Carlos* is very like Calderon's similar reading in his astonishing psychological study of the patriarchal father–son relationship, *Life is a Dream*.[80] Calderon's play depicts a son effectively enslaved by his father (in violation of every person's natural right to "[s]weet and beautiful freedom"[81]) because of his father's fears, and how the father's fear-ridden break in relationship to his son creates the monster he feared (cf. the comparable fear of the parents of Oedipus and its similar consequences). For Verdi, like Calderon, the patriarchal father–son relationship so divides fathers and sons into hierarchy and submission that it breaks any relationship based on personal voice, and constructs a father–son pair based on misunderstanding, fear, and hatred. It is not only,

---

[77] See Giuseppe Verdi *Don Carlos*, recording, Claudio Abbado, conductor, Deutsche Grammophon, libretto, at pp. 206–7.

[78] See Julian Budden, *The Operas of Verdi, Volume 3*, p. 125.

[79] See, on this phenomenon, Mark Juergensmeyer, *Terror in the Mind of God*; for the link to patriarchy under threat, see, especially, pp. 182–97.

[80] See Pedro Calderon de la Barca, *Life is a Dream*, John Clifford, trans. (London: Nick Hern Books, 1998).

[81] See *id.*, at p. 8.

as Verdi saw in his early operas, that fathers and sons consequently can barely read, let alone understand and act on, their love, but that sometimes the consequence of patriarchy becomes a destructive Oedipal hatred, which may in turn corrupt politics, ethics, and religion with a murderous intolerance.

There remains to consider Posa, whom both Philip and Carlos desperately want as a friend. Posa is a free man of integrity. As Philip explains to the Inquisitor his emotional need of Posa:

| | |
|---|---|
| "Pour traverser les jours d'epreuves ou | To endure these trying times in which |
| nous sommes, j'ai cherche dans ma cour, | we find ourselves, I sought in my court, |
| ce vaste desert d'hommes, | that vast desert of men, |
| Un homme, un ami sur . . . J'lai trouve! | For a man, a sure friend . . . I found him!" [82] |

Posa's appeal for Philip and Carlos is that he is outside the patriarchy: he accepts no patriarchal hierarchy or subordination to men or women. The anthem that recurrently blares out to mark the attachment of Posa and Carlos, "Dieu, tu semas dans nos ames" ("God, Thous sowest in our spirits") yokes their voices together as "they vow to live and die together in brotherly love for the cause of freedom."[83] The Italian version, an epigraph of this book, puts the sentiment in particularly arresting form:

| | |
|---|---|
| "Vivremo insiem e morremo insiem | "We will live and die together! |
| Sara l'estreme anelito, | Our last breath |
| Sara, sara un grido, un grido: | Will be a cry: |
| Liberta!" | Liberty!" [84] |

The homoerotic analogy of David and Jonathan seems psychologically correct here: a son, resisting his patriarchal father and seeking solace from the losses his father has imposed on him, finds the love he lacks from his father with an open-hearted man who defiantly remains free of the strictures of patriarchy. It bespeaks something like blinding sexual passion, albeit appropriately masked by political idealism, at least on the part of Posa for Carlos, that Posa should so extravagantly have idealized Carlos's capacity for intelligent, courageous political action. From the point of view of coldly

---

[82] See Giuseppe Verdi *Don Carlos*, recording, Claudio Abbado, conductor, Deutsche Grammophon, libretto, at pp. 204–5.

[83] See Julian Budden, *The Operas of Verdi, Volume 3*, p. 64.

[84] Duet of Carlo and Rodrigo, Act II, scene 1, *Don Carlos*, pp. 98–9, libretto to CD, Italian version, Verdi, *Don Carlos*, conducted by Carlo Maria Giulini, EMI classics.

deliberated political idealism, Posa's sacrificing his life for Carlos seems unreasonable in the extreme; Carlos is sensitively portrayed musically by Verdi as anxious, volatile, emotionally erratic, in a word, as a deeply neurotic young man (but certainly not the possibly mentally ill Carlos of history[85]). Posa's ascription of realistic political ability to Carlos is not a rational act. From the point of view of passionate homoerotic love (conscious or unconscious) of Posa for Carlos, however, the sacrifice at least makes psychological sense. Verdi shows us that the same destructive idealization of women that cut men off from appreciating their sexual voice exists as destructively in relationships between men, including a gay man, who uncritically defines his relationships in idealized terms that fail to respect free and equal voice in relationship. It is surely of interest that here, as also in *Un Ballo in Maschera* (as we shall see), a possibly gay man (Gustavo) is portrayed as a person of integrity precisely because he lives so conscientiously, even defiantly outside patriarchy. Such a man can still, for Verdi, be tragically tripped up by patriarchy to the extent his resistance to patriarchy is defeated by failure to know his emotions and their relation to his ideals. To this extent, Posa is yet another of Verdi's tragic lovers.

The emotional range and depth of Verdi's study of the tragedy of patriarchy embrace all aspects of human sexual and emotional psychology, including the variations of sexual orientation. No doubt, the great appeal of Verdi's art is the way in which his vision thus embraced with such complex truthfulness the range of human sexuality, including gay sexuality. There is, of course, no necessary relationship between any expression of sexuality and support for or resistance to patriarchy; homosexuality has, like heterosexuality, certainly sometimes historically expressed itself in highly patriarchal forms.[86] But Verdi brilliantly explores here, as elsewhere, how gay feeling may express itself in resistance to patriarchy, and how the reactionary forces of patriarchy may still crush it. Gay men, myself included, often hear a resonance for the dignity of gay love, in "Dieu, tu semas dans nos ames" (or, in Italian, "Vivremo insiem e morremo insiem") – an anthem for the transformative moral powers of gay love, understood and lived in a certain way. In *Don Carlos*, Verdi puts this human need in the general perspective of the ways in which patriarchy isolates not only fathers from sons but men in general from one another in rigidly hierarchical patterns of dominance and submission, a threat as much to straight as gay relation-

---

[85] See, in general, Henry Kamen, *Philip of Spain* (New Haven: Yale University Press, 1997); Geoffrey Parker, *Philip II*, Third Edition (Peru, IL: Open Court Publishing, 1995).

[86] See, on this point, Craig A. Williams, *Roman Homosexuality: Ideologies of Masculinity in Classical Antiquity* (New York: Oxford University Press, 1999).

ships. Philip II's hunger for Posa is the emotional hunger of the human psyche for relationship with an equal that all men, heterosexual and homosexual, feel, as do all women. The Inquisitor's response homophobically degrades this need as unworthy:

| "Pourquoi | Why |
| Un homme? Et de quel droit vous | a man? And by what right |
| Nommez-vous le Roi, | do you call yourself King, |
| Sire, si vous avez des egaux? | Sire, if you have equals?"[87] |

The Inquisitor exemplifies a psychology of patriarchal manhood in which universal human needs for relationship are theocratically bullied into silence as unmanly.

### (3) Mothers and Sons

The structural injustice of patriarchy crucially entrenches its power, as we have seen (chapter 2), in terms of mythologically idealized gender stereotypes whose political power derives from the suppression of the voices that might reasonably contest such stereotypes. From this perspective, the Italian idealization of mothers (on the model of the madonna) may no more describe reality than, as I earlier suggested (chapter 2), calling foundlings "children of the madonna." Such idealization mythologizes mothers as not only lacking a sexual self or voice, but as engaged in a total maternal devotion to their sons that demands the sacrifice of whatever self she has. It does not bring any realism or sense of justice to women's perspectives, as persons, on their roles as mothers. To the contrary, mothers are accorded patriarchal privilege to the extent they impart to their sons their sexist privileges, which includes not attending to the emotional and sexual life and voice of women, including their mothers. Southern Italian husbands and fathers thus spend little time at home with their wives, seeking friendship with other men outside the home; and boys gravitate to other groups of boys outside the home. The Southern Italian idealization of women thus covers a double loss, the breaking of personal relationships not only to their sons, but to their husbands as well.[88] The idealization of mothers thus psychologically covers a traumatic break in relationship with them.

The patriarchal mother's role may include, as in ancient Rome,[89] an active

---

[87] See Giuseppe Verdi *Don Carlos*, recording, Claudio Abbado, conductor, Deutsche Grammophon, libretto, at pp. 204–5.

[88] I am indebted for this point to conversations with Carol Gilligan and Donald Levy.

role in securing her son's compliance with patriarchal demands, a theme brilliantly investigated in Shakespeare's *Coriolanus*. Only his mother, Volumnia, is able to bring Coriolanus back into patriarchal line with Rome's demands on him, essentially through shaming him before women and children (including his mother and wife and young son):

"Down, ladies; let us shame him with our knees.
To his surname Coriolanus 'longs more pride
Than pity to our prayers. Down! An end,
This is the last. So, we will home to Rome,
And die among our neighbors. – Nay, beyhold 's!
This boy, that cannot tell what he would have,
But kneels and holds up hands for fellowship,
Does reason our petition with more strength
Than thou hast to deny't . . . "[90]

Volumnia is portrayed herself in a patriarchally hierarchical relationship to her son, whom she has brought up in the code of honor with whose demands she now bullies him into compliance though, as he points out to her, it will probably mean his death. In the only relationship to a woman (his wife, Virgilia) that might putatively be more egalitarian and voiced, we have nothing of the sort: Coriolanus greets her thus, "My gracious silence, hail."[91] Coriolanus – the classic armored military man brilliant in war but in peace vulnerable to shame and violence in reponse to the democratic dialogue republican Rome demands of its leaders – is psychologically imprisoned by idealizations of his honor. In vowing to resist all pleas to forebear vengeance on the Roman republic that unjustly exiled him, Coriolanus claims to:

" . . . stand
As if a man were author of himself,
And knew no other kin."[92]

But, in Shakespeare's devastating psychological portrait of the patriarchal mother–son relationship, Coriolanus is in fact in a highly dependent, even symbiotic patriarchal relationship to his own mother, who can proudly (as a matter of her honor) control and use him to her own patriarchal purposes.

Verdi's musically forceful portrait of Lady Macbeth certainly depicts a

---

[89] See Judith P. Hallett, *Fathers and Daughters in Roman Society*.

[90] William Shakespeare, *Coriolanus*, V, iii, in G. Blakemore Evans, ed., *The Riverside Shakespeare* Second Edition (Boston: Houghton Mifflin Company, 1997), pp. 1440–1488, at pp. 1481–2.

[91] See *Coriolanus*, II, i, *id.*, at p. 1456.

[92] See *Coriolanus*, V, ii, *id.*, at p. 1480.

woman who would be a mother of this sort, but he touches on the mother–son relationship itself only incidentally in two Risorgimento operas, *I Lombardi* (Sofia, the Sultana, is the mother of Oronte, who loves Giselda) and *La Battaglia di Legnano* (Lida is portrayed as having a son by Rolando). Among his mature operas, *Un Ballo in Maschera* depicts Amelia as having a young son. When Renato, her husband, threatens to kill her because of suspected adultery with Gustavo, Amelia's plea to see her son gives moving musical expression to the devastating effects of her death on their son in these terms:

| | |
|---|---|
| "Non rifutarlo ai prieghi | Do not reject the pleas |
| Del mio materno cor | Of a mother's heart. |
| Morro, ma queste viscere | I shall die – but this body |
| Consolino I suoi baci, | May be consoled by his kisses, |
| Or che l'estreme e giunta | For the end is in sight |
| Dell'ore mie fugac | Of my fleeting hours. |
| Spenta per man del padre, | Put to death by his father's hand, |
| La man ei stendera | His hand he will extend |
| Sugli occhi d'una madre | To close the eyes of his mother |
| Che mai piu non vedra! | Whom he will never see again!"[93] |

Verdi thus gives striking musical expression to the impact of patriarchy's breaking of relationship through the voice of a mother speaking of her son's prospective traumatic loss. In general, however, in Verdi's operas, natural mothers of sons are psychologically absent from their son's lives, which suggests exactly the kind of psychology of mother–son relationships which patriarchy requires, namely, no relationship at all.

The strength of patriarchy is shown by the ways in which, even when mother–son relationships in fact importantly exist, it is often difficult for sons to give voice to these relationships, as we saw earlier in the case of Mario Puzo (chapter 3). Both the culture and psychology of patriarchy are importantly sustained by the suppression of such voice, which shows itself in the difficulties sons from even quite non-patriarchal families sometimes have in acknowledging their relationship to their mothers in a way free of patriarchal stereotypes that often demonize such mothers. What might happen if there were a relationship of mothers to sons is the subject of two of Verdi's most fascinating operas.

The only operas in which Verdi found an adequate musical dramatic form to represent the issues of a voice of relationship in mother–son relationships that resist patriarchy are the ones, I shall argue, in which the relationship

---

[93] Verdi, *Un Ballo in Maschera*, libretto to recording by Georg Solti, National Philharmonic Orchestra, pp. 166–7.

is not in fact between a natural mother and her son, namely, the relationship between Azucena and Manrico in *Il Trovatore* and the relationship between Ulrica and Gustavo in *Un Ballo in Maschera*. In both cases, the women in question are ethnically different (a gypsy, black) and not really the natural mothers of the sons they care for. Verdi could only find a way of giving musical expression to a mother's voice in relationship to a son obliquely in women who, in defiance of ethnic stereotypes of them as women, actually exercised choice in deciding to care for men as sons (rather than regarding themselves as doing so as required by patriarchy). Azucena and Ulrica are women who resist patriarchy by choosing to stay in relationship to men they care for as sons.

*Il Trovatore* begins with a scene that musically expresses the irrational terror of soldiers of the Count di Luna over the stories told by Ferrando, an officer, about the burning of a gypsy for alleged witchcraft that led her daughter, in revenge, to kidnap the infant child of the then count and apparently burn him in a pyre. The premise of the opera is thus the study of a violent political culture, riven by civil war among various factions in Spain, in which irrational witchcraft beliefs can terrorize grown men into the murder of innocent outcast women of color (in this case, gypsies). The music here "has a bizarrerie, a counterpoint of accent and contour that suggests Meyerbeer, except for the quality of spontaneous combustion that Meyerbeer never achieves but which informs every note of *Il Trovatore*."[94]

We are shortly introduced to the gypsy woman, Azucena, who so terrifies this band of soldiers. After the famous anvil chorus, Azucena gives voice to her obsessional "Stride la vampa" in which she relives the traumatic experience of seeing her mother burned at the stake – the crackling flames, the cries of the victim, the cruel joy of the persecutors. The gypsies find the terrifying song depressing, and leave; Azucena pays no attention to them. Utterly absorbed she murmurs "Avenge me", and Manrico, her son, demands finally to be told the story of his grandmother. Her story begins where Ferrando's left off. Azucena saw her mother dragged to the stake; she followed, carrying her own infant son. The old women's last words to her daughter were, "Avenge me." "And did you avenge her?" Manrico asks. "I stole the Count's son," she resumes, "and brought him to the spot where the flames were still burning" (we must assume that, gypsy-fashion, she carried her infant with her on all occasions); Manrico cries with horror. There is a pause, then an emotional *non sequitur*, but deeply human, "as Azucena remembers how the sight of the Count's baby weeping desperately

---

[94] See Julian Budden, *The Operas of Verdi, Volume 2*, p. 74.

moved her to pity. Flute and piccolo depict the whimpering child, turn into the G major Azucena's sudden upsurge of maternal feeling."[95] At that moment a vision of her mother appeared to her, crying: "Mi vendica!" ("Avenge me!"). In a daze Azucena had seized a child and thrust him into the flames. The vision faded; she saw the fire devour its victim; and there beside her was the Count's son; she had murdered her own child. As Manrico expresses horror, Azucena repeats in a blood-curdling voice that strikes terror in listeners, "My son! It was my own son that I had burned!"

> "There is an eight-bar cadence centred on a dominant minor ninth like a shriek of agony, then a subsidence of twenty-two bars that allows Azucena to descend into the hollow register of her voice ("Sul capa mio le chiome sento drizzar ancor") . . . Experienced with this degree of force and dramatic truth the story of the wrong baby consigned to the flames no longer makes us smile."[96]

Manrico is understandably bewildered. If Azucena burned her own son, who was he? She interrupts that, of course, he is her son, and that she was confused in telling her mother's narrative. Had she not nursed him to health after his injuries from battle with true maternal devotion? In fact, as we learn later, Azucena, after her own traumatic murder of her son, had chosen lovingly to bring up Manrico, son of the man who murdered her mother, as her own son.

Strikingly, *Il Trovatore* presents two different conceptions of women, embodied in Leonora – a noble woman who loves Manrico, and Azucena. The two women never meet on stage, which dramatizes that these women move, literally, in different worlds. In her gorgeously lyrical poetic aria, "Tacea la notte placida" ("It was a peaceful quiet night"), Leonore expresses her ecstatic, life or death romantic passion for her troubadour, "a potent symbol for the romantic age: the lonely outcast, the champion of freedom whose love-lorn melancholy songs were a constant reproach to the heartless society that would have none of him."[97] When she thinks he has been killed, she withdraws into a monastery to take her vows as a nun. Her soaringly beautiful last act aria, longing for the rescue of her condemned lover, speaks not only of her love, but her nobility of feeling for the wretched and oppressed:

> "Aura, che intorno spiri,                    Enveloped in the darkness
>   Deh, pietosa gli arecca I mieri sospiri!    In pity bear my plaint to him!

---

[95] See *id.*, at p. 84.

[96] See *id.*, at p. 85.

[97] See *id.*, at p. 78.

| | |
|---|---|
| D'amor sull'ali rosee | Go forth, said sigh, |
| Vanne, sospir dolente, | on the rosy wings of love |
| Del prigoniero misero | and soothe the afflicted mind |
| Conforta l'egra mente . . . | of the wretched captive. |
| Com'aura di speranza | Like a breath of hope |
| Alleggia in quella stanza, | flutter in that cell, |
| La desta alle memorie, | and rouse dreams of love |
| Ai sogni dell'amor! . . . | in his memory! |
| Ma. Deh! Non dirgli improvvido | But spare him and tell him not |
| Le pene del mio cor! | Of the pain in my heart! " [98] |

At the end of the opera, she makes a deal with the Count that he will save Manrico's life in exchange for Leonora's love. But Leonora, herself a woman of honor (very much on the pedestal), prefers to kill herself rather than comply with her agreement.

But if Leonora reflects an image of the idealized woman on a pedestal, Azucena reflects its racialized other. As earlier observed, the code of honor mythologizes its control of women in terms of a racialized pedestal that sharply distinguishes the virtues of one's own women from the vices of women of the racialized other. Verdi is certainly dealing in *Il Trovatore* with the impact of the racialized pedestal in separating women from one another (marked by their never meeting though they both love Manrico, as he does each of them) and its role as well in rationalizing racial and ethnic hatred, quite clearly dealt with in the burning of Azucena's mother and, at the end of the opera, the arrest and burning of Azucena. His psychology of patriarchy unites, as in *Don Carlos* later, a personal and political psychology that is as destructive of personal life as it is of public life (whether the religious intolerance of *Don Carlos* or the ethnic hatred and misogyny of *Il Trovatore*). But while Verdi is dealing with the underlying stereotypes of gender and ethnicity, he is also forging musically expressive voices that contest and rebut such stereotypes, and no voice in the opera more powerfully does so than that of Azucena. Verdi insists that we musically hear her trauma, its desolating breaking of relationship to her mother and son, in its full, almost unimaginable horror, including her ambivalence about the son of her enemy that she mistakenly saved; but we also hear as well her maternal love for this man who is not her son. As Verdi insisted in a letter to his librettist:

"Do not make Azucena a mad woman. Broken down by fatigue, sorrow, terror, and wakefulness, she is incapable of speaking coherently. Her feelings are overwhelmed, but she is not crazy. *We must maintain until the very end the*

---

[98] See Verdi, *Il Trovatore*, recording, James Levine, conductor, Metropolitan Opera Orchestra, libretto, at p. 142.

*two great passions of this woman*: her love for Manrique and her desperate need to avenge her mother."[99]

In the last scene of the opera, both emotions are given expression. Azucena and Manrico are both in prison. Azucena already feels death upon her. When they come to take her to the pyre she will already be lifeless:

"All at once she is seized with hallucinations. The scene of fifteen years ago rises before her: the fierce crowd, the flames, her mother's screams. She gives a despairing cry and fall convulsed into Manrico's arms. It is a magnificent scena."[100]

Manrico tries to soothe her so she can sleep with a lovely lullaby, "Riposa o madre", which then turns into an entirely new, unforgettable melody, sung by Azucena, the famous "Ai mostri monti":

"Ai nostri monti ritorneremo . . .    Let us return to our mountains
L'antica pace ivi godremo            and recover our old happiness!
Tu canterai sol tuo liuto . . .        You shall sing to your lute . . .
In sonno placido io dormiro . . .    Then I shall sleep in peace . . . "[101]

Verdi thus musically portrays not only Azucena's trauma, but her capacity for relationship, as a mother, with a man she regards as her son; Azucena quite rightly says of her love for her son:

"Qual per esso provo amore     Such love I feel for him
Madre in terra not provo.        As no other mother ever felt."[102]

His art of musically expressive voice thus opens our imaginations to a mother–son relationship that might resist patriarchy. Verdi's Azucena has, in this connection, surely been read correctly as such a model for women who resist patriarchy, as Sean O'Casey in *Juno and the Paycock* has the mother and daughter, who will stand together in resisting the patriarchal violence of the men in the family in the midst of the Irish civil war, sing together as a kind of anthem of female solidarity against patriarchy: "Home to our mountains" ("Ai mostri monti"), Azucena's duet with Manrico from *Il*

[99] Quoted in Pierluigi Petrobelli, *Music in the Theater: Essays on Verdi and Other Composers*, Roger Parker, trans. (Princeton: Princeton University Press, 1994), at p. 103.
[100] See Julian Budden, *The Operas of Verdi, Volume 2*, at p. 104.
[101] See *Il Trovatore* recording, James Levine, conductor, Metropolitan Opera Orchestra, liberetto, at p. 164
[102] See *Il Trovatore* recording, James Levine, conductor, Metropolitan Opera Orchestra, liberetto, at p. 124.

through his armored wit to suggest the very real risks of tragedy that lie, in her view, conspicuously about him. He dismisses her worries, giving her a purse of gold and revoking her decree of banishment. Touched, Ulrica warns him to be on his guard, since among his followers there is a traitor – "more than one perhaps." Gustavo cuts her short with a curt "Non piu" ("No more now"). Ulrica does not appear again in the opera, but, strikingly, when Amelia learns that her husband means to kill Gustavo, she mentions Ulrica as the one person who might help her in saving his life.

Verdi's remarkably astute and sensitive musical portrait of Gustavo is of a personality and context very like those of Oscar Wilde later on: a generous public man, very conscious of his presence as a witty performer, giving pleasure to others, on the public stage, sexually gay but also gay in his carefree, laughing attitude to life.[114] But, a man who can speak only in that voice cannot speak in the voice of the full range of his emotions and needs. We know, because we have heard "La rivedra nell'estasi" ("With rapture I shall look upon her"), that Gustavo has tender longings for an inaccessible love object; and we know as well, from his great Act II duet with Amelia, that he is capable of passionate love, guilt, and renunciation. But his laughing public voice compulsively walls him off from any voice that might express these or other emotions. Not knowing these emotions in himself renders him emotionally stupid in not reading them in others. Like Posa in *Don Carlos*, Gustavo, unlike most of Verdi's tragic heroes, lives free of patriarchy. He imposes no patriarchal demands on others, nor does he conform his life to patriarchal demands on others. But like Posa, this free and generous man does not know himself and thus cannot know others. In particular, he cannot take seriously that he lives in a patriarchal world, reflected in the homicidal jealousy of his friend, Renato, who is willing to kill Gustavo merely on suspicion of adultery, which we in fact know did not and will never take place; Renato's remorse wonders at the inexplicable emotions, later to be explored by Verdi in the similar psychological vulnerability to suspicion of Othello, which led him to murder his best friend and most generous of sovereigns on the basis of suspicion alone:

| | |
|---|---|
| "Ciel! Che feci! E che m'aspetta Esecrata sulla terra! . . . | O Heaven! What have I done? And What is left for me, despised on earth! . . . |
| Ei qual sangue e qual vendetta M'asseto l'infausto error! | For what taste of blood and revenge Did this unholy mistake let me thirst!"[115] |

---

[114] See, in general, Richard Ellmann, *Oscar Wilde* (London: Penguin, 1987).

[115] See Verdi, *Un Ballo in Maschera*, recording, Georg Solti, conductor, National Philharmonic Orchestra, libretto, at pp. 222–3.

Gustavo cannot understand the limits of others, including the ways in which the psychology of patriarchy renders them capable of such blinding violence and murder.

Ulrica fully understands this dark world, and chooses to speak to Gustavo about it and its risks to him. As in *Il Trovatore*, Verdi musically portrays a voice that speaks against the stereotype of the racialized pedestal (Ulrica is black, as Azucena is a gypsy), as we hear not only the dark emotional world Ulrica knows, but her capacity for relationship and relationship, as a caring person, with a man she comes to care for as one might a son. His art thus opens our imaginations yet again to a kind of mother–son relationship that might resist patriarchy. The gypsy, Preziosilla, plays an analogous role in Act III of *La Forza del Destino* in response to the sadness of young Italian recruits to the war, who in touching musical terms voice their loneliness in separating from their mothers:

| | |
|---|---|
| "Povere madri deserte nel pianto | Our poor mothers wept as we left them, |
| Per dura forza dovemmo lasciar, | snatched by cruel war. |
| Della belta n'han rapiti all'incanto, | They have torn us away from all we love, |
| A'nostre case vogliamo tornar. | Our only wish is to go home again." [116] |

Preziosilla, like Azucena and Ulrica, shows maternal concern as she tries to lift their spirits:

| | |
|---|---|
| "Che vergogna! Su, coraggio! | Shame on you! Come, be brave! |
| Bei figliuoli, siete pazzi? | Handsome lads, have you gone mad? |
| Se piangete quai ragazzi | If you blubber like babies, |
| Vi farete corbellar. | Your comrades will laugh at you." [117] |

Earlier, in Act II, Preziosilla was able, like Ulrica, psychologically to see under the disguise of Carlo; and she also, later in Act III, saves Father Melitone from violence at the hands of the soldiers angered by his rebarbative homilies, distracting them from their anger. Similarly, in *Les Vêpres Siciliennes*, Henri emotionally resists his father's patriarchal demands strikingly by appealing to "L'image de ma mere, qui s'interpose entre nous!" ("The shadow of my mother, who stands between us"),[118] a racialized

---

[116] See Verdi, *La Forza del Destino*, libretto to recording conducted by Riccardo Muti, Orchestra e Coro del Teatro alla Scala, at pp. 146–7.

[117] See *id.*, at pp. 146–7.

[118] See Verdi, *I Vespri Siciliani*, libretto to recording conducted by Riccardo Muti, conducting Orchestra e Coro del Teatro alla Scala, at p. 133.

Sicilian woman forcibly sexually taken by Montfort and who brought her son up to resist French rule. It is striking that Verdi is able to forge such anti-patriarchal maternal voices precisely by giving musically expressive voice to the racialized bad woman who is the mirror image of the idealized good woman. It is by giving a morally and emotionally compelling voice to such women that Verdi contests the very structure of the racialized pedestal that holds patriarchy in place, resting, as it does, on the repression of such voices. Verdi thus fundamentally and radically questions the idealized image of the mother (for example, Shakespeare's portrait of Volumnia) that is so fundamental in the historically entrenched pattern of Italian patriarchal culture. It is, Verdi suggests, only women who refuse their patriarchally assigned roles that can be emotionally and morally in relationship to the men they choose to be their sons. Carol Gilligan's study of recent forms of such mother–son relationships suggests how radically anti-patriarchal they may be, as sons relate to their mothers not as idealizations but as persons to whose intelligence and emotions they are and remain relationally attuned.[119] Verdi's mature creative art, perhaps rooted in his own relationship to women (Strepponi, his mother), represents the psychological possibility of such relationships between mothers and sons in terms of women who are marginal outsiders to the conventional patriarchy.

## (4) Mothers and Daughters

The same mythological idealization of mothers under patriarchy that rationalizes the break in a relationship of mother and son applies equally to the relation of mother and daughter that must be broken as a real relationship between persons in order ideologically to align the symbolism of motherhood as such with the demands of patriarchy.[120] Verdi explores the personal and political psychology of such a breaking of the mother–daughter relation under patriarchy by representing a daughter's relation to her mother, with one notable exception, in terms of the mother's psychological absence from her daughter's life, in particular, in any context where a mother might reasonably support her daughter's resistance to the unjust demands patriarchy places on her. Only in one early opera, *I Lombardi*, does a mother–daughter pair appear on stage, and then only briefly. The mothers of the tragic women in Verdi's operas are usually dead and emotionally

---

[119] See Carol Gilligan, *The Birth of Pleasure*, at pp. 36, 38, 42–3, 44–5, 70–3, 108–9, 135–6.
[120] See, for feminist analysis along these lines, Adrienne Rich, *Of Woman Born: Motherhood as Experience and Institution*, 10th anniversary edn. (New York: W.W. Norton, 1986).

present in the lives of their daughters, to the extent they are present at all, as idealized objects of prayer. To mention just a few notable examples, Luisa in *Luisa Miller*, Lina in *Stiffelio*, Gilda in *Rigoletto*, Azucena in *Il Trovatore*, Amelia in *Boccanegra*, Leonora in *La Forza Del Destino*, Elizabeth in *Don Carlos*, and Desdemona in *Othello*, are in relationship to their absent mothers often in prayers either to them or to a proxy for them (the Virgin Mary or God). Indeed, appeals to dead idealized mothers are patriarchal weapons of terror against wayward women in Verdi's mature tragic operas. Stiffelio's violent rage against his adulterous wife, Lina, is thus suddenly unleashed when he discovers that she no longer has his mother's ring that he gave her when they married; and, one of the few musical improvements in *Aroldo*, Verdi's later adaptation of *Stiffelio*, is Verdi's remarkably effective innovation of a musical voice for the terror of the wayward wife (here, Mina) aroused by the thought of the condemnation of her dead mother, set to:

| | |
|---|---|
| "Ah, dal sen di quella tomba | Ah, from the depths of that tomb |
| Cupo fremito rimbomba! | There echoes a sinister trembling! |
| Scellerato fu l'accento | It was your wicked voice |
| Che lo giunse a provocar. | That caused it do sound.. |
| Di mia madre l'ombra irata | The angry shade of my mother |
| Gia ne sorge, su me guata! | Rises up and glares at me! |
| Oh terrore! Gia mi sento | Oh, terror! I hear |
| Dal suo labbro fulminar. | My condemnation from Her lips."[121] |

Dead idealized mothers are also invoked by fathers, as by Amonasro in *Aida*, as the ultimate psychological weapon to bring a daughter into line with the demands of the patriarchy. Verdi artistically frames such psychological absence in these ways to give musical voice to the effects on women of the unjust enforcement of gender stereotypes whose force depends on the suppression of the voices that would most reasonably contest their injustice. Such voices pivotally include the sexual voices of mothers and daughters, repressed by an honor code that imposes on them mythological idealizations that deny sexual voice or feeling in service of patriarchal hierarchy and control. Patriarchal mothers and daughters conform to these gender idealizations, competitively enforcing them on one another and on all other women by means of the intrusive surveillance, competition, and hostility among women typical of such cultures. Patriarchy thus enforces an absence of sexual voice in relationship between mothers and daughters, as persons, which explains a psychology of women under patriarchy, as Carol

---

[121] See Verdi, *Aroldo*, libretto to recording of Fabio Luisi, conducting Orchestra e coro del Maggio Musicale Fiorentino, at pp. 92–3.

Gilligan's recent work is at pains to make clear,[122] that uses psychological violence between women in support of accepting the structural injustice of sexism as in the nature of things. Verdi's tragic operas dramatize this psychology by the role the absent idealized mother plays in the psychology of daughters, keeping daughters tragically in line with the demands placed upon them by patriarchy.

There is one remarkable exception to this rule, and it is the exception that decisively proves the rule, namely, Verdi's one comedy of genius, his last opera, *Falstaff*. In *Falstaff*, unlike any other Verdi opera, relationships between women, including the relationship between a mother and daughter, are pivotal to the narrative. The honor of both Alice Ford and her friend, Meg Page, both married women, have been impugned by the untoward sexual advances of the aging, fat knight Falstaff. But Alice and Meg do not respond to the matter patriarchally, by calling upon the violent intervention of their husbands; rather they decide to handle the matter themselves, with the help of their friend Mrs. Quickly and Alice's daughter, Nannetta, through strategies of humorous public ridicule, the last of which finally brings Falstaff to his senses. At the same time, Ford, the husband of Alice, has decided patriarchally that his daughter, Nannetta, shall marry the man of his choice, not the man she is in love with, Fenton. But, in the masquerade that ends the opera, Alice assists her daughter in wearing a costume that allows her to marry Fenton, not the man chosen by her father. The ongoing relationship between mother and daughter is thus crucial in enabling the mother to handle Falstaff and empowering the daughter to act on her own desires in choosing the young man she loves as her husband. In both cases patriarchal authority is circumvented by the moral agency of a mother and daughter who stay in relationship to one another's aims and desires, as persons, and do not accept the roles imposed on them by the patriarchy. The resistance of these women to the patriarchy is crucially empowered by mothers and daughters who stay in relationship. It is surely striking that Verdi and his librettist, Boito, chose to underscore this theme of a mother–daughter alliance in the opera which is not in Shakespeare's *The Merry Wives of Windsor*, in which the Nannetta-character is the daughter of Mrs. Page who as strongly resists her daughter's choice of Fenton as does her husband.[123]

The scintillating score that Verdi wrote for *Falstaff* gives musical expression to its devastating deconstruction of the code of honor that Verdi had

---

[122] See Carol Gilligan, *The Birth of Pleasure* (New York: Knopf, 2002).

[123] See William Shakespeare, *The Merry Wives of Windsor*, in G. Blakemore Evans, ed., *The Riverside Shakespeare* (Boston: Houghton Mifflin Company, 1997), pp. 320–60, at pp. 351–6.

tragically studied so obsessively throughout his creative life. The deconstructive turn is unforgettably marked in the opening act by Falstaff's great outburst attacking honor, "Onore! Ladri!":

> "L'onore!
> Ladri! Voi state ligi all'onor vostro, voi!
> Cloache d'ignominia, quando, non sempre, noi
> Possiam star ligi all nostro. Io stesso, si, io, io
> Devo talor da un latto porre iltimore di Dio
> E, per necessita, sviar l'onore, usare
> Stratagemmi ed equivoci, destreggiar, bordeggiare,
> E voi, coi vostri cenci e coll'occhiata torta
> Da gatto-pardo e i fetidi sghignazzi avete a scorta!
> Il vostro onor! Che onore? Che onor? Che onor! Che ciancia!
> Che vaia! Pur l'onore riempirvi la pancia?
> No. Puo l'onor riempirvi la pancia?
> No. Puo l'onor rimettervi uno stinco? Non puo.
> Ne un piede? No. Ne un dito? No. Ne us capello? No!
> L'onor non e chirurgo. Ch'e dunque? Una parola.
> Che c'e in questa parola? C'e dell'aria che vola.
> Bel costrutto! L'onore lo puo sentire chi e morto?
> No. Vive sol voi vivi? Neppure: perche a torto
> Lo gonfian le lusinghe. Io corrompe l'orgoglio.
> L'ammorban le calumnie; e per me non ne voglio!
> Ma per tornare a voi, furfanti, ho atteso troppo
> E vi discaccio!
>
>
> Your honour!
> Scoundrels! You dare to talk about your honour! You!
> You sewers of debasement tell me of honour.
> Who can always live by honour? Not even I, I can't even.
> Ever so often I must go in the fear of Heaven
> When I am forced by want to veer from honour with hellish lies
> And half-lies and strategems; to juggle, to embellish.
> And you, with rags and tatters, the look of half-dead owls,
> And live for comrades, who go through life surrounded by scornful howls,
> Talk honour now! What honour? You swine! You filth!
> How funny! What rubbish! Can this honour fell your paunch
> When you're hungy? No. Can this honour heal a leg that's broken?
> Not so. A shoulder? No. A finger? No. Nor a thumbnail? No!
> For honour's not a surgeon. What is it then? Six little letters.
> What's in his word of six letters? There is a vapour that scatters.
> What a structure! This honour, think you a dead man feels it?
> No. Lives it with the living? Not either,
> Our lust congeals it,
> Our vanities corrupt it, our enjoyments infect it,
> And calumnies debase it; as for me I reject it! Yes!

Will I miss it? No! But to come back to you, you scoundrels!
Now I am full up and I dismiss you!"[124]

As Julian Budden observes,

"Boito had skilfully stitched the text of Falstaff's famous outburst from three
sources: successively, his speech to the repentant Pistol in the *Merry Wives*,
Act II, scene ii; his self-catechism in *King Henry IV*, Part I, Act V, scene I;
and finally the *Merry Wives*, Act I, scene iii, the equivalent of its present
context, where Nym and Pistol are ordered out of the Garter Inn. Each of
these passages forms a separation section of piece in which declamation and
motif are fused in a wholly original manner. Stanford aptly described it as
the smiling sister of Iago's Credo."[125]

The brilliantly orchestrated, luminous polyphony of voices in the next
scene captures the sense of anger and hilarity among the women as they
begin to plan their comic strategies against Falstaff, which is counter-
pointed to a similar polyphony among the men, including Ford who is
being told by Falstaff's disgruntled men about his threat to Ford's honor.
For a moment, Fenton and Nannetta are left on the stage, and they

"now emerge in their true guise as Verdi's most poetic pair of young lovers.
This is in itself a departure from Shakespeare whose Fenton honestly admits
that his first reason for wooing Ann Page was her father's wealth . . . The
Fenton of the opera would be incapable of such pragmatism. He and
Nannetta are far closer to Ferdinand and Miranda. Their love is bathed in the
pure radiance of a youth transfigured by the imagination of age."[126]

A similar pattern of brilliantly voiced polyphony is used in a later scene of
Falstaff's humiliation (he is put in a laundry hamper and dropped in the
Thames), which is interrupted by the amorous kisses of the two lovers who
are in their own world.

Only once in the opera is this extraordinarily imaginative comic and
erotic musical invention interrupted and that is when Ford, the patriarchal
father and husband, reflects on his jealousy and grief as he believes (wrongly)
that his wife is having an affair with Falstaff in his "Is this a dream . . . or
reality" ("E sogno? O realta"); "it is the only passage to recall the world of
tragedy that was once Verdi's domain."[127]

Verdi portrays the wreckage of patriarchy in the character of Falstaff, who

---

[124] See Verdi, *Falstaff*, recording, Leonard Bernstein, conductor, Vienna Philharmonic
Orchestra, libretto, at pp. 60–2.

[125] See Julian Budden, *The Operas of Verdi, Volume 3*, pp. 453–4.

[126] See *id.*, pp. 465–6.

[127] See *id.*, p. 482.

rails, as we have seen, against the honor code as the rationale of any knavery, but who still lives in the illusion of his own patriarchal privilege over women's sexual availability on command. His disillusionment is twofold: first, with the code of honor itself; and second, with his illusion that his sexual desirability commands satisfaction from women. At the very end of the opera, Falstaff points out, beginning the great polyphonic chorus that brings Verdi's career to a close, that his own folly is the folly of the other men in the opera (including Ford who tried, unsuccessfully, to impose a patriarchal marriage on his unwilling daughter):

| "Tutto nel monda e burla | Life is the joke we make it. |
|---|---|
| L'uom e nato burlone, | Jokes are ever in season. |
| La fede in cor gli ciurla, | If reason refuse to take it. |
| Gli ciurla la ragione. | Gaily make wisdom of reason. |
| Tutti gabbati! Irride | Wisdom is laughter! And man is |
| L'un l'altro ogni mortal. | A clown easing his fall. |
| Ma ride ben chi ride | Laughter is all his plan is, |
| La risata final. | Laughing last at you all." [128] |

The honor code draws its support from male illusion, which includes all men subject to it. Patriarchy cuts men off, as it did Oedipus, from self-knowledge of who they are, let alone from knowing the sexual and emotional lives of women. As the women in *Falstaff* exemplify, the tonic of self-knowledge comes with free voice and association in place of silence, broken relationship, and disassociation.

At the very end of his creative life, Verdi has found creative resources to turn from the obsessional tragedy of patriarchy he had been exploring throughout his career to writing a comedy that laughs at the alleged inevitability of this tragedy as an illusion fed by a failure of imagination. At the end of the *Symposium*, Socrates is portrayed as arguing: "that knowing how to compose comedies and knowing how to compose tragedies must combine in a single person and that a professional tragic playwright was also a professional comic playwright." [129] Shakespeare had combined the two forms throughout his creative life, but Verdi only in his most mature works explored how the two forms might, as Socrates suggested, come from the same impulse.

Verdi had earlier musically explored this issue in the remarkable balance of comic and tragic elements in *Un Ballo in Maschera* in which Verdi self-

---

[128] See Verdi, *Falstaff*, recording, Leonard Bernstein, conductor, Vienna Philharmonic, libretto at p. 264.

[129] See Plato, *The Symposium*, Robin Waterfield, trans. (Oxford: Oxford University Press, 1994), at p. 71.

consciously counterpoints a musical style sometimes reminiscent of Offenbach[130] to set off his maturing musical voice expressive of an underlying private and public tragedy. Gustavo, noted earlier, wilfully turns any threat of tragedy into an occasion for comedy, a theme echoed by the conspirators who, believing that Amelia had not met (as they had expected) her adulterous lover but her husband, laughingly observe:

| "Ah! ah! ah! | Ha! Ha! Ha! |
|---|---|
| E che baccano sul caso strano | What an uproar about such a strange affair, |
| E che commenti per la citta . . . | What comment there will be in the city . . . |
| Ve, la tragedia muto in commedia | See, the tragedy has turned to comedy."[131] |

*Ballo* brilliantly suggests how unstable the line can be between the tragic and comic reading of a narrative, how much depends on circumstances but also on ourselves. *Falstaff* carries this insight further as Verdi gives brilliant musical expression to a comic telling of the narrative of patriarchy that theretofore he had always treated as inexorably tragic.

The impulse in Verdi is telling the truth about the psychological power that patriarchy imposes over both our personal and political lives. That Verdi had come to take the view that this power could be represented not only tragically but comically suggests what his art had always assumed: that, whatever the cultural depth of patriarchy in our institutions and psychology, we have always humane choices to make and we are responsible for the choices we do make. Both tragedy and comedy address this domain of humane imaginative choice, including our divided consciousness about the archaic pressures of the inherited past and our reflective moral competence to learn from the past and sometimes imagine and even take a different path. If tragedy frames this consciousness as often doomed to repeat the archaic patriarchal patterns of the past, comedy may frame the very absurdity of such a sense of doom. The remarkable achievement of *Falstaff* must be read against the background of Verdi's life-long obsession with the tragic hold the code of honor had over the lives of men and women, dividing them in their most private as well as public lives from any possibility of relationship based on free and equal voice. If anything, Verdi's more musically mature operas portrayed the psychology of resistance to patriarchy as almost

---

[130] As in the musical setting of the chorus that concludes Act I, scene 1.

[131] See Verdi, *Un Ballo in Maschera*, libretto to recording of Georg Solti, conducting National Philharmonic Orchestra, at pp. 158–9.

doomed to failure, either doomed by a heart-broken fatalism (*La Forza del Destino*), or the implacable demands of theocratic religion corrupted by patriarchy (*Don Carlos*, *Aida*), or a fundamentally polar masculine and feminine psychology divided between an armored, emotional stupidity and a vulnerable, self-sacrificing masochism (*Otello*). At the very end of his career, Verdi reflects on this sense of doom in the characters of both Falstaff and Ford, both apparently locked in variant forms of narcissistic illusion that disable them from emotionally reading the women they claim to desire or love. But, the women here, for the first time in all of Verdi's long output, confront these illusions themselves with shrewdly resisting, collaborative voice that expose these illusions to public scrutiny for what they are – fantasies of emotional control that cannot in their nature take seriously the epistemic role of free and equal voice in any relationship based on reciprocity and mutual respect. Verdi demands, at the end of his creative life, that we see a comic absurdity in the illusions on which the very sense of the necessity of patriarchal tragedy, as tragedy, rests. In asking us, at the end of *Falstaff*, to laugh at ourselves, he asks us to imagine, as moral agents, a way out of patriarchy, and suggests we have the answer already at hand if we have the wit and emotional intelligence to grasp it.

# Chapter 6

# Siblings

Sons and daughters live under patriarchy not only in relation to their parents, but often in relation to one another as siblings. Relations among siblings are in their nature much more egalitarian than parent–child relations, and thus present opportunities of both relationship and resistance that could powerfully destabilize the demands imposed by patriarchy. This psychology of resistance was evident as early as Attic tragedy. In Sophocles' *Antigone*, Antigone resists the tyrannical order of her uncle, Creon, refusing to bury one of her dead brothers, on the basis of "reverence" for "a brother whom I love."[1] A brother–sister relationship, resisting patriarchy, precisely because it challenges the patriarchally constructed gender binary, offers particularly powerful resources of egalitarian voice in relationship for a personal and political psychology living outside patriarchy. On the other hand, the demands of patriarchy, consistent with its other disruptions of relationship, often strains and even breaks such relationships and thus distorts and even sometimes destroys the opportunities they offer. There are three relationships among siblings whose psychic geography we should examine from these perspectives in Verdi's operas: brother to sister, brother to brother, and sister to sister.

## (1) Brother to Sister

Verdi deals with the implications of brother–sister relations for resistance to patriarchy in two of his mature operas, *Les Vepres Siciliennes* and *La Forza*

---

[1] Sophocles, *Antigone*, in Sophocles, *The Theban Plays*, E. F. Watling, trans. (Harmondsworth: Penguin, 1973, pp. 126–62, at p. 128.

*del Destino. Les Vepres* explores some of the psychological complexities and tensions that the brother–sister relation, as a ground for resistance, imposes on a sister; *La Forza*, in contrast, examines such complexities but in the psychology of a brother and sister, whose resistance to patriarchy brings upon her not the support, but the homicidal hatred of her brother.[2]

Helene in Verdi's *Les Vepres Siciliennes* is in mourning for her brother, Frederick, unjustly executed by Montfort, the patriarchal leader of the French occupying forces in Sicily. Helene aligns herself with her brother's just cause of expelling the French from Sicily, and she imposes on Henri as the condition of her love support for such resistance, a condition he proves (after he discovers that Montfort is his natural father) psychologically unable to discharge, at least when it calls for assassination. The opera centrally explores, as earlier discussed, the psychology of the conflict between Montfort and Henri, but it also examines the tension within Helene of her resistance (based on her relationship with her idealized, dead brother) and her love for Henri. This tension is exquisitely musical represented at two points in the opera. First, in Act II there is the musical expression in the tenor/soprano duet after Henri declares his love for Helene:

> "Helene's reaction is reserved for the second movement. Hitherto she has shown nothing but the cold inflexibility of a Donna Anna. Her reluctant yielding to gentler emotions is beautifully realized in this 'dissimilar' cantabile with its progress from E flat minor to major. She is not Giovanna d'Arco, however, to abandon herself completely; on the contrary like Donna Anna once more she makes Henri swear an oath to avenge her brother. But in three successive musical ideas we can see tenderness for her suitor gradually taking possession of her thoughts."[3]

The music shifts magically from its previous hollow harmonies "like an unexpected shaft of sunlight,"[4] and Helene sings an uncannily moving long descent suggesting the thought of her dead brother at her top range but ending in her now admitted love for Henri in her lower register. As sung by Montserrat Caballe in one of those unforgettable vocal performances that haunt one's emotional memory heard at the Metropolitan Opera some years ago, this descent captures a woman's movement from the disassociated

---

[2] Verdi deals with a brother–sister relationship incidentally in the last act of *Rigoletto* when Sparafucile's sister, Magdalena, persuades her assassin brother not to kill her new lover, the Duke, but rather the first person who comes to the tavern that night; but, as the brother–sister pair does not resist the patriarchal vengeance as such, but only its object, their relation is hardly one of resistance to patriarchy as such.

[3] See Julian Budden, *The Operas of Verdi, Volume 2,* at p. 204.

[4] See *id.*

idealized emotions of grief for her brother to her psychological presence in the emotion of love she finally admits for Henri, moving from a voice of identification to a voice of relationship. The second such musical moment comes later in Act IV of the opera when Helene, once Henri explains to her his reasons for saving Montfort from assassination (namely, he is his son), again emotionally moves from grief to an expression of love, albeit doomed love (the same long vocal descent is movingly repeated, as Helene again moves from disassociated grief to love, also unforgettably sung by Caballe).

Helene's voice of political protest in *Les Vepres* is very much in the line of powerful resisting women of the early Risorgimento operas (for example, the overtly militaristic Giovanna in *Giovanna d'Arco*, Odabella in *Attila*), including her own abortive assassination attempt on the life of the French leader. Her resistance, however, largely centers on the role she plays in prompting men (including Henri) to a sense of their national duty of expelling the unjust French occupation from Sicily. *Les Vepres* prominently uses French sexual aggressiveness against Sicilian women as a way of making its point about the injustice of the French occupation, an aggressiveness at one point fomented by Helene and the Sicilian revolutionary leader, Procida, to prod Sicilian men to take arms against the French. It is because the French undermine the traditional patriarchal authority of Sicilian men that it is a matter of national honor that Sicilians must expel the French. The conventional code of honor is thus, as in *La Battaglia di Legnano*, very much being used here (albeit, in the case of Helene and Procida, cynically and opportunistically) to advance the case for a legitimate sense of nationalism. Helene's patriotic idealism, based on her feeling for her dead brother, defines a sense of personal honor that requires her to master her feelings for Henri unless and until Henri can serve her political ideals. Verdi's exquisite musical art precisely explores the underlying emotional strain and sadness that such resistance may require.

Verdi's most sustained study of the psychology of the brother–sister relationship under patriarchy is Carlos and Leonora in *La Forza del Destino*. The opera opens with Leonora's decision to resist the patriarchal claims of her father, and to elope with Alvaro, the man she loves. However, the father of Carlos and Leonora, as noted earlier, is killed accidentally from a gun thrown to the ground in surrender by Alvaro when he and Leonora were about to elope. Carlos, the ultimate patriarchal brother, takes as his mission to be executor of the vengeance required by the code of honor of his sister and her lover. As noted earlier, Verdi powerfully explores musically the emotional price that both Leonora and Alvaro pay for their resistance to patriarchy, as each assuages their remorse by withdrawal into forms of idealism (political and religious) that solace them for their broken hearts and dreams. Carlos, the vindictive brother, follows Alvaro and Leonora to the monastery where Alvaro lives as a monk and nearby Leonora (unknown to Alvaro) lives as a hermit. Carlos provokes Alvaro to a duel by a racist insult about Alvaro's honor, "Desso splende piu che gemma" ("It is coloured by your half-breed's blood."). Carlos is mortally injured in the duel, but, when his sister goes to minister to him, he kills her.

There is, however, one moment earlier in the opera when Carlos at least shows some sense of resistance and conflict over his course, which Verdi musically explores as an alternative path of association as opposed to disassociation within Carlos's divided consciousness. Carlos and Alvaro (both under different identities) form a close relationship under the circumstances of their common military service in Italy in the War of the Austrian Succession; indeed, at one point, Alvaro saves the life of Carlos, and they swear an oath of eternal friendship. However, after Alvaro is seriously injured, Carlos promises him the order of Calatrava, and is shocked by Alvaro's horrified reaction. In a duet that for such a blend "of lyrical and dramatic freedom within a structure of classical poise one can only look to Mozart,"[5] Alvaro then swears his friend never to open a packet he gives him, and to burn it if Alvaro dies. Alvaro is then taken away for medical care. In a long declamatory scene, Alvaro "reveals the obsession which has poisoned his life."[6] He is about to open the packet when he remembers his sworn oath. He finally throws down the packet, and addresses himself to the cantabile "Urna fatal" ("Fatal vessel"):

> "More than its dramatic force the quality that Verdi exploits in the baritone voice is its ambivalence; and nowhere more powerfully than in the course of this double-aria. . . . Don Carlo's chief trait is his fixity of purpose, reflected in a tendency at first for each phrase to cling to one note. But as he persists in his resolution not to tempt his fate and break his work, so the line becomes increasingly flexible and the accompanimental texture begins to loosen. By the time he has reached the final cadenza he would seem to have put all thoughts of revenge behind him."[7]

However, Carlos continues to search in Alvaro's case and finds a container with a picture of Leonora in it.

> "In the elaborate coda with its surprise modulation to G sharp minor Carlo seems literally to be panting for vengeance. From now on he is a lost soul."[8]

Carlos nurses Alvaro back to health, but then challenges "Don Alvaro,

---

[5] See Julian Budden, *The Operas of Verdi, Volume 2*, p. 482.
[6] See *id.*, p. 483.
[7] See *id.*, pp. 483–4.

the Indian" to a duel. Alvaro refuses to fight with a man to whom he has sworn friendship, and reasonably pleads the accidental nature of the Marquis of Calatrava's death and claims Leonora is dead as well. When Carlos tells him she is alive, Alvaro calls for his marriage to her immediately. Carlos implacably responds that he must kill Alvaro and then Leonora, which provokes a duel. They are, however, separated by soldiers.

Verdi's psychological portrait of this patriarchal brother–sister relationship is of a complete absence of relationship between brother and sister, dramatized by the fact that they meet only at the very end of the opera. Carlos is obsessionally driven to kill his sister for an alleged breach of the code of honor; he responds even to her attempt to help him with murder. The only relationship in the opera that breaks, however temporarily, his obsession is his friendship, whose music suggests love, with Alvaro. The intimate association between Carlos and Alvaro could, Verdi's musical art makes clear, have given them both some reparative solace from their loveless, violent, and haunted lives, the easy friendship of comrades in war. But even that relationship is psychologically broken, finally, by the demands of the code of honor. Carlos pursues his savage course unto his own death and the death of his sister, and the heart-broken grief of Alvaro.

## (2) Brother to Brother

The potential for resistance arising from a relationship of brother to brother is musically portrayed in Verdi's operas as psychologically blunted by patriarchy in two ways: first, by competition over the love and authority of the father; and second, by competition over a woman irrespective of her wishes.

The patriarchal competition of two brothers over the authority of their father as well as for the love of a woman is the subject of Verdi's relatively early work, *I Masnadieri*. Based on Schiller's *Die Rauber* (*The Robbers*), *I Masnadieri* is a kind of retelling of the Edmund–Edgar–Gloucester trio in *King Lear*. Francesco, the villainous brother, fraudulently separates his brother, Carlo, from their father by misrepresenting the father's intentions to Carlo, leading to Carlo being leader of a bandit gang. Francesco later falsely tells his father that Carlo has died, leading to his collapse, upon which Francesco imprisons him in appalling conditions, and succeeds to his position. Carlo undertakes to rescue his father. The musically expressive high points of the opera come when Francesco contemplates in terror his

---

[8] See *id.*, p. 486.

wrongdoing and accountability,[9] and when Carlo, yet unknown to his blind father, consoles him.[10] Unlike, however, Verdi's more mature work dealing with the tragedy of patriarchy, there is little complexity in the musical representation of Carlo, let alone in his relationship to the woman he claims to love. Carlo is himself rather one-dimensional and self-obsessionally patriarchal. Once Carlo reveals his evil life to his father, he accepts prison as punishment and, presumably as part of his punishment, kills the woman he loves.

Fraternal tension over a woman is the subject of both *I Lombardi* and the opera based on it for Paris, *Jerusalem*, but achieves its starkest tragic resonance in *Il Trovatore*. Both *I Lombardi* and *Jerusalem* deal with the breaking of fraternal bonds but incidentally as a problem that politics and religion can heal. In *I Lombardi*, one brother tries to kill the other, in order to claim his wife, but mistakenly kills his father; in *Jerusalem*, one brother (feeling incestuous feelings for his niece) attempts to kill his rival but nearly kills instead his brother. In both operas, religious service in the Crusades redeems the moral stain, but the homicidal brother in question dies from wounds in battle. *Il Trovatore*, in contrast, interprets such fraternal competition as the tragic consequence of patriarchal obsession rooted in traumatic loss.

Manrico and the Count are, unknown to either, brothers, sons of a noble father who barbarously had Azucena's mother burned at the stake as a witch. The brothers have been separated since childhood when Azucena, crazed by grief over the burning of her mother as a witch, mistakenly in vengeance killed her own son, instead of Manrico, and adopted Manrico as her son in his place. The Count's father had died in grief, swearing his son to an oath to find his brother. Manrico and the Count are in love with the same woman, Leonora. Manrico and Leonora are, however, in love, and the Count is musically portrayed as tyrannically controlling, emotionally desperate, and obsessionally jealous, effectively musically portrayed in his famous apostrophe to Leonora, "Il balen."[11] The Count's patriarchal jealousy shows itself not only in his willingness to abduct Leonora but, later, his admittedly unjust imprisonment and plan to execute Manrico. His patriarchal passion for control leads him to agree with Leonora to save Manrico's life if she marries him. In fact, she poisons herself. The Count orders Manrico's execution, learning too late (from Azucena) that he has killed his own brother.

The brothers in *Il Trovatore* move, like Leonora and Azucena, in different worlds; Manrico feels some sense of a connection between himself and the

---

[9] See Julian Budden, *The Operas of Verdi, Volume 1*, pp. 333–5.

[10] See *id.*, pp. 335–7.

[11] See *id.*, p. 88.

Count, a psychological inhibition ("un grido vien dal cielo", "a voice from heaven"[12]) he appeals to in order to explain to Azucena his refusal to kill the Count in a duel in single combat, but the brothers are radically separated psychologically by their different relations to patriarchy. The Count is an obsessionally controlling patriarchal man driven by insatiable emotional needs arising from traumatic loss. Manrico, a troubadour artist, was, as in Verdi's own life as an artist, separated from his patriarchal family, and lives outside patriarchy, loving and loved by both Azucena (a woman who chooses to be his mother) and Leonora. Verdi gives musically expressive voice to the subjective feelings of both women in marvelously beautiful and compelling ways that, between them, bridge a broad range of the feelings of women's love for men. Such love, including Azucena's anti-patriarchal mother's love, gave Manrico a psychological road out of patriarchy. In contrast, his brother, the Count, experienced the full brunt of the tragedy of patriarchy – broken relationships to his father and brother that led to an aching loss, a loveless desolation – that fuels his obsessional need to control, his violence, his emotional and moral blindness to the feelings and concerns of others, culminating in the suicide of Leonora and the murder of his brother.

## (3) Sister to Sister

Carol Gilligan's *The Birth of Pleasure*[13] calls, in a self-consciously contemporary feminist spirit, for a rethinking of personal and political psychology in terms of the women-centered spirit of "The Story of Cupid and Psyche" in Apuleius' *The Golden Ass*.[14] The great psychological interest of the Apuleius myth is its focus on the interlinked relations both between Cupid and Venus, his mother, and between Psyche (Cupid's lover) and Venus. The antagonistic relationship between women like Psyche and Venus under patriarchy (including the antagonistic relationship to Psyche of her two jealous and competitive sisters) divides women stereotypically into idealized good and devalued bad women. Such stereotypes rest on a psychology of disassociation not only of women but of the men they love, disabling both from living in relationship to one another as persons. Rather, idealization cuts them off from a sense of loving relationship based on embodied sexual

---

[12] Verdi, *Il Trovatore*, libretto to recording conducted by James Levine, at p. 88.

[13] See Carol Gilligan, *The Birth of Pleasure*.

[14] See Apuleius, *The Golden Ass*, E. J. Kenney, trans. (London: Penguin, 1998), at pp. 71–106.

voice, mutual knowledge and desire, and conviction and the pleasure to which such love gives birth. Gilligan argues that new kinds of relationships between women (including relations between sisters) are crucial features of the personal and political psychology required for men and women to resist the structural injustice of sexism. Verdi, in contrast, studies the personal and political psychology of the tragedy of patriarchy, a world in which his tragically broken women lack not only relations to mothers but to sisters as well.

The only sustained examination of the sister–sister relationship under patriarchy is Verdi's early opera, *Nabucco*, which patriarchally divides two sisters as the tragedy of patriarchy requires. The psychology portrayed in the opera is of two sisters divided by a struggle for the love of a man and for the authority of their father, who is the king of Babylon. Women are thus divided patriarchally: first, over a putative male lover–husband; and second, over their father's authority. Fenena, the good daughter, is the natural daughter of Nabucco; Abigaille, the bad daughter, is believed to be the eldest daughter of Nabucco, but is adopted, daughter of a slave. Fenena and Abigaille love the same man, the Israelite, Ismaele; but Ismaele loves Fenena. Abigaille's frustration in love turns, however, to despotic political ambition, which is brilliantly musically voiced as Abigaille, who learning she is a slave, decides that, with the support of the priests of Baal, she shall try to take power.[15] After Nabucco is struck down as mad by his blasphemous statement that he is God, Abigaille takes power (vowing imperious revenge for her former slavery) and gets her confused and broken father to sign the death warrant of Fenena, of which he immediately piteously repents:

> "Nabucco pours out his grief in an F minor melody which owes something to Guillaume Tell's 'Sois immobile' not only in its dignified restraint but in its moving key change to D flat and back again. Abigaille, nourishing her dreams of glory, seems to inhabit a different world. Where he is submissive she is imperious; while his line is smooth-moving within a restricted compass hers is jagged and moves by leaps. His tonality is F minor, hers is D flat. Inevitably when the two voices sing together they do so in her key, not his, yet they retain their individual character till the end. Previous Italian composers just did not write this kind of duet movement."[16]

Verdi's art gives Abigaille in this and earlier scenes a musical voice unforgettably expressive of darker emotions of anger, rage, and indignation not

---

[15] See *id.*, pp. 102–3.
[16] See *id.*, p. 106.

only at her lovelessness (both from Ismaele and Nabucco), but at her sense of herself as a slave and the child of slaves. Verdi, even at this very early stage of his artistic development, insists that we hear in its full ferocity the murderous rage of a woman resisting the humilitating indignities imposed on her by patriarchy.

*Chapter 7*

# Lovers

The gender binary, formed as we have seen by the requirements of the patriarchal family, shapes a larger personal and political psychology of relations among adults. Nothing is more compelling in Verdi's mature art than the ways in which he explores the connections between the impact of patriarchy on private and on public life, in particular, on how its disruption of all forms of personal relationship is the psychological fuel for unjust violence in both private and public life. We earlier saw (chapter 3) how the Attic tragedians Aeschylus and Sophocles framed the tragedy of patriarchy as the necessary price for democratic citizenship, which was very much defined by the demands of military service that the Athenian democracy imposes on its exclusively male citizens; and we observed as well how Euripides more skeptically framed the tragedy as responsible for the unjust imperialistic wars that destroyed the Athenian democracy. It is a remarkable cultural universal in all societies (democratic and non-democratic) that the gender binary has been importantly structured by the psychological demands placed on men to fight in wars.[1] Tragic art offers an interpretation of the psychology of the gender binary supposed to be required for democratic citizenship, including fighting in war. Verdi's mature art exquisitely studies how the personal and political psychology that sustains patriarchy (including militaristic and religious idealization that covers traumatic loss) renders all forms of democratic relationship, public and private, unsustainable. There are three relationships among adults we should examine from this perspective in Verdi's operas: relations between men, between women, and between men and women.

---

[1]  See, for an important defense of his view, Joshua S. Goldstein, *War and Gender: How Gender Shapes the War System and Vice Versa* (Cambridge: Cambridge University Press, 2001).

## (1) Male–male Relationships

Relationships between adult men are in Verdi's operas, both in his earlier and later works, divided either along lines of patriarchal competition for the love of a woman (as in *Ernani*, *Alzira*, *Attila*, *La Battaglia di Legnano*, *Stiffelio*, *Ballo in Maschera*, *La Forza del Destino*, *Don Carlos*, *Otello*) or along lines of such competition over a daughter and granddaughter (*Simon Boccanegra*). Even when divisions between men are mainly political, as in *Macbeth*, the struggle is conceived patriarchally in terms of whose children will succeed to supreme political authority. It is Verdi's standard view that breaks arising from personal life always transmute into larger breaks in political life, rendering, in *Simon Boccanegra*, for example, the politics of the Genoese republic permanently factionalized along lines deriving from the personal hatred of Fiesco for Simon. Patriarchal men, set against each other by the demands of the code of honor, become the fratricidal citizens of the Genoese republic. Certainly, such men, like Fiesco, sometimes are permitted to experience gnawing remorse for their honor-obsessed political opposition to men like Simon, one of the very few political leaders with a humane and liberal vision depicted in Verdi's operas. But the remorse comes too late, as enforcement of the honor code destroys the foundation of liberal political fraternity as it already has the possibility of a humane intimate life.

Some of Verdi's most penetrating observations of the psychology of the relations of mature men under patriarchy come in his later operas in which the poignant breaking of friendship becomes a central issue, as in the relationship of Gustavo and Renato in *Un Ballo in Maschera*, Alvaro and Carlos in *La Forza del Destino*, Philip and Posa as well as Carlos and Posa in *Don Carlos*, and Cassio and Othello and Iago and Othello in *Otello*. Verdi gives marvelously compelling musical expression to the deep emotional need for love between men under patriarchy as an alternative to the intrinsic tragedy, as Verdi sees it (see below), of relations between men and women under patriarchy. Verdi sometimes frames these relationships, as we have seen, as having homoerotic elements (as in Gustavo in *Un Ballo in Maschera*, or Posa and Carlos in *Don Carlos*).[2]

In *La Forza del Destino*, he starkly portrays this desperate emotional need in the two men, Alvaro and Carlos, who, not knowing each other's identi-

---

[2] There may be such homoerotic elements in Shakespeare's play, *Othello*, on which Verdi's *Otello* is based, suggested certainly by Iago's speech beginning "I lay with Cassio lately," in Shakespeare, *Othello*, III, iii, l. 413 ff., in G. Blakemore Evans et al., *The Riverside Shakespeare*, pp. 1251–96, at p. 1272, and, more indirectly, as an explanation (namely, repressed homosexuality) for Iago's malice against Othello and Desdemona. Boito's setting of the relevant

ties, bond as friends in the comradeship of heroic military service. The beautifully scored musical opening to Act III with clarinet solo and the similar scoring of Alvaro's succeeding rumination on his emotional plight, opening with the words, "La vita e inferno all'infelice" ("Life itself is hell to the sorrowful"), speak of "a world of dreams and nostalgia,"[3] broken by traumatic separation both from his executed parents and from Leonora. His similarly scored following prayer to Leonora, "O tu che in seno agli angeli" ("O you who dwell among the angels") (at this point he believes her to be dead), expresses his desire to die, and turning to military service as a way of achieving this end. Alvaro does not apparently draw distinctions between just and unjust ends and means of war that preoccupy Montfort and Henri in *Les Vepres Siciliennes* and Gaston in *Jerusalem*.[4] War serves a depressed emotional need for death but heroically valued death, and he rationalizes such needs in terms of an idealized image of his supposedly dead lover, now conceived as an angel. Alvaro's emotional bond with Carlos fills this vacuum, and, as Alvaro thinks he lay dying, Verdi gives powerful musical expression to the love between the friends in the duet:

"ALVARO

| Or muoio tranquillo; | Now I can die in peace |
| Vi stringo al cor mio. | I embrace you with all my heart. |

CARLO

| Amico, fidate nel cielo! | My friend, trust in Heaven."[5] |

Carlo also, as we earlier saw, experiences genuine moral conflict as he struggles between his patriarchal sense of honor and his feeling for Alvaro. Once, however, he decides for patriarchal honor, he implacably resists Alvaro's moving pleas both in Act III and in Act IV (given powerfully eloquent musical expression in both cases). The emotional need of men for the love of one another is thus portrayed starkly as broken by patriarchy.

---

speech of Iago from Shakespeare is much less explicitly homoerotic, see Verdi's *Otello* libretto to recording conducted by Georg Solti, Chicago Symphony Orchestra, at p. 63, and Boito and Verdi seem much less interested in the psychology of Iago than was Shakespeare. But a homoerotic interpretation of the Iago–Cassio and Iago–Othello relationships in Verdi's *Otello* cannot be ruled out as implausible.

[3] See Julian Budden, *The Operas of Verdi, Volume 2*, at p. 477.

[4] In the opening scene of *Jerusalem*, Gaston complains to Helene of her father: 'Il a tue le mien/dans une injustice guerre!" ("He killed my father/in an unjust war!"), in Verdi, *Jerusalem*, libertto to recording conducted by Fabio Luisi, L'Orchestra de la Suisse Romande, pp. 36–7.

[5] See Verdi, *La Forza del Destino*, libretto to recording conducted by Riccardo Muti, at pp. 124–5.

Relationships between adult men under patriarchy are always emotionally fragile relationships, because they turn on a code of honor whose demands on men require the violent breaking of any relationship that threatens patriarchally defined honor.

There is a notably subtle exploration of the impact of patriarchy on male psychology in Alvaro in *La Forza del Destino*. Once Alvaro's relationship to Leonora is broken by grief and remorse over the accidental killing of her father, Alvaro covers over his desolating loss in relationship by two alternative masculine idealisms, the one political, the other religious: military service as a war hero, religious service as a monk. In both cases, the psychological fuel of such idealism is traumatic loss in relationship, feelings and vulnerabilities buried under a defensive psychological armor in service of a collective military or religious discipline. In the case of war, as we have just seen in Alvaro's rumination on his emotional plight, Verdi's musical art powerfully expresses the naked need of a man, once intimate relationship has been broken, for some form of patriarchally validated political violence, whether just or unjust, in which, strikingly, the mythological image of his absent, putatively dead beloved rationalizes such violence (violence against the French is similarly rationalized in terms of the patriarchal protection of women in *Les Vepres Siciliennes*). Verdi's art exquisitely explores the psychology of even a good man, like Alvaro, under patriarchy, in which such military service reenforces patriarchy because such service is here rooted in patriarchally inflicted emotional losses whose justice has been removed from discussion precisely by the loss of voice and feeling. Violence replaces voice.

The central tragedy of *Otello* is the relation of a husband and wife (see the following discussion), but the tragedy includes as well the breaking of a friendship between Cassio and Othello (as Othello orders his former friend and confidante, Cassio, to be killed) and Othello's crazed trust in a friendship with Iago which never exists. Othello's tragic failure to read his wife is rooted in his tragic trust in Iago. Patriarchy breaks real relationships between men and between men and women, replacing it with a mythology of gender and sexuality which, as in the case of Iago and Othello, allows a false male friend to be trusted more than either a true male friend or a true and loving wife (see the following discussion on male–female relationships).

## (2) Female–Female Relationships

As Carol Gilligan's recent work suggests, living under a burden of stereotypes disables women and men from knowing themselves or from knowing the person they love. Verdi's operas limn the same psychology in the relations of adult women to one another. Both in his earlier and later works, any relationship between women is emotionally broken by the demands of patriarchal competition for a man, often explained in terms of a blinding, competitive jealousy that is ultimately self-destructive. Verdi deals with such broken relationships in an earlier work like *Il Corsaro* and in two mature works, *Don Carlos* and *Aida*. The treatment of the issue in *Il Corsaro* is schematic at best.[6] The treatment in the mature operas is a different matter.

*Don Carlos* explores the competitive relationship between Princess Eboli and Elisabeth, the Queen, both over Don Carlos and Philip II himself. Elisabeth has accepted fatalistically her loveless marriage as required by her patriarchal duty to her father and country, and had rejected Don Carlos's attempts to revive their former love; she is, in terms of the patriarchal division of women, a good woman (both her mother and father are psychologically absent throughout the opera). As we saw earlier in chapter 5 – Parents and Children – in the section on Fathers and Sons, she withdraws into a religio-political idealism that, in their last act duet, supports the withdrawal of Don Carlos into political idealism. Eboli, in contrast, is introduced to us in the musically expressive uncontrolled sensuality and dalliance of her "Chanson Du Voile" ("The Veil Song"), a beautiful woman in love with being loved; she is, in terms of the patriarchal division, a bad woman. Verdi's musical art powerfully explores their different worlds, and how their division from one another destroys them both as well as the man (Don Carlos) they both love. Elisabeth is emotionally and intellectually locked into the terms of her patriarchal marriage, cut off by her sense of duty from her family in France, from the man she loves, and from her husband, whom she never loved. Her dignified unhappiness, which finds solace in religion, cuts her off from any human relationship, but morally empowers her actively to support Carlos's political ideals. Eboli's isolation, in contrast, is rooted in her narcissistic objectification of her own beauty and desirability, which cuts her off not only from other women but from men (there is no suggestion she loves Philip and she misreads the man, Don Carlos, she does love). Her narcissism leads her to wrongly interpret Don Carlos's emotional unbalance when he is with Eboli and his stepmother as love for Eboli. When Eboli realizes the truth, she supposes that Elisabeth has been unfaithful

---

[6] Medora and Gulnara, both of whom love the pirate Corrado, only meet in the brief last scene, at which time Medora dies and the hero, Corrado, throws himself off a cliff; there is thus no relationship between the women as such for Verdi to explore.

with her stepson and turns her rage furiously on the morally innocent Elisabeth as a hypocrite:

| | |
|---|---|
| "Et moi qui tremblais devant elle! | And I who used to tremble before her! |
| Elle voulait, cette sainte nouvelle | She wanted, that new saint, |
| Des celestes vertus, conservant | while preserving an exterior |
| Les dehors, | of heavenly virtue, |
| S'abreuver a pleins bords | to drain to the last drop |
| A la coupe ou l'on boit | the cup of life's pleasures! |
| Les plaisirs de la vie! | |
| Ah! sue mon ame, elle etait hardier! | Ah! By my soul, she was daring!"[7] |

Eboli discloses to Philip II, with whom she has been having an affair, Elisabeth's secret casket, which contains evidence of Elisabeth's love for Carlos before her father, the king of France, married her to Philip instead. When Eboli realizes that her accusation of Elisabeth's adultery is false, she confesses her own adultery to Elisabeth, who curtly dismisses Eboli from her service. In her musically powerful following aria, "O don fatal et deteste" ("O fatal and detested gift"), Eboli mourns her loss of her relationship to Elisabeth and the curse of her beauty that tempted her proudly to betray the Queen with her own husband and then falsely accuse Elisabeth of an adultery of which only Eboli was in fact guilty. She determines, having recognized her folly, to save Carlos from Philip's revenge. Verdi portrays Eboli's narcissism – living only in the desire she believes her beauty inspires in all men – as cutting her off not only from any real relationship to men (shown in her misconstrual of Don Carlos's feelings) but from women as well. She not only fails to understand the dignified sadness of Elisabeth in a loveless marriage, but she disastrously endangers both Elisabeth and Carlos by ascribing to them motives that reflect not their psychological reality, but mirror her own nescient passions. Eboli is as much caught up in the illusions of a patriarchal psychology of objectified beauty as Falstaff, illusions which can, as Verdi's art shows, either be the basis of broken relationship and tragedy or, if resisted by women and men in relationship, the stuff of comedy.

Verdi's *Aida* very much centers its musically expressive exploration of the psychology of women under patriarchy in terms of the triangular relationship of Amneris, daughter of pharaoh, and Aida to the man they both love, Radames. Aida is a black slave to Amneris, which adds yet the further dimension of the racialized pedestal to their emotionally tense, competitive

---

[7] See Verdi, *Don Carlos*, libretto to recording conducted by Claudio Abbado, at pp. 180–1.

relationship. The psychological contrast of Amneris and Aida is of two daughters of monarchs, but one, Amneris, very much on her patriarchal pedestal, and the other, Aida, after the experience of slavery and loving relationship with a man, much more resistant, as we earlier saw, to the patriarchal demands imposed on her by her father. Amneris is not completely without feeling for Aida's plight, but her feelings are covered over by her patriarchally defined sense of honor. After Radames's victory over the Ethiopians, Amneris glories in his achievement; but, when Aida enters, Amneris initially musically expresses sadness at what Aida must be feeling at the defeat of her people:

> "Silenzio! Aida verso noi s'avanza      Silence! Aida comes toward us . . .
> Figlia de' vinti, il suo dolor m'e       Daughter of the vanquished; I
> Sacro                                     respect her sorrow." [8]

But, torn by her worries about the relationship between Radames and Aida, Amneris shuts down such feelings, and then callously tests her slave's emotions by falsely reporting that Radames has been killed to see what her reaction would be. When Aida's reactions (to the report, first, of death, then, life) are despair, then joy, Amneris has learned what she wished to know, and turns on her slave with insult and contempt. Verdi's art thus centrally explores the patriarchally required division of women from one another, a psychology that Carol Gilligan's recent work regards as critically central to the power of patriarchy.

It is Amneris's tragedy that she believes she can get what she wants (the love of a man like Radames) by playing good daughter on the terms of the patriarchal theocracy of Egypt (her father is patriarchal god–pharaoh), marrying Radames as pharaoh commands after his victory over the Ethiopians. But the patriarchal psychology of Amneris disables her from understanding the man she believes she loves, precisely because she cannot understand that for a free man like Radames love exists outside patriarchy. Her emotional blindness leads her to indulge her own patriarchal rage at Radames for his love of Aida and political betrayal of his country's secrets; she exposes his treason to the priests and thus is responsible for his eventual condemnation to death. The last act of *Aida* contrasts the remorse and rage of Amneris in the first scene, to the love and death of Aida and Radames in the second, concluding scene. Verdi powerfully musically expresses Amneris's rages at the priests who inexorably condemn Radames, who will not defend himself, to death. She is finally caught in the spider's web of the patriarchal system of theocratic power on which she had depended to secure

---

[8] See Verdi, *Aida*, libretto to recording conducted by Claudio Abbado, at pp. 82–3.

Radames as her husband, a web that cuts her off from any emotional understanding of either the man she believes she loves or the woman she regards as her competitor. Aida and Radames, in contrast, die happily in love and in a sense of the meaning of their love, a meaning that each of them has earned by their respective struggles to stay in relationship against a background of patriarchy which pulled them apart. Verdi musically sets their dying in an exquisite duet of tender, caring relationship, counterpoised to Amneris's remorseful loneliness, which, as is usual in Verdi's abandoned women, is expressed in religious prayer, as Amneris begs for peace of mind in the chapel above the tomb of the man she loved and destroyed.

## (3) Male–Female Relationships

We turn, at last, to the relationship – adult women to men – that was, for Verdi, at the patriarchal heart of darkness. From the very beginning to the end of his long career as a composer of musical tragedies, Verdi portrays personal sexual love between a man and a woman as tragically vulnerable to defeat by the demands of patriarchy that crush and silence the personal voice and conviction of free and equal women and men, who are in love. Whenever in Verdi a man and woman fall or are in love, tragedy looms as in *I Lombardi* (Giselda and Oronte), *Ernani* (Elvira and Ernani), *Giovanna D'Arco* (Giovanna and Carlo), *Alzira* (Alzira and Zamoro), Macbeth (Lady Macbeth and Macbeth), I *Masnadieri* (Amalia and Carlo), *Il Corsaro* (Medora and Corrado), *La Battaglia di Legnano* (Lida and Arrigo), *Luisa Miller* (Luisa and Rodolfo), *Stiffelio* (Lina and Stiffelio), *Rigoletto* (Gilda and the Duke), *Il Trovatore* (Leonora and Manrico), *La Traviata* (Violetta and Alfredo), *Les Vespres Siciliennes* (Helene and Henri), *Simon Boccanegra* (Maria and Simone), *Un Ballo in Maschera* (Gustavo and Amelia), *La Forza del Destino* (Leonora and Alvaro), *Don Carlos* (Elizabeth and Carlos), *Aida* (Aida and Radames), and *Otello* (Desdemona and Othello).

Verdi's most profound studies of the tragic vulnerabilities of such relationships are those where the psychic geography of the tragedy arises from within the psychology of the relationship, as in his two settings of Shakespearean tragedy, his early, later revised *Macbeth* and his late *Otello*. Verdi was interested in men "in whom an inner conflict between good and evil soars and plummets with each new situation."[9] He was fascinated with *Macbeth* because the conflict arises within the relationship of husband and

---

[9] See Julian Budden, *The Operas of Verdi, Volume 1*, p. 279.

wife who love each other, and he grew remarkably as a musical dramatist through struggling to give a musical representation of the struggle this play depicts:

> "That even Macbeth should retain our compassion is the incredible achievement of Shakespeare the dramatist. Not only that, but he devised for him the perfect partner in crime – perfect because her qualities are the converse of her husband's. Outwardly cold and ruthless, with nerves of steel, Lady Macbeth is rotting inwardly, like a diseased elm. While Macbeth retains to the end all the energy of a gored bull, she goes into a decline the nature of which she does not understand herself. Macbeth gains strength and courage from the ability to look into the abysses of his own soul, even when his nerves are shattered. Lady Macbeth's falterings are like unconscious reflexes. She herself would have murdered Duncan if only he had not looked like her father when he slept. The result is not only psychologically convincing; it produces also a state of equilbrium between the two characters which remains until the end." [10]

Verdi brilliantly depicts Lady Macbeth's ferocious goading of her husband's ambitions, presenting "Lady Macbeth as Abigaille enriched by the musical experience of five years." [11] But the rot within Lady Macbeth is harrowingly portrayed in her "Gran Scena del Sonnambulismo," "a scene unique in all Italian opera of the time." [12]

It was in his last operatic tragedy, *Otello*, however, that Verdi, inspired by Shakespeare's achievement, turned to his closest psychological study of the vulnerabilities to tragedy implicit in love under patriarchy. As I earlier suggested, Verdi took as his challenge as a music dramatist to depict the deeper truths of psychological reality:

> "As early as 1876, before the idea of setting *Otello* had even been hinted at, Verdi wrote a famous letter to the Countess Maffei about the necessity of 'inventing truth' . . . 'Ask Papa,' he wrote, meaning Shakespeare. 'It is quite possible that he, Papa, might have come across a Falstaff of some kind; but it's most unlikely that he ever met a villain quite so villainous as Iago, and he could never had met women as angelic as Cordelia, Imogen or Desdemona, etc. Yet they are so true." [13]

*Otello* is Verdi's last, most exact, microscopic study of the psychology of men and women ostensibly in love under patriarchy. We know from the

---

[10] See *id.*, p. 280. See also, on Verdi's artistic growth through study of Shakespeare, De Van, *Shakespeare's Theater*, at pp. 75–6.

[11] See Julian Budden, *Ther Operas of Verdi, Volume 1*, 285.

[12] See *id.*, p. 308.

[13] See Julian Budden, *The Operas of Verdi, Volume 3*, p. 317.

very wildness of the storm that opens the opera, leading to Othello's glorious entry with "Esultate!",[14] that emotional chaos and this armored war-hero with his piercing opening high note are no strangers. The opera explores the emotional desolation and disassociation of the psychology that supports and sustains the inexorable demands the code of honor makes on men and women.

The opera explores, in particular, the emotional vulnerabilities of an ethnically other man (a Moor) in love with a beautiful Venetian woman to seduction by a patriarchal demon, Iago, into murdering the woman he loves by the mere appearance of things. Iago's seduction stimulates Othello's internal doubts based on why Desdemona could not have loved him, doubts that include his age and race:

| | |
|---|---|
| "Forse perche gl'inganni d'arguto amor | Happy because I am not practised |
| forse perche discendo | in the deceits of love |
| nella valle degli anni, | or that I am declined |
| forse perche ho sul viso | into the vale of years |
| quest'atro tenebror | or that my complexion |
| | is of this dusky hue."[15] |

He is, of course, musically portrayed as experiencing these doubts in a duet with his innocent wife who is sincerely expressing her love for him. Othello, a black man who has married in violation of the racialized pedestal, is himself seduced by the mythological stereotypes that sustain the pedestal: Desdemona cannot have sincerely desired and wanted him as a man and husband. Othello cannot hear his wife's love: he more easily can believe Iago because Iago speaks in the terms of the code of honor and its racialized pedestal, which shape reality in their own image.

Verdi and Boito importantly make Iago, in his "Credo", effectively state patriarchy as an ultimate metaphysical principle of evil:

"Iago's creed has four articles of belief: in a cruel God who has created him in his own image; that to do evil is to fulfill his destiny; that virtue is a lie and the good man a contemptible dupe; and that man is the plaything of fate and can hope for nothing in this life or after death – 'for death is nothingness and heaven an old wives' tales'."[16]

As we have seen, in the remarkable third act of *Luisa Miller*, Rodolfo

---

[14] See Julian Budden, *The Operas of Verdi, Volume 3*, pp. 337–8.
[15] See Verdi, *Otello*, recording, George Solti, conductor, Chicago Symphony Orchestra, libretto, at p. 56.
[16] See Julian Budden, *The Operas of Verdi, Volume 3*, at p. 358.

deems what he has done (poisoning himself and the woman he loves) as serving a monstrous god, the inhuman demands of patriarchy of which he has become the unwitting instrument and dupe, in the same way the Count di Luna in *Il* Trovatore responds to Leonora's pleas for pity with: "My only god is vengeance" ("E sol vendetta mio Nume").[17] This theme is carried much further in *Don Carlos* in which the patriarchal Inquisitor transforms religion and morality into the demands of patriarchy. Verdi's Iago carries Rodolfo's, the Count, and the Inquisitor's point to its metaphysical conclusion: God is now created in the image of patriarchy, a cruel father bent on hierarchy and subordination as the metaphysical reality of things which is in the nature of things so that resistance is pointless. Verdi, unlike Shakespeare, is not interested in Iago psychologically. Rather, he is using Iago as a way of stating the evil power of patriarchy to transform not only religion and morality into its own image (already studied in *Don Carlos*), but the very nature of reality itself so that we must, in the nature of things, accommodate ourselves to its demands. It is that reality-transforming nihilistic power of patriarchy that Iago forthrightly states for us as our fate.

It is this metaphysical image of the power of patriarchy which explains why Desdemona barely exists as a person in the opera – "not a woman," Verdi wrote on a later occasion, "but a type. She is the type of goodness, resignation, self-sacrifice. There are beings who are born for others, who are quite unaware of their own egos."[18] Patriarchy, which rests on fundamental structural injustice, rationalizes the injustice as in the nature of things by suppressing the personal voice and conscience that might contest its unjust demands. In particular, mythologized images of gender and sexuality, thus contested, remake reality in their own stereotypical image. Verdi goes to great musically expressive lengths to create a tenor voice for Othello of a complexity and range he had not used since *Stiffelio* in order to portray the scope of Othello's subjective experience, his heroism, his sensual tenderness, his despair, his rage. But Desdemona barely exists as a person in the opera because Othello thinks of her stereotypically. When she does voice her fears and hopes in the last act in her exquisitely beautiful "Willow Song", she shows piercing emotional intelligence when, near its conclusion, she summarizes the meaning of the song for her in terms of incommensurable conceptions of manhood/womanhood, then immediately hears a cry (portrayed musically as one of wrenching terror) as it were under such conceptions:

---

[17] See Verdi, *Il Trovatore*, recording, James Levine, conductor, Metropolitan Opera Orchestra, libretto, p. 150.

[18] See Julian Budden, *The Operas of Verdi, Volume 3*, at p. 322.

| "Povera Barbara! | Poor Barbara! |
| Solea la storia con questo | The story used to end |
| Semplice suono finir: | with this simple phrase: |
| "Egli era nato per la sua gloria, | 'He was born for glory, |
| io per amar . . . ' | I to love . . . ' |
| (ad Emilia) | (to Emilia) |
| Ascolta. Odo un lamento. | Hark! I heard a moan."[19] |

Desdemona, not understanding intellectually the ostensible grounds for her husband's violent rage at her, nonetheless accurately reads his psychology, his sense of patriarchal masculinity so realistic in war cannot realistically read love. There are no more harrowing moments in Verdi than his musical depiction of moments when women (whether Dedemona thus hearing a moan, or Violetta in *La Traviata* begging Alfredo to love her, or Amelia in her great Act II aria in *Un Ballo in Maschera* hearing inner weeping which terrifies her) come to a sense of their inner weeping at not being able to be loved as they love. Desdemona has the emotional intelligence to read her plight.

However, in the equally beautiful prayer that follows, "Ave Maria", this intelligent woman disappears before our eyes into her idealization of the Virgin Mary, sacrificing her life on the pedestal that has suppressed her voice and conviction (as Violetta disappears into an idealized angel by force of her self-sacrifice at the end of *La Traviata*), praying even for the man who loves her and is wrongfully about to kill her ("the powerful man, who also grieves"):

"Ave Maria, piena di grazia,
eletta a fra le spose e le vergini sei tu
benedetto il frutto, o Benedetta
di tue materne viscere, Gesu,
Prega per chi, adorando te, si prostra,
Prega del peccator, per l'innocente,
E pel debole oppresso e pel possente,
Misero anch'esso, tua pieta dimostra,
Prega per chi sotto l'oltraggio piega la fronte,
E sotto la malvagia sorte;
Per noi, per noi tu prega,
Prega sempre,
E nell'ora della morte nostra,
Prega per noi, prega per noi,
Prega!

---

[19] See Verdi, *Otello*, recording, George Solti, conductor, Chicago Symphony Orchestra, libretto, at p. 102.

Hail Mary, full of grace,
Blessed amongst wives and maids art thou,
And blessed is the fruit, o blessed one,
Of thy maternal womb, Jesu.
Pray for those who knelling adore three,
Pray for the sinner, for the innocent
And for the weak oppressed; and to the powerful man,
Who also grieves, thy sweet compassion show.
Pray for him who bows beneath injustice
And 'neath the blows of cruel destiny;
For us, pray thou for us,
Pray for us always,
And at the hour of our death
Pray for us, pray for us,
Pray!" [20]

We are left, after Othello is confronted with the reality of what he has done, with his "'Gloria . . . Otello fu' – a blaze of woodwind and brass followed by a void," and then his voiced agony over what he has done, in which Desdemona, dead, coldly disappears for Othello into her purity:

"E tu . . . come sei pallida!
E stanca, et muta, e bella,
Pia creatura nata sotto maligna stella.
Fredda come la casta tua vita,
E in cielo assorta.
Desdemona! Desdemona!
Ah! Morta! Morta! Morta!

And thou . . . how pale thou art!
And weary, and mute, and beautiful,
Pious creature, born 'neath an evil star.
Cold, even like thy chastity,
And gathered into heaven.
Desdemona! Desdemona!
Ah! . . . Dead! Dead! Dead!" [21]

Suicide follows, and he expires with a tender "Un bacio . . . un bacio ancora . . . un altro bacio." [22]

Verdi's musically exquisite psychological exploration of the vulnerabili-

---

[20] See Verdi, *Otello*, recording, George Solti, conductor, Chicago Symphony Orchestra, libretto, at p. 103.

[21] See *id.*, at p. 113.

[22] See Julian Budden, *The Operas of Verdi, Volume 3*, p. 398.

ties of Othello shows how under patriarchy one may ostensibly be in love but not be in relationship to the person one loves. Patriarchy, defined by the code of honor, divides men from women because its force and stability depend on the sexist suppression of women's voice and conviction, indeed justifies violence in the place of voice. It is enough for Othello that his wife should appear to have been unfaithful to unleash a homicidally violent retribution on her which Othello calls justice. To frame this psychology, Verdi goes to extraordinary lengths musically to represent the emotional frailty and disassociation of the armored war-hero, a kind of emotional child in the body of a general. The man who has such military courage and command against a realistic enemy cannot read the love of his wife. Mere suspicion, as an insult to his fragile honor, rationalizes homicidal violence not only against his wife but his political compatriot, Cassio. Verdi insists that we see patriarchal men as psychologically vulnerable to such tragedy in private and public life because patriarchy, when permitted to remake reality in its own metaphysical image, rests on self-perpetuating illusions that, in their nature, break relationship. On the one hand, it forges a violent armor capable of killing other men in largely hand-to-hand wars, whether just or, as was much more often the case, unjust. On the other hand, the same breaking of relationship between and among men is systematically linked to the breaking of relationship between men and women. Locked in illusion, such men lack the elementary resources of emotional intelligence, voice and conviction, to relate to persons, both men and women. Love and friendship under patriarchy must for this reason be vulnerable to tragedy, a theme Verdi obsessionally investigates in his tragic operas from *Oberto* to *Otello*.

Verdi shows that there may be an alternative path in *Falstaff* in which, for the first time in all his work, patriarchally resisting relationships are systematically portrayed. As we have seen, these relationships crucially include a mother to her daughter and women friends supportive of one another. But they also include the luminous musical moments accorded the tender love play of Nannetta and Fenton, which the free voices of women and men, joined in resistance to the illusions of patriarchy, finally make possible.

Verdi's last musical thoughts were, I believe, of the pivotal psychological importance of such relationships between men and women in his *Quattro Pezzi Sacri* (Four Sacred Pieces).[23] Three of them address Mary, the mother of Jesus ("Stabat Mater", "Laudi alla Vergine Maria", "Ave Maria");

---

[23] For a different but equally secular reading, see De Van, *Verdi's Voice*, pp. 343–4.

the fourth, God Himself ("Te Deum"). After a lifetime of exploration of the psychology underlying the tragedy of patriarchy and the resistance thereto, Verdi chooses in his last work to set three texts about a mother, and one about a father, but a father who is equally father, son, and holy spirit. Verdi, one of the deepest students of the psychology of men and women under patriarchy, always innovates musically expressive voice from a certain person's point of view situated in some psychological relation to patriarchy. He had earlier often used prayers to the Virgin Mary (culminating in Desdemona's "Ave Maria" in *Otello*) as the expression of the disassociated psychology of women bending sacrificially to the demands of patriarchy. But the image of Mary is subject to less patriarchal interpretations,[24] which, in the wake of *Falstaff*, may have come to interest Verdi both as an artist and man. If *Falstaff* enabled him finally critically to examine his own patriarchal illusions, such self-examination may have included a sense of remorse for the grief his affair with Stoltz caused Strepponi, and a freshly understood sense of what he creatively owed to Strepponi's voice as support and resonance for his deepest artistic ambitions and perhaps for similar reasons to his own mother earlier (Strepponi, now an invalid, was nearing the end of her life). From this perspective, I hear in the three Marian settings of the *Quattro Pezzi Sacri* Verdi creating an acoustic space for us to hear the pious voice of Strepponi and probably also Verdi's mother, depicted in vulnerable and loving resonance for Verdi's pain, rooted in early trauma and loss, relationships which had been a loving resonance for hearing his own creative voice (as Mary tenderly witnesses the pain and death of Jesus in "Stabat Mater"). It is particularly suggestive that Verdi's creative interest was arrested by Dante's exquisite "Laudi alla Vergine Maria" from the *Paradiso* (set in a Palestrina-like, hushed, a capella style), which begins with the remarkable phrase, "Vergine madre, figlia del tuo Figlio" ("Virgin mother, daughter of Thy son") in which the metaphorical placing of mother and son in the relationship of son and his daughter suggests an egalitarian reciprocity of mutual dependence; the poem then acknowledges Mary's seminally creative goodness:

" . . . che l'umana natura . . .     who so ennobled
nobilitasti si, che 'l suo Fattore     human nature that its Creator
non disdegno di farsi sua fattura.     did not disdain to make Himself its
    creation."[25]

---

[24] See, for discussion of this point, David A. J. Richards, *Italian American*, at pp. 210–11.
[25] See Verdi, *Pezzi Sacri*, libretto to recording conducted by Myung-Whun Chung, Coro e Orchestra dell'Accademia Nazionale di Santa Cecilia, at p. 8.

Verdi tenderly acknowledges the creative moral force in men's lives of their relations to women. The musical setting of the "Te Deum" is, in contrast, in Verdi's much less pious and more personally operatic musical voice as a man and artist, addressing a God who "did not abhor the Virgin's womb" ("non horruistic Virginis uterum"),[26] a creator, like Verdi, who realizes his mature creative powers only as, equally, father, son, and holy spirit, and then only in relationship to a woman, and whose powers gloriously dignify the best humane traditions of his people. Strepponi dies after Verdi sends the *Quattro Pezzi Sacri* for publication in 1897. Verdi dies in 1901.

---

[26] See Verdi, *Requiem*, *Quattro Pezzi Sacri*, conducted by Carlo Maria Giulini, Philharmonia Orchestra, libretto at pp. 42–3.

# Part III

## Between Patriarchal and Democratic Manhood

# Chapter 8

# Tragedy as the Dilemma of Democratic Manhood

This work has examined the idea of tragedy in two new ways: its main example is not drawn from literature or the stage, but from music drama; and its analysis proceeds in terms of the contested place of feminism in political liberalism. The focus on music drama raises the same question Nietzsche raises about why Attic tragedy makes its distinctive point, in contrast to Greek philosophy and politics, in musical forms of drama. Nietzsche answers his question in terms that indict the Greek rationalism he despised in Socrates and Euripides. I agree with Walter Kaufmann that philosphical reason is among Greece's most valuable enduring contributions to human thought and that, nonetheless, the greatest Attic tragedies (including, *pace* Nietzsche, Euripides) are often more truthful about the human situation than the philosophers were.[1] Tragedy is, like philosophy, another enduring contribution of Greece to the human search for truth, one required, in my view, to deal truthfully with issues of life under democracy that could not otherwise be even exposed for discussion. To understand such truthfulness we need not indict, as Nietzsche did, either Socratic philosophy as such or democracy as such, but rather to take seriously what the subject matter of tragedy is.

The argument of this book has been that the tragedy has been and is as important to democracy as philosophy or other forms of rationalistic inquiry into truth. It offers us a way into the complexities of human psychology under democracy with which more rationalistic forms of inquiry (including empirical psychology) cannot adequately deal. It is the nature of trauma, the psychology that tragedy studies, that it cripples voice and memory,

---

[1] See Walter Kaufmann, *Tragedy and Philosophy* (Garden City, NY: Doubleday, 1968).

(157)

effects which explain why it may be difficult reasonably to even acknowledge, let alone discuss. If there is a scientifically reliable approach to human psychology under democracy, tragedy must be regarded as a branch of this science. Of course, its insights must be checked and validated against other forms of inquiry once psychology has, as it has today, embraced trauma and its effects as important features of human psychology.[2] Its insights, when thus validated, can, of course, be politically interpreted in quite different ways, some quite conversative, others liberal and even radical. But tragedy is an indispensably important mode of inquiry into the truth of our complex psychology under democracy. I have argued that the very truthfulness of its inquiry sometimes requires *musical* voice, as the required mode of revealing the trauma and its consequences. Music, on this view, is integral to sound methods in a human psychology that aspires to truth, as much as Leonardo's breathtaking art of human anatomy was a way into a more truthful understanding of our complex bodies than the medical science of his period or even the science of periods long after.[3] Great artists and historians, as Freud, Erikson, and Gilligan have recognized, reveal our complex psyches in ways scientific psychologists ignore at their peril. There are very good reasons why this should be so, as the context and aims of tragedy show.

Tragedy arises and flourishes in Attic Greece as an art for democratic citizens, reflecting on the new responsibilities of citizenship required in transition from the previous rule of kings. Its subject matter is the kind of manhood now required. But since manhood is defined by its gender binary, womanhood, tragedy often uses portrayals of women under the rule of kings (Klytemnestra, Cassandra, Iphigenia) to make its points about the shift in gender roles that democracy requires. The subject matter of tragedy is the shifts in gender (both manhood and womanhood) supposedly required by democracy as a more defensible form of government than the rule of kings.

Both Aeschylus and Sophocles were patriots of the Athenian democracy, very much committed to its institutions as a defensible form of government (in this, they both contrast sharply to philosophers like Plato and Aristotle, both of whom were critical of the democracy). The Athenian democracy was, however, not only limited to men, but placed new kinds of normative and psychological demands on men, including not only service in the participatory institutions of the democracy, but, more importantly, military

---

[2] See Judith Herman, *Trauma and Recovery* (New York: Basic Books, 1997); Bessel A. van der Kolk, Alexander C. McFarlane, and Lars Weisaeth, eds., *Traumatic Stress* (New York: The Guilford Press, 1996).

[3] See, on this point, Sherwin B. Nuland, *Leonardo da Vinci* (NY: Lipper/Viking, 2000).

service not in the mode of the kingly heroes of *The Iliad* but in the inter-dependent male-bonded phalanxes of hoplite armies.[4] The tragedies portray the shifts in gender (both manhood and womanhood) required both to legit-imate and psychologically to sustain such new responsibilites.

There was, however, both a normative and psychological problem that such shifts raised, a problem whose representation gave rise to tragic art. The normative problem is the egalitarianism on which the political appeal of democracy rests. The Athenian democracy was certainly not egalitarian in the terms we today regard as required, but Athenian democrats under-stood its normative appeal, in contrast to kingship, as preferable because more egalitarian. That egalitarian appeal crucially included not only equality of voting rights, but equal rights of voice. But the Athenians certainly knew, as the tragedies display so clearly, that women had a compe-tence in voice at least the equal of men, something men have always known from their intimate relationships to women, whether as mothers, sisters, lovers, or wives. The terms of Athenian democracy required men not only not to give democratic expression to women's equal rights of voice, but effectively to silence such voices in the public life of the democracy. At this point *The Oresteia*, as we have seen (chapter 2), resorts to a mythology of gender that rationalizes such silencing (as the Furies are domesticated in the *Eumenides*). It is, however, a feature of the kind of democratic voice and dialogue that Athenian democracy required that such voice questions the legitimacy of mythologies that cannot bear reasonable criticism and discus-sion, as both its philosophers and the tragedian, Euripides, clearly show. There would in such circumstances always be psychological space for doubt about the egalitarian legitimacy of the democracy. Indeed, such doubt plays as a kind of figured base in the musical texture of *The Oresteia*, as the very mythological terms required to resolve the play's sense of contradiction rhetorically blares out over the relentless music of democratic doubt beneath.

The correlative psychological problem is the shifts in gender psychology required by the democracy, in particular, that boys and men must break any relationships to women or their voices that would threaten the forms of male-bonded associations among men required to sustain the democracy. The psychological point of *Oedipus Tyrannus* is along these lines: the need for democratic boys to break relationships to their mothers, and align them-selves with the patriarchal voice of their fathers (see chapter 2). The trauma of such breaks in relationship for young boys psychologically serves the ends

---

[4] See Simon Goldhill, *Reading Greek Tragedy* (Cambridge: Cambridge University Press, 1986), at pp. 91–2, 120, 143–5.

of the democracy, because the effects of trauma (loss of voice, and disassociation) allow them to identify with the requirements of the new conception
of manhood that the democracy requires.

Athens innovated not only democracy but, as we have seen, new forms
of democratic voice, dialogue, and inquiry, whose tendency was demythol-
ogizing. Democratic citizens in such a cultural milieu would be open to
both the problems of legitimacy and psychology centering on what I call
the dilemma of democratic manhood. On the one hand, democracy calls
for equal citizenship and voice, but limits both only to men, who must
frame a sense of citizenship that can live with a sense of this normative
contradiction. On the other, democracy requires of manhood traumatic
breaks and loss of voice in intimate relationships to women, showing itself
in identification with gender idealizations that rest on disassociation and
loss of voice. Tragedy arises and flourishes in Athens because it truthfully
acknowledges the dilemma of manhood in a way philosophers certainly
did not. It does not attack the democracy, as philosophers often did, but,
in terms democratically open to all citizens, both tries to show why it is
more legitimate than kingship and why men must accordingly bear its
burdens, including the sense of tragic loss that the psychology of democratic manhood requires. Attic tragedy uses music to make its tragic points
because music truthfully acknowledges and expresses the emotional
depths of trauma and loss of voice that democratic citizens hold in their
psyches, but cannot give voice to. The truthfulness of tragedy is that it
acknowledges the terrifying losses that a more normatively legitimate
form of government apparently requires. It both acknowledges doubts of
legitimacy and the psychology of loss required to overcome them, and
urges resolution of doubts and acceptance of loss as heroic requirements of
manhood under democracy.

The idea and practice of tragedy arise from a sense, in artists and audiences, of what I have described as the dilemma of manhood, which is also
the dilemma of womanhood. It flourishes in periods of transition to more
egalitarian values and institutions, exploring the sense of contradiction
between patriarchal forms of manhood (and womanhood) and more egalitarian values. For example, in a period of transition of British culture to
more democratically egalitarian values, Shakespeare's mature tragedies –
*Hamlet*, *Othello*, *King Lear*, *Macbeth* – study this divided patriarchal psychology in men, crippled by a skepticism that cuts them off from all the
human relationships they value.[5] My concern in this book has been to

---

[5] See Millicent Bell, *Shakespeare's Tragic Skepticism* (New Haven, CT: Yale University Press,
2002).

introduce into the discussion of the idea of tragedy an example, Verdi's music dramas, almost never discussed in this context, and yet an example quite like the Attic tragedies, since the tragic forms in Athens and in Verdi's Italy arise in quite similar contexts and appeal to music in tragic expression.

Like Aeschylus, Sophocles, and Euripides in the not dissimilar circumstances of democratic Athens, Verdi forged a democratically open and accessible art that represented to the Italian people, during a period of struggle for some form of democratic unity, both the archaic heroes of their past and the new responsibilities of democratic citizenship. Verdi had early supported Mazzini's advocacy of liberal republicanism as the ultimate aim for an Italy reunited from its various forms of colonial occupation, but had come to accept the constitutional monarchy of Piedmont's Cavour as the vehicle for a reunited Italy as the only feasible alternative (at Cavour's insistence – Verdi was that strongly identified in the Italian public mind with democratic unification – Verdi served in the parliament of the constitutional monarchy). The constitutional monarchy had a limited democratic franchise and gave powers of war and peace to the monarch that were to prove unfortunate,[6] leading eventually to unjust wars and Mussolini's dictatorship.[7] But Verdi accepted its institutions as a form of liberal constitutionalism on the model of Great Britain that might, like Britain, become more democratic over time but within a broadly liberal conception of limited government. Verdi's tragic art addresses the same question as that of the Attic tragedians: How could the Italians, like the Greeks before them, critically learn from their past so as to avoid its mistakes and understand the new responsibilities of democratic citizenship? Verdi's life-long obsession with the historically entrenched power of the code of honor in Italy played the same role for him in the understanding of contemporary Italian democratic responsibilities as the archaic heroes played in Attic tragedy for the Athenian democracy, namely, as anachronistic practices and attitudes that must be critically evaluated if a more legitimate form of democratic government was to be feasible. It is from this perspective that we can understand how and why the development of his art moves so seamlessly between private and public life, linking patriarchal relations of fathers and daughters or fathers and sons within families to larger themes of political oppression, personal and political violence, civil war, unjust wars between nations, and factionalized republican politics. Verdi saw the role

---

[6] On these powers, see David A. J. Richards, *Italian American: The Racializing of an Ethnic Identity* (New York: New York University Press, 1999), at pp. 86–7.

[7] See, on these points, *id.*, pp. 85, 97.

of patriarchy in both personal and public life as what had importantly balkanized and divided Italians and what had to be superseded if a better form of polity was to be possible.

Indeed, the long trajectory of Verdi's creative output dealing with these themes may, within one artist's creative lifetime, be analogized to the development from Aeschylus to Euripides earlier discussed, namely, from Aeschylus' triumphalist celebration of the founding of the Athenian democracy in *The Oresteia* to Euripides' skepticism about abuses in the democracy, for example, its imperialistic wars. Verdi's artistic development moves from his unqualified defense of the struggle for Italian nationalism (the Risorgimento which triumphs in the unification of Italy under constitutional monarchy) to his growing concerns in his later operas from *Simon Boccanegra* to *Otello* with the corruption of political power as such by faction, by religious intolerance, by ethnically motivated imperialism, and by sexist violence. As we have seen (chapters 5–7), the patriarchal system which, in private life, divided parents from children, husbands from wives, and siblings from one another also divided citizens from one another by faction, by religion, by ethnicity, and by gendered sexist violence in ways that undermined the psychology of tolerant fraternity within nations required for democratic citizenship. Indeed, Verdi astutely portrays such divisions as the root of public and private violence, including the psychological needs that fuel wars that are unjust in their ends and means.

The subject matter of Verdi's tragic art is the normative and psychological dilemma of manhood (and womanhood) under democracy in the same sense it was for the Greek tragedians. The terms of democratic citizenship under Italy's constitutional monarchy were limited to men on terms that conflicted with its egalitarianism. If anything, the normative contradiction was much more obvious in this period than in ancient Greece because political liberalism in Britain, the United States, France, and elsewhere had by this time given rise to feminist argument by both women and men (for example, John Stuart Mill[8]) that regarded the contradiction as a fundamental political injustice.[9] On the other hand, the Mediterranean honor code was, if anything, much more strongly in place in Italy than other countries in ways that we know Verdi, like other Italian liberals, criticized (notably, Italian intolerance of the background

---

[8] See John Stuart Mill and Harriet Mill, *Essays on Sex Equality* edited by Alice S. Ross (Chicago: University of Chicago Press, 1970).

[9] See, for the historical development of feminism, David A. J. Richards, *Women, Gays, and the Constitution: The Grounds for Feminism and Gay Rights* (Chicago: University of Chicago Press, 1998).

of Giuseppina Strepponi, Verdi's mistress and later wife – see chapter 2). The force of this code in Italian cultural life rested on the same gender psychology of trauma, disassociation, and gender idealization studied by the Attic tragedians. It was a psychology to which Verdi himself would appeal in the Risorgimento operas calling for the Italian people to struggle for reunification (see chapter 4), and his own psychology as an Italian man of his time was described by people who best knew him in terms of an armored sense of honor very much in line with this gender psychology (see chapter 2). On the other hand, Verdi's unusually intimate creative relationship to Giuseppina opened him to a more democratic conception of manhood (chapter 2). Verdi was thus repelled by and in thrall to the psychology of patriarchal manhood.

Verdi's music dramas are the modern period's closest approximation to the tragic force of the Attic dramatists because both artist and audience were living in a particularly acute sense of normative and psychological contradiction over the apparent requirements of democracy and manhood. The tragic force of Verdi's art is the way it explores its subject matter, the dilemma of manhood (and womanhood), in terms of an obsessional focus on the impact of the patriarchal Italian honor code on the psychology of men and women. It is because that impact was unspeakably traumatic that its tragic force is expressed, indispensably, through *musical* voice. Verdi's art, for example, enables us to hear the voices – screaming with pain – of persons often burdened by unjust stereotypes: Rigoletto, the hunchback, howling over the loss of his daughter; Azucena, the gypsy, screaming over her lost son; Violetta, the courtesan, facing death and the loss of love; Gustavo, the gay man, who yearns for an inaccessible beloved; the aged Philip II, who mourns his lovelessness; Aida, the black slave, who grieves for her homelessness; Othello, the Moor, who howls with grief when he realizes he has unjustly killed the woman he loved. The revelatory power of Verdi's art is indispensably expressed through his innovations in musical voice which communicate the disassociated emotions of traumatic breaks that it is a mark of trauma cannot usually be remembered let alone verbalized.[10] It is precisely the power of Verdi's *musical* art that we hear a tragic truth that under patriarchy cannot be spoken.

Verdi, the tragic musical dramatist, creates a new kind of expressive voice to speak of different forms of these emotions in men and women living

---

[10] See, on these features of trauma, Vessel A. van der Kolk et al., *Traumatic Stress*, at pp. 279–302, 565.

[11] See Paul Robinson, *Opera and Ideas From Mozart to Strauss* (New York: Harper & Row, 1985), pp. 168–9.

under patriarchy, what Paul Robinson has called "power voices", in particular, "the high baritone and the dramatic soprano."[11] But he also, as Rodolfo Celletti observes, increasingly called for male voices detached:

"from the ornate and florid vocal tradition. Verdi adopted this attitude and . . . extended it to female voices. But his action was not limited to the gradual suppression of vocalized, ornate singing and its replacement by syllabic singing, nor to the requirement that his performers, in moments of greatest tension, give a more vigorous, stentorian, and dramatically credible vocal characterization that those of his predecessors' operas. He did not even limit himself to accentuating these moments of tension by raising the voices further up into the higher registers and having them sing in unison with each other or in unison with the orchestra (the so-called instrumental doubling). He did more. He insisted that the vocal writing had to provide an immediate reflection of the psychology of the character, with a rapidity unknown to earlier opera composers."[12]

In contrast to Rossini's vocal art, Verdi innovated much more emotionally resonant and more mobile expressive voices to expose the range of darker, often unspoken, if not unspeakable emotions, that his subject matter required.[13]

Verdi's innovations in musical voice (including his increasingly subtle orchestration) give expression to two kinds of voice analogous to the two voices of Iphigenia earlier discussed (chapters 2–3): Iphigenia's voice of relationship (as she expresses a girl's love for her father) and her voice of idealizing identification (identifying with her father's sacrificial image of her, thus accepting her murder). These two voices – the one of relationship, the other of identification – give expression to the psyche before and after the impact of patriarchy on it. The first voice is the psyche in real relationship to another person, a truthful communication based on affection or love. The second voice is the voice required by a gender stereotype (manhood or womanhood) whose force depends on the suppression of any real personal voice in conflict with the terms of the stereotype. Such stereotypes involve idealizations of those who conform to their terms, or denigrations of those who do not conform. Verdi, consistent with the subject matter of his art, not only finds expression for both voices, but for the underlying suppressed voice that a person, subject to gender stereotypes, still holds in her or his psyche. Verdi's mature musical art from *Stiffelio* forward, as argued in chap-

---

[12] Rodolfo Celletti, "On Verdi's Vocal Writing," in William Weaver and Martin Chusid, eds., *The Verdi Companion*, pp. 216–38, at 232–3.

[13] On the contrast to Rossini's vocal style, see John Potter, *Vocal Authority: Singing Style and Ideology* (Cambridge: Cambridge University Press, 1998), at pp. 58–9.

ters 5–7, gives precise and increasingly subtle expression to often sudden shifts one voice to another, for example, from the disassociated voice of identification to the voice of relationship and underlying loss in the interview of Stiffelio and Lina after their divorce in *Stiffelio*; or, the similar sudden shifts in Violetta's interview with Germont in *La Traviata*; or, Otello's sudden shifts from tender lover to crippling, despairing doubt to murderously vengeful patriarch; or, Helene's shift from the voice of identification with her dead brother to a voice of loving relationship to Henri in one remarkable descending vocal line in *Les Vêpres Siciliennes* (discussed in chapter 6, section 1). Sometimes, Verdi's art marks shifts among these voices in terms of shifts from a bullying, public voice of tribal identification (dominated by patriarchal codes of honor) to a personal voice of broken relationship. The public voice is an aural world of compulsive, distracting merriment (for example, the ball scenes that begin *Rigoletto* and *La Traviata* and end *Un Ballo in Maschera*) or brutal religious and military triumphalism (the auto-da-fé scene in *Don Carlos*, the march of triumph in *Aida*); a personal voice then takes us into the most intimate recesses of personal feeling of traumatic loss and desolation (for example, Philip II's and Aida's arias of conflicted loyalties, longing, and despair).

We are confronted with the psychological impact of such gender idealizations on voice in Verdi's increasingly subtle explorations of the tragic voice of women under patriarchy, as their loving sexual voices are disrupted and silenced, and covered over by idealizations of feminine self-sacrifice whether for their lovers (Violetta in *La Traviata*, Leonora in *Il Trovatore*), or their children (Amelia in *Un Ballo in Maschera*), or their sense of religious obligation (Leonora in *La Forza del Destino*, Elisabeth in *Don Carlos*, Desdemona in *Otello*). Verdi powerfully underscores such emotionally crippling desolation in Desdemona's earlier discussed (chapter 7) "Willow Song" with its rigid gender stereotypy (men destined for glory, women for love) and underlying terrifying scream of anguish:

| | |
|---|---|
| "Povera Barbara! | Poor Barbara! |
| Solea la storia con questo | The story used to end |
| Semplice suono finir: | with this simple phrase: |
| "Egli era nato per la sua gloria, | 'He was born for glory, |
| io per amar. . .' | I to love . . ." |
| (ad Emilia) | (to Emilia) |
| Ascolta. Odo un lamento. | Hark! I heard a moan." [14] |

---

[14] See Verdi, *Otello*, recording, George Solti, conductor, Chicago Symphony Orchestra, libretto, at p. 102

Desdemona with remarkable emotional intelligence understands how her husband's patriarchal masculinity, so brilliant in war, could be so stupid in love; yet she herself, emotionally alone and disassociated from her intelligence, in her following "Ave Maria" literally sacrifices her life to such stupidity, even embracing in her pieteous prayer:

"... e pel possente,        ...the powerful man,
Misero anch'esso        Who also grieves" [15]

Desdemona still feels and pities the grief underlying her husband's armored, patriarchally homicidal rage, as she self-consiously faces imminent death at his hand.

We experience the tragic psychological impact of gender idealizations on men's voices in Verdi's comparably subtle explorations of the suppression of their loving sexual and human voices, a heat and cooling that psychologically anneals the masculine armor of the often destructive and/or self-destructive masculine ideals of political or religious heroism (Alvaro in *La Forza Del Destino*; Carlos, Philip II, Rodrigo in *Don Carlos*; Othello in *Otello*). Such identification in men psychologically fuels exactly the kind of war hero, combining armored violence in public life with emotional immaturity and violence in private life, that are at the heart of how Verdi describes the tragic impact of patriarchy on the psychology of men. Consider, in this connection, the war heroes of Attic tragedy (Agememnon in *Iphigenia at Aulis*) or of Shakespearean tragedy (Lear, the father, or Othello, the lover), or Verdi's tragic fathers (Rigoletto, Montfort, Philip II) and husbands (Othello), all of whom have this character. On the one hand, they are capable of whatever level of violence is required to achieve their public ends (including hand-to-hand combat in unjust wars of racist imperialism like the Trojan War); on the other, they are in private life emotionally walled off from the sons, daughters, lovers, or wives they ostensibly love – unable to read love, they often turn to or are responsible for violence against the ostensibly beloved. Montfort in Verdi's *Les Vepres Siciliennes* and Alvaro in *La Forza del Destino* illustrate this point exactly. Montfort craves a relationship with his son, Henri, the offspring of Montfort's violent abduction of Henri's Sicilian mother, now dead; but Montfort, insisting that Henri break faith both with the memory of his beloved mother and with the Sicilian noblewoman Henri loves, defines his aims for Henri completely in terms of a patriarchal conception of honor that regards control of his son and victory in war as ends in itself, whether unjust

---

[15] See Verdi, *Otello*, recording, George Solti, conductor, Chicago Symphony Orchestra, libretto, at p. 103.

or just; his conflict with his son is over his son's conception that only aims of justice are honorable. We may say of Monfort like our other examples that they define their public and private lives in terms of patriarchal codes of honor that render hierarchy and subordination the terms of all relationships, unleashing violence in public or private life whenever such codes are violated, irrespective of the injustice of such violence. Analogously, Alvaro in *La Forza del Destino*, traumatized by the break with his parents and Leonora, seeks solace in heroic military service in war as an end in itself (whether just or unjust), rationalizing his violence in terms of a mythological idealization of Leonora herself. Psychologically, violence takes the psychological place of suppressed voice.

Political and cultural support for such a personal and political psychology of manhood may at least make adaptive sense in some circumstances: for example, in the transition from the Roman Republic to the Empire, when service in the Roman armies required breaking of personal relationships (soldiers could not marry) and such service called for especially close bonds among soldiers required for both the organized military formations and ferocity which made the Roman armies the terror of the ancient world. The narrative of Virgil's *The Aeneid* importantly validates this development, as Aeneas, the tender lover of Dido, breaks his relationship with her to serve his dynastic patriarchal destiny and is psychologically hardened by such loss to become the homicidal killing machine of the last books of the poem, that is, the psychologically armored Roman warrior the Empire needed as the instrument of relentless aggressive imperialistic war and enslavement that were required to achieve and maintain its imperial ends.[16] Similarly, Augustine of Hippo's argument in *The Confessions*, calling for a similar break in sexual relationship to women, at least makes adaptive sense if the Roman Catholic Church is now institutionally to replace the authority of the now collapsed Roman Empire, and priests (who are, in Augustine's own language, soldiers of the new order[17]) are psychologically to replace the soldiers of the Empire. Augustine strikingly expresses his new armored self in righteous hatred of the enemies of

---

[16] See, on these points, Richard Alston, "Arms and the Man: Soldiers, Masculinity and Power in Republican and Imperial Rome," in Lin Foxhall and John Salmon, eds., *When Men Were Men: Masculinity, Power and Identity in Classical Antiquity* (New York: Routledge, 1998), at pp. 205–23. On the centrality of imperialistic aggressive war and enslavement to Rome's expansion and stability, see Aldo Schiavone, *The End of the Past: Ancient Rome and the Modern West*, Margery J. Schneider, trans. (Cambridge, MA: Harvard University Press, 2000).

[17] See Saint Augustine, *Confessions*, Henry Chadwick, trans. (Oxford: Oxford University Press, 1991), at pp. 140, 206.

[18] See *id.*, at pp. 160, 254.

Scripture,[18] and famously is the first major Christian thinker, in a thitherto remarkably tolerant religion of free belief, to make an argument for persecution of heretics.[19]

Verdi's extraordinary understanding of this personal and political psychology is at the center of *La Forza del Destino*. Once his relationship to Leonora has been traumatically broken, Alvaro turns to the two alternatives of patriarchal manhood defended, respectively, by Virgil and Augustine – heroic military service and the celibate priesthood. Both armor a man against the desolating loss of relationship, and fuel obsessional devotion to military service or monastic discipline as such sometimes without concern with their justifying ends of justice or charity. Relationship to women is replaced by their mythological idealization, in which they become symbols that rationalize violence (as Alvaro appeals to the idealized image of Leonora as the rationale for his heroic military service) often in service of injustice (as in the American South's honor code that rationalized slavery and, later, racism in such terms).[20] Thus, the traumatic breaks in relationship, inflicted by patriarchy, fuel the violence and injustice that keep men unreasonably in thrall to its sometimes inhuman demands.

Verdi's art quite precisely shows us both the psychological mechanism and consequences of such suppression of our human needs for a loving sexual voice when we see how some of his most clearly humane women and men (Alvaro and Leonora in *La Forza del Destino*; Elisabeth, Rodrigo, Carlos in *Don Carlos*) are, because of the patriarchal disruption of intimate sexual voice, poignantly alone and thus out of realistic relationship not only to their own needs but to doing anything that might realistically help others, as their humane idealism requires. The psychology, arising from the suppressed voice of trauma, is one radically alone, a psychological solipsism that deprives even the most humane idealism of elementary emotional and intellectual intelligence (Alvaro and Leonora take no realistic steps to find one another, rather losing themselves in political or religious self-sacrifice; Elisabeth, Rodrigo, and Carlos sacrifice themselves, but futilely: they ultimately do nothing to help free Flanders). Verdi's mature art shows us men and women under patriarchy as poignantly alone and homeless, haunted, as Elisabeth clearly is, by debilitating fears and anxieties of even being under suspicion for violating the honor code, incapacitating them, even when they

---

[19] See, on this point and the pivotally important arguments of Locke and Bayle to refute him, David A. J. Richards, *Toleration and the Constitution* (New York: Oxford University Press, 1986), pp. 85–102.

[20] See, for a brilliant disagnosis of this pathology by Ida Wells-Barnett, Richards, *Women, Gays, and the Constitution*, pp. 185–90.

have a humane sense of justice, of acting on it with even minimal intelligence. Thus, our very sense of justice is, as Verdi's art shows, corrupted by the underlying trauma that patriarchy has inflicted on intimate sexual voice. Even the most humane people, injured by the way patriarchy mindlessly disrupts intimate relationships, are caught in a repetition compulsion, as their very attempts to resist injustice self-destruct because they are so out of touch with their own intelligence.

Verdi's life-long obsession with the tragic impact of patriarchy is shown, as I have now argued at length, by the psychic geography of personal relations under patriarchy that were his subject matter throughout his long career. Verdi, as he said of Shakespeare, aimed to create the psychological and moral truth of how men and women lived under patriarchy, giving an unsparing view of the trauma and loss which it inflicted. Verdi was fascinated by the yawning abyss between the essentially external demands of the code of honor so historically entrenched in Italian life and the inner psychic lives of the men and women whose lives were lived under the inexorable pressure of such demands. The code of honor is, in its nature, a political system that enforces its demands by forms of physical and psychological violence directed at anyone who deviates from its demands. Its psychological force derives from the way in which its demands are developmentally inscribed into the human psyche by traumatic separations that suppress voice precisely at the points where such voice might reasonably contest the justice of the honor code's demands. Verdi's art of musically expressive voice is so illuminating of the psychology of gender that supports patriarchy because it enables us to hear such inner psychic lives, including not only the lives of the sons and daughters whose lives have been wrecked by patriarchy but the desolation of the patriarchs themselves as, like Rigoletto and Philip II, they face their loveless loneliness.

Verdi was certainly not a neutral, detached observer to the psychic geography of disrupted relationships under patriarchy he studied so closely. From his earliest Risorgimento operas (like *Nabucco, Giovanna D'Arco, Attila, La Battaglia di Legnano*) to later works like *Les Vepres Siciliennes* and *Aida*, Verdi aligned himself with unjustly oppressed peoples struggling to throw off rule by their colonialist oppressors. He clearly gives voice in his operas to his own convictions about various forms of injustice: religious intolerance (*I Lombardi* to *Don Carlos* and *Aida*), ethnic hatred (*Alzira* to *Il Trovatore, La Forza del Destino, Aida*, and *Othello*), intolerance for sexual lives that deviate from marital norms (*Stifellio, La Traviata, Un Ballo in Maschera*), irrationalist misogyny in witchcraft beliefs (*Il Trovatore*), and hatred of the physically deformed (*Rigoletto*).

Moreover, resistance to injustice is itself a continuing theme in his operas from *Nabucco* on forward. Even in his early operas, Verdi portrays such resistance to injustice as psychologically difficult, sometimes pitting resisting daughters against fathers (*I Lombardi*, *Giovanna D'Arco*), or a son against his father (*I Due Foscari*). Sometimes these resisters have to become outlaw bandits (*Ernani*, *I Masnadieri*) or pirates (*Il Corsaro*). In *Luisa Miller*, Verdi begins his closer examination of the psychological difficulties of resistance, as bullying threats are made to Luisa, including of her father's death, that she cannot reasonably resist. In *Stiffelio*, the threats are those of Lina's patriarchal father, bullying her into not, as she wishes, disclosing to her husband the truth of her infidelity. In *Rigoletto*, Gilda's resistance to her father's iron patriarchal control, both in loving as she chooses and later deciding to die in the Duke's place, lead to her death. In *La Traviata*, Violetta tries to resist Alfredo's father, but is psychologically vulnerable to his patriarchal pleas. In *Les Vêpres Siciliennes*, Henri is committed to resistance against the French occupation of Sicily, but his father undermines his resistance. In *La Forza del Destino*, Leonora resists her father's patriarchal will, but the accidental death of her father psychologically crushes her and Alvaro (who are morally noble to a fault) with a remorse and traumatized disassociation that separate them not only from one another for most of the opera but from themselves as moral agents as opposed to pitiable pawns of fate. Both Leonora and Alvaro speak at different points of their depressive desire for death, and withdraw into forms of idealism that enable them to make sense of their depressions. Alvaro's traumatized desolation, for example, psychologically fuels his life-threatening heroic military service as an end in itself whether the wars in question are just or unjust in their means or ends. In *Don Carlos*, Carlos, Posa, Philip, and Elizabeth all at various points make attempts to resist what they take to be injustice that founder on a combination of conflicting emotions (including religious and political idealism) and circumstances. In *Aida*, Aida tries to resist her father's plea to betray her lover for her country, but cannot resist his claims of justice. And in *Otello*, Othello's initial attempts to resist Iago collapse under the weight of his own emotional vulnerabilities and doubts.

For Verdi, the personal and political psychology that sustains patriarchy brings all its force to bear against resistance, either by external forms of coercion (including violence) or by inculcating internal vulnerabilities and doubts that psychologically cripple resistance. It is part of the expressive power of his tragic art that his life-long study of the psychology of patriarchy should, like Shakespeare's comparable studies of a Hamlet or Macbeth or Lear or Othello, focus so closely on how this psychology bears on understanding the difficulties of resistance. Hamlet, for example, explores in his five great soliloquies his resistance to the patriarchal obligation of revenge that is imposed on him by the dead ghost of his father at the opening of the play, but cannot ultimately resist the patriarchal pressures arrayed against him. Verdi interpreted this psychology, as we have seen, in terms of a psychic geography of patriarchal relations in family life that mapped onto similar relations in public life. The psychology of patriarchy drew its power from this public–private geography of relations structured by gender stereotypes of hierarchy and subordination that break relationships between parents and children, siblings, and adults. To the extent such patriarchally mandated relations remain uncritically fixed as if in the nature of things, its underlying psychology will, as Verdi clearly saw, cripple resistance.

Verdi's art confronts the democratic mind with the trauma and loss that patriarchy imposes on private and public life and its corruption of democratic values of tolerance, freedom, and equality, and raises the fundamental question: whether and how patriarchy might be resisted to achieve democratic values in private and public life. One view, which Verdi's later art sometimes suggests, is that such tragic loss is in the nature of things, and that men, in particular, as part of the legitimate burden of manhood in democratic citizenship, must accept such loss as the price of civilized order, as Aeschylus, for example, clearly argues at the end of *The Oresteia*. Verdi's art, however liberal and humane in its inspiration, did not stop Italians from being the first European state to embrace the patriarchally reactionary fascism of Mussolini, nor can it reasonably ensure that Italian patriarchal patterns are responsibly politically addressed in contemporary circumstances. Opera, including Verdi's great humane tragic art, can no more in itself guarantee that a people not make tragic political mistakes than the Attic tragedies could save Athens from the political tragedy of the Peloponnesian War. Art can never substitute for an ethically responsible liberal democratic politics.

But, though Verdi's art probably should be read as largely consistent with the Aeschylean view of tragic demands of patriarchal manhood,[21] there are two reasons that suggest Verdi had continuing doubts about this view: first, the value he placed on an intimate life based on free and equal voice in relationship, and second, *Falstaff*.

Both Verdi's life and art show an extraordinary value placed on the free choice of two persons to love one another and share their lives in defiant resistance to conventional norms of patriarchal control and intolerance. As we have seen, Verdi's most important, life-long personal relationship was to Giuseppina Strepponi, a remarkably independent, experienced, highly

---

[21] See, for a reading along these lines, De Van, *Verdi's Voice*.

intelligent, well-read, and spirited nineteenth-century Italian woman –
artistically, economically, sexually. Their union was, by the standards of the
age, an unusually intimate and creatively collaborative relationship, and one
which Verdi defended with an integrity rooted in liberal indignation
against all-comers, including family and friends. It is suggestive of how
much Verdi may have come to distinguish patriarchal marriage from intimate relationship that he did not marry Strepponi for well over a decade,
living with her in defiance of conventional patriarchal opprobrium,
including of Verdi's parents. He writes during this period two remarkable
operas, *Stiffelio* and *La Traviata*, which musically express the brutal
demands of patriarchy, whether made by a father or husband, on a sexually
experienced woman to break relationship to the man she loves and the
harrowing consequences. In these works, loving relationship flourishes only
outside patriarchal marriage. In Verdi, the fact that patriarchy breaks such
relationships is not portrayed, as it was by Aeschylus, as a grim necessity of
democratic masculinity as such, but at best in some circumstances as justified by independent considerations of justice (as in *Aida*, where her betrayal
of her lover is required to do justice to her people). Rather, such patriarchal
demands are more often portrayed as breaking the heart of the patriarch
himself (Rigoletto, Philip II, Othello), a psychology of desolating emptiness and lovelessness that, in turn, rationalizes personal and political
atrocity.

If there were any doubt about this matter, Verdi's *Falstaff* (a work "written . . . for my own pleasure and on my own account"[22]) makes quite clear
what his final views were on the tragedy of patriarchy. Anyone who has read
through the remarkable letters of Giuseppina Strepponi in Frank Walker's
*The Man Verdi*[23] – intelligent, witty, sometimes hilarious, devoted to her
husband's art as a combination artistic advisor, business manager, and intermediary with the outside world – may reasonably suspect that the portrait
of women in *Falstaff* is very much a tribute, after the turmoil of the Stoltz
affair, to Giuseppina's endurance, hard work, wit, and good humor, and that
the portrait of Falstaff may well be of the patriarchal follies of Verdi himself. Verdi's description of the kind of singing actress he wanted for Alice
certainly suggests a witty, highly intelligent, resisting woman of considerable emotional range and flexibility he knew intimately:

> "above all an actress and a person who has *the devil inside of her* [diable au
> corps]. Alice's role is not as extended as Falstaff's, but theatrically she has as
> much [to do]. It is Alice who manages the entire intrigue of the comedy.[24]

---

[22] See Julian Budden, *The Operas of Verdi, Volume 3*, at p. 430.

[23] See, in general, Frank Walker, *The Man Verdi*.

For the first time in all Verdi's operas, a natural mother (Alice Ford) of a child, a daughter (Nannetta), is centrally portrayed, and portrayed in double resistance to her husband's patriarchal authority. First, her husband's patriarchal right to reject Falstaff's sexual advances to his wife is usurped by his wife herself, because she knows her patriarchally jealous husband would respond with violence, not, as Alice prefers, with a comic voice which would teach Falstaff the lesson he richly deserves. Second, her husband's patriarchal right to make his daughter marry a man she does not love is resisted by Alice, who stage manages Nannetta's marriage to the man she loves. The tragedy of patriarchy becomes, Verdi shows, a comedy if mothers and daughters stay in relationship with one another and other women (Meg, Mistress Quickly) and the men who love them (Fenton), and use their voice and conviction intelligently to challenge and resist patriarchal authority. In his last opera, "written . . . for my own pleasure," Verdi not only questions, in terms we may reasonably call feminist, the inevitability of the tragedy of patriarchy in both private and public life, but shows us a way out of tragedy into comedy. As mentioned earlier, Carol Gilligan's *The Birth of Pleasure*[25] calls, in a self-consciously contemporary feminist spirit, for the same turn from our telling and retelling of tragic narratives of trauma and loss as the Aeschylean price for democracy to the creative invention of comic narratives.[26] Verdi's dominant view may have been more pessimistic, but his last opera suggests that finding a way out of the tragedy of patriarchy may be as important for democratic men as for women.

## Between Patriarchal and Democratic Manhood

What of us? The argument of this book appeals to my own experience of Verdi's voice over my lifetime as a way of understanding the appeal of his art for me and so many others, namely, offering us a more truthful understanding of human psychology against the distorting impact on public representations of unjust gender stereotypes. I earlier discussed one example of this disjunction (chapter 3): the appeal to unjust gender stereotypes to

---

[24] Letter cited in Martin Chusid, "Verdi's Own Words: His Thoughts on Performance, with Special Reference to *Don Carlos, Otello*, and *Falstaff*," in William Weaver and Martin Chusid, *The Verdi Companion*, pp. 144–92, at p. 168.

[25] See Carol Gilligan, *The Birth of Pleasure*.

[26] See Apuleius, *The Golden Ass*, E. J. Kenney, trans. (Penguin, 1998), at pp. 71–106.

bully Italian Americans into telling a mafia narrative that, in fact, is not only false to their ethnic experience, but falsely inverts gender relations from that ethnic experience in order to comply with the dominant gender stereotypes (Mario Puzo). The example is not only of local interest to Italian Americans, because the bullying appeal of these gender-linked stereotypes is quite general. Indeed, Verdi's art may today have deeper appeal than it has ever had because we more fundamentally question, on grounds of constitutional principle, the role that stereotypes of gender (like those of religion and race) have traditionally played in shaping both public and private life. To this extent, we are more – not less – alive to the questions about the tragedy of patriarchy that obsessed Verdi.

We are, as a culture, much more in transition between patriarchal and democratic manhood than the age of the Attic tragedians or of Verdi. Certainly, many of us see that the tragic psychology Verdi describes does not serve the ends of the values of free and equal voice fundamental to constitutional liberal democracy as a defensible form of government nor does it serve the aims of free and equal loving relationship in our intimate lives. The Attic tragedies, as we have seen, may have validated this psychology in ways that corrupted Athenian democracy, including its disastrous propensity for imperialistic wars. And this psychology may importantly explain the acceptability of aggressive imperialism, enslavement, and intolerance, practices that many now repudiate on grounds of constitutional and ethical principle. For example, Augustinian intolerance has been a central object of criticism by the tradition of liberal constitutionalism in Europe and America, calling for a new conception of constitutional principles that insures equal respect for all persons irrespective of religious or irreligious convictions.[27] We are, if anything, constitutionally much more self-consciously democratic, egalitarian, and respectful of basic human rights than Athens and certainly than imperial Rome (in both its secular and religious forms), and much more skeptical for the same reasons of aggressive wars, so that this psychology is, if anything, much more deeply corrupting of our values and practices. War plays a much less central role in our lives, and to the extent it does, the justice of its ends and means are subject to lively debate and question; its increasingly technological character no longer reasonably correlates, in the way it once did, with ostensible gender differences.[28] Finally, the traditional political power of patriarchy is now contested and contestable, in the United States and elsewhere, on grounds of fundamental constitutional principle that

---

[27] See, in general, Richards, *Toleration and the Constitution*.
[28] See, in general, Joshua S. Goldstein, *War and Gender*.

condemn sexism directed against both men and women.[29] For all these reasons, patriarchal manhood is today much more questioned and questionable as a requirement of democracy. But, men today may often remain much more vulnerable to the psychology of Aeneas and Augustine than is any longer defensible as a matter of democratic political philosophy and practice.

As we have seen, the developmental psychology that makes possible a conception of manhood that can sustain patriarchal demands requires traumatic separation of young boys from their mothers in contrast to the developmental continuity in such relationships allowed to girls until early adolescence.[30] The marks of such trauma are not only loss of intimate voice and memory, but the kinds of disassociation from intimate relationship that, as we have seen, patriarchal manhood requires. Idealizing stereotypes are, in their nature, objectifying, supported by such a psychology of disassociation that lends itself to the forms of violence required to hold such stereotypes in place in patterns of structural injustice.

The honor code, thus understood, is held in place by a system of physical and psychological violence triggered by deviance from its demands; such external demands enter into the psyches of men and women through their loss of protesting voice and their consequent vulnerability to shaming by any appearance of deviation from the honor code and the expression of such shaming in violence, whether physical or psychological. The psychology of such shaming is in conflict with a democratic ethics of reciprocity based on the free and equal voice of all persons, an ethics that expresses itself in ideals of equal respect as the foundation of friendship and love expressive of free and equal voice. The requirements of this ethics enters into our psyches through the experience of love and respect consistent with its demands, and shows itself in guilt and remorse when one culpably violates the demands of equal respect and the forms of love it makes possible.[31] Both the honor code and its psychology of shaming are in fundamental conflict with this ethics and psychology because the shaming demands of honor enter into our psyches through a violent repression of voice that is condemned by an ethics of equal respect. Indeed, the power of the political psychology of honor must

---

[29] For fuller discussion of this constitutional development, see David A. J. Richards, *Women, Gays, and the Constitution: The Grounds for Feminism and Gay Rights in Culture and Law* (Chicago: University of Chicago Press, 1998).

[30] See, on these points, Carol Gilligan, *The Birth of Pleasure*, at pp. 14–17, 89–91, 161–3, 178–9, 204.

[31] I explore both this ethics and its associated moral psychology in David A. J. Richards, *A Theory of Reasons for Action* (Oxford: Clarendon Press, 1971).

in large part derive from the degree to which it succeeds in marginalizing or suppressing that part of our moral psychology that rejects its demands. Conversely, a psychology awakened to the demands of equal respect (as through the experience of a love based on free and equal voice) may fundamentally question the codes and psychology of honor heretofore taken to be axiomatic.

It is this alternative in developmental psychology that underlies what I call democratic manhood. We can see a form of it in advocates of nonviolence like William Lloyd Garrison, Leo Tolstoy, Mohandas Gandhi, and Martin Luther King.[32] The story is by no means the same in each case, and several of them certainly live in some degree of contradiction between their overall protest of structural injustice and the forms of patriarchy they still allowed to dominate parts of their lives. But there is a remarkably similar alternative developmental psychology in their lives, one that made psychologically possible for them a more democratic conception of manhood, one much more sensitive to issues of suppressed voice (including the voices of women) than patriarchal manhood. What is remarkably discernible in the case of each of them is, instead of the developmental trauma of early boyhood separation from mothers, a staying in significant intimate relationship to the loving moral voice, care, and concern of persons (biological mothers or an aunt, as in the case of Tolstoy) and placing continuing value and weight on their voices and insights as a significant counterweight to traditional patriarchal demands. How should we understand this common experience and its links, if any, to their turn to nonviolence?

Certainly, Virginia Woolf in *Three Guineas* had suggested links between women's claims to voice and resistance to political violence: "[we] fighting the tyranny of the patriarchal state as you are fighting the tyranny of the Fascist state."[33] Sara Ruddick has recently refined Woolf's insight in her pathbreaking inquiry into the voices of mothers that have been traditionally patriarchally silenced.[34] Ruddick is well aware that such loving care is, has been, and should be done by men, but chooses, for reasons of exposition, to call all such care "maternal work."[35] Such work has, for Ruddick, three tasks: preservation, growth, and acceptability – all of which require a loving care that Ruddick, drawing on Iris Murdoch and Simone Weil, calls

---

[32] See David A. J. Richards, *Disarming Manhood: Roots of Ethical Resistance in Jesus, Garrison, Tolstoy, Gandhi, King, and Churchill* (forthcoming, Ohio University Press, 2005).

[33] Virginia Woolf, *Three Guineas* (Harcourt Brace & Company: San Diego, 1938), at p. 102.

[34] Sara Ruddick, *Maternal Thinking: Toward a Politics of Peace* (Boston: Beacon Press, 1989), at p. 38.

[35] See *id.*, at p. 41.

"attentive love."[36] Ruddick certainly sees the complex strands in such work, some of which may be distorted by narcissism and others guided by patriarchal aims. But she insists that we take seriously at least those strands of such maternal practice of intimate voice and responsiveness in which mother and child can read one another's human world well after the mother–child attunement of infancy.[37] Ruddick's brilliant insight is to identify in such maternal care practices of nonviolence required to maintain connection in the right developmental way, including sustaining life and growth,[38] renouncing one's lethal powers to nurture the vulnerably powerless,[39] limiting aggression to maintain connection,[40] and even willingness to suffer oneself as a developmental strategy of moral education.[41] Such practice has implicit in it four ideals of nonviolence: renunciation, nonviolent resistance, reconciliation, and peacekeeping.[42]

My hypothesis about the alternative developmental psychology of the four advocates of nonviolence is that they shared a common developmental psychology that, in contrast to the traumatic break with mothers required by the Oedipal patriarchal story in early boyhood, prominently included staying in significant relationship to the loving voice and care of maternal caretakers, understood as displaying the features of attentive love and implicit ideals of nonviolence that Ruddick describes so well. This story may be much more common than even in his own period Freud supposed, let alone today when, as Ruddick's work shows, feminist women are bringing their convictions to bear on both their private lives as mothers and their public lives as citizens. The unjust political demands of patriarchy would, to the extent patriarchy is hegemonic or at least still very powerful, show themselves by the attempt to suppress or marginalize the kinds of developmental experiences that would psychologically threaten the stability of patriarchy. This might show itself in reading this alternative developmental story as a narrative of the aetiology of homosexuality. In my view, it would be a developmental strength in gay men if their development includes a maternal care like that described by Ruddick, but it is clear that not all gay men come from such a background, and it is certainly quite

---

[36] See *id.*, at pp. 119–23.
[37] See, on this phenomenon in infancy, Daniel N. Stern, *The Interpersonal World of the Infant: A View from Psychoanalysis and Developmental Psychology*, pp. 148–51.
[38] See Sara Ruddick, *id.*, pp. 148–51.
[39] *Id.*, p. 166.
[40] *Id.*, pp. 182–3.
[41] *Id.*, pp. 169–70.
[42] See *id.*, p. 176.

clear that many straight men (including the four advocates of nonviolence) also profit from such backgrounds.[43]

But, of course, not all persons with this background will make of it what the advocates of nonviolence did. The demands of patriarchy can lead people to repudiate or deny or marginalize psychological propensities that do not appear to have any legitimacy or ethical appeal. To make sense of why some men rather unusually (for men) acted on their sense of psychological truth, we need to address how and why they held onto their sense of lived truth in relationship, as one among life's most enduring and sustaining humane values, and were motivated for this reason to resist unjust patterns of structural injustice.

My hypothesis is that these four nonviolent men resist such disassociation by holding onto the psychological truth of loving association experienced in their relationships of loving care to maternal caretakers. If patriarchal manhood armors itself through disassociation against the voices and feelings that reasonably contest gender idealizations, these nonviolent men self-consciously disarm themselves of the role violence plays in traditional manhood as a way of remaining truthful to personal voice, relationships, and experiences with sometimes remarkable consequences to themselves and others. The psychology of nonviolent resistance to injustice thus is rooted in the protection of the psychological truth of such intimate relations. The move to nonviolence is both a way of giving expression to what one learns from those relationships and what is required to sustain them, namely, a free and honest voice. It is the insistence on the importance and authority of such voice, including women's and men's voices that are traditionally silenced, that explains the sense of skepticism about the force violence plays in a politics dominated by patriarchal manhood. Such men are of continuing interest to us because they are pioneers in the development of a conception of democratic manhood and womanhood, and their transformative consequences for both the theory and practice of constitutional democracy.

It is this sense of psychological truth against the lies of violence that explains how and why these men were able to make the discoveries they did about how nonviolent resistance might speak to an underlying human moral psychology more complex and nuanced than the patriarchal conceptions of gender that use honor and shame to sustain patterns of structural injustice. If I am right about the sources in developmental psychology of

---

[43] For one plausible view of the character of close relations to their mothers of gay men, see Richard Green, *The "Sissy Boy Syndrome" and the Development of Homosexuality* (New Haven: Yale University Press, 1987).

the turn to nonviolence, it would explain how and why nonviolent resistance, though sometimes met with repressive violence, has also spoken to an underlying human psychology developed in and through loving care and respect for persons. Whereas patriarchal manhood is tied to hierarchy and a rigid gender binary, democratic masculinities work "within a paradigm of connectedness (mind in body; body in mind; self in relationship, relationship in self; thought in feelings, feelings in thought) and reflecting the perception that men and women are inseparably connected (man in woman, woman in man). Freed from hierarchy and from loss, gender becomes more variable, more improvisational, and the shaming of manhood less explosive."[44] Verdi himself may have had a relationship to his mother and later Giuseppina which placed him, at least to some extent and degree, in a creatively fertile psychological transition between patriarchal and democratic manhood, enabling him through creative musical voice to explode the gendered paradigm of his age (thought versus feelings) and thus show us through his analytics of musical voice truths (the impact of patriarchy on traumatized voice) no other thinker of his generation could even acknowledge, let alone explore.

Men today are, as a general matter, also pulled between both patriarchal and democratic manhood. Unjust gender stereotypes retain a particularly ferocious impact on the psychology of men, rigidly holding them into conformity with the requirements of patriarchal authority (authority deriving from the hierarchical relationships of sons to fathers). Yet this psychology is now more visibly than ever deeply antagonistic to the aims of our democratic constitutionalism. We veil this truth from ourselves because men have been silenced so early and so pervasively about these issues by the continuing force that the psychology of patriarchy enjoys over their lives as men. Even when our development has been less blighted by such trauma, as may be more often the case today than ever before as parents (including feminist women and men) resist the terms of patriarchy, we cannot, because of the force of gender stereotypes (for example, the mafia stereotype, among others), acknowledge the reality of such personal relationships (for example, of sons to mothers) and the psychological strength such relationships give us in leading better lives. We are alienated from a truthful sense of our relationships across the divide of gender, and thus do not call upon the relational complexity of such relationships to resist the force that the simplifications of gender stereotypes impose on our lives. We crave the truth that great tragic art brings to our divided and conflicted

---

[44] Carol Gilligan, "Knowing and Not Knowing: Reflections on Manhood," p. 12 (Gender Lecture on Masculinities, University of Cambridge, May 22, 2003).

lives as conscious moral beings; yet our theories of tragedy, like those of Schopenhauer and Nietzsche, ascribe its power to empty and distracting metaphysical abstractions rather than face what men have such difficult facing, the psychology of patriarchy that still so compels them like a repetition compulsion, as it compelled Verdi both in his life and in his art. At every point, men are emotionally silenced in speaking about issues central to their most basic convictions of justice in both public and private lives. It is that silence that psychologically fuels the compulsion to repeat the unjust demands of patriarchy from generation to generation, rendering patriarchy so stable and so apparently resistant to change. We cannot break the silence because we cannot, as men, hear the cry within. Verdi's tragic operas reveal our lives in the same way his *Requiem* studies our humanity before death – beneath the sentimentality and bravado of our patriarchal pieties and practices, we hear the trauma and the terror of broken relationship and loss and a voice crying for humane recognition and love.

We can see through Verdi's exquisite art the consequences of this heart of darkness in intimate life. Fathers and sons are cast in a rigid hierarchy of domination and submission that models authority as intrinsically insensitive to democratic voice. Fathers are walled off from the free sexual voices of their daughters whom they come to regard as symbols, rather than persons, in the sexist mythology underlying codes of honor. Mothers are not present in their relationships either to their sons or daughters, but rather ghostly absences to whom men or women desperately appeal as idealizing rationalizations of either, for men, violence to others or, for women, violence to self. Brothers are cut off from the free sexual voices of their sisters as their fathers are. Women regard other women as competitors in a sexist struggle, and men regard other men as objects of violence to be conquered. And men and women structure intimate life on terms of a gendered inequality that destroys loving voice in relationship, an inequality that also destroys voice in gay relationships. The insight of Verdi's tragic art is that patriarchy in these ways rests on traumatic breaks in anything that could reasonably count as a loving relationship based on free and equal voice, indeed suppresses such voice, rationalizing violence (physical and psychological) against such protesting voice as the model for authority in both personal and political life. The death of the voice is the death of the psyche, a deadness in thoughts and feelings no longer responsively alive either to outer reality or to inner need.

If we still carry this psychology within ourselves (uncritically defined as the natural terms of intimate life), it shows itself in the incoherence of our very sense of justice and of the constitutional law that gives expression to such justice, for the psychology rests on acceptance of the tragic loss of voice as the price of democratic manhood, cutting us off from the free resisting voice of justice. A patriarchy still uncritically dominant in intimate life explains the still widespread failures of public intelligence underlying the rather striking gaps between our practices and our democratic principles, mentioned in the introduction (chapter 1), including our failure reasonably to extend liberal principles of equality to family life.[45]

Like the Attic tragedians, Verdi's art studies the transition from the rule of kings and tyrants to democratic rule, and explores this transition in terms of a psychology of the democratic manhood of equal citizens that reinscribes patriarchy as the tragic but necessary condition of democratic equality. Hierarchical rule by kings is rejected, but a new form of hierarchy (patriarchy) is inscribed in the psychology of democratic manhood, as if the overthrow of hierarchy psychologically necessitates a return of the repressed (patriarchy). There is no good normative argument here, but rather the betrayal of the ideals of free and equal voice that justify democracy as a legitimate form of government. But the personal and political psychology that motivates this betrayal are all too real. The great interest of Verdi's tragic art is its acute sensitivity to the personal and political psychology underlying this contradiction within the theory and practice of political liberalism, in particular, its roots in the role gender stereotypes play in the personal and political psychology regarded as necessary for democracy. For Verdi, the code of honor was, in its nature, a political system – fundamental to the family, politics, and religion – that enforced its demands by forms of physical and psychological violence directed by men and women at anyone who deviated from its demands. Its psychological force derived from the way in which its demands were developmentally inscribed into the human psyche by traumatic separations that suppress voice precisely at the points where such voice might reasonably contest the justice of the honor code's demands. His art diagnoses the contradiction within liberalism as starting psychologically where political liberalism was least inclined to look, namely, in the relations of fathers and mothers to sons and daughters and men and women to one another in intimate life, precisely the areas that political liberalism had walled off from critical attention. To the extent these relationships are still uncritically framed by the terms of patriarchal stereotypes, there remains intact a personal and political psychology that cannot acknowledge, let alone resist, the unjust terms patriarchy imposes not only on our private but on our public lives as well.[46] The continuing tragic appeal of Verdi's art, in a culture like others much less blatantly patri-

---

[45] See Susan Moller Okin, *Justice, Gender, and the Family*.
[46] See *id.*

archal than that of nineteenth-century Italy, is that it demands that we hear how much the terms of intimate life, both between parents and children and lovers with one another, remain unjustly burdened by sexist stereotypes that rest on the suppression of the democratic demands of equal voice in relationship. It is precisely because such patriarchal demands remain still invisible to us in this domain that we are more absorbed than ever by a tragic art, like Verdi's, that enables us at least to hear emotions and voices that we could not otherwise even acknowledge. Hearing such emotions within ourselves is a condition of acknowledging them as real losses, raising questions about injustice we cannnot otherwise acknowledge because the injustice has been naturalized in terms of what love must be, a psychology stuck in contradiction between our practices and our democratic principles.

Verdi's artistic voice arose, as we have seen (chapter 2), from the ambition to represent the gap between popular stereotypes (of the crippled hunchback, or the courtesan, or the gypsy witch) and the subjective human feelings and ambitions of individual persons burdened by such stereotypes. His mature art, as we have seen (chapters 4–7), offers us a remarkably acute psychological investigation of the ways in which such stereotypes draw their popular force precisely from the failure to hear the individual human voices of the persons thus stereotyped and thus rationalize traumatic breaks in intimate relations between fathers and daughters, fathers and sons, mothers and daughters, mothers and sons, and lovers with one another. Gender idealizations thus cover and are psychologically motored by loss that the idealizations, by suppressing voice, cut off from self-knowledge.

Verdi's art systematically represents to us the force and consequences of such idealizations in terms of a gender binary that enforces the injustice of patriarchy as the price of democracy. But since patriarchy organizes all forms of authority (both public and private) in its unjust image of hierarchy and submission, Verdi's art systematically explores the role of suppressed voice throughout the patriarchal system, including not only the family and politics, but religion and ethics. Democracy, which arises from overthrow of the patriarchal rule of kings, reinscribes patriarchy as the condition of democracy. Verdi offers us nothing less than a psychic geography of the full range of impacts on suppressed voice, the voice both of women and men, that the stability of such continuing patriarchy unjustly requires. It is the unjust division of the gender binary that, on Verdi's psychologically acute reading, makes possible a personal and political psychology of disassociated emotional stupidity that supports not only sexism, but the full range of dehumanizing prejudices (including extreme religious intolerance and racism), all of which Verdi closely studied throughout his long career. Masculinity and femininity are, as it were, psychologically constructed in the terms required by patriarchy, masculine armored heroism and control corresponding to feminine emotional vulnerability and self-sacrificing malleability, two kinds of human sacrifice mythologically idealized as the terms of a good man and good woman under patriarchy. Our humane ethical resources of intellectual and emotional depth and complexity are stultified into separate and rigidly defined departments of the mind marked male or female that deprive us of knowledge of one another and of ourselves. The structural injustice of patriarchy rests, I have suggested, on the violent suppression of dissenting conviction and voice of both women and men. Verdi's invention of musically expressive voice explores such unexpressed convictions and voices of both men and women, revealing the emotional stupidity, turmoil and vulnerability under the masculine armor and the frustrated intelligence, desolation, and moral rage under the feminine vulnerability.

I have argued in this work that Verdi's great artistic gift to our democratic generation is to have given us the most musically expressive representation of the tragedy within democracy that still threatens us, the tragedy of patriarchy. It has been a tragedy of manhood under democracy since the Athenians forged tragic theatre as they self-consciously forged democracy and a conception of the democratic citizen. It compels us to face the psychological contradictions in ourselves, including our disassociation from the traumatic loss that fuels the psychology of patriarchy that corrupts us as democrats and as lovers. The spirit of music serves such tragic insights because it speaks truthly to and of the disassociated emotions of the alienated mind and body that patriarchy psychologically inflicts on men and women.[47] Indeed, the indispensable power of music in truth telling about a tragedy as culturally entrenched as patriarchy may be that it speaks of these issues in a way in which our dominantly patriarchal language still cannot – very much in the spirit of the remarkable tribute of Proust (a gay man) to the powers of music:

> "And, just as certain creatures are the last surviving testimony to a form of
> life which nature has discarded, I wondered whether music might not be the
> unique example of what might have been – if the invention of language, the
> formation of words, the analysis of ideas had not intervened – the means of
> communication between souls."[48]

Such "certain creatures" are, I believe, much more common than Proust may have supposed. Certainly, many gay men have, like Proust, found in

---

[47] See, on this function of music, Anthony Storr, *Music and the Mind* (New York: Ballantine Books, 1992), pp. 149, 183–4.

[48] Cited at Anthony Storr, id., p. 71.

music in general and opera in particular a resonance for an embodied sexual voice that the dominant culture brutally, even savagely repressed.[49] But the issues of repression of voice extend quite generally to all subordinated groups afflicted by a history of structural injustice, which include, as I have suggested, groups afflicted by sexism, which include not only women (straight and lesbian) but men (straight and gay). Indeed, it may be precisely because the traditional political power of patriarchy is now more contested and contestable that our imaginations are more not less needily open to exploring the ways in which the injustice of patriarchy remains still uncritically entrenched in our practices and ways of life, often because of the impact of reactionary fundamentalist political movements (at home and abroad) that are overtly or covertly antifeminist.[50] Verdi's voice is for this reason as absorbing a resonance as ever for the ways in which patriarchal patterns continue to enjoy support on the basis of the unjust suppression of resisting voice. Men, in particular, need its resonance now more than ever, in particular, as they face forms of violent religious fundamentalism abroad and at home motored by reactionary forms of patriarchy, based on codes of honor, that war on women and men for the advances in feminist justice they have achieved.[51] Verdi's contemporary appeal for men in particular is for this reason perhaps stronger than it has ever been, which explains what I undertook the argument of this book to explain: Why such operas – written for a different time and place – have the enormous appeal to contemporary audiences that they do. The voice Verdi's operas insist we hear is a voice culturally all around us and personally within us.

Verdi forged his astonishing art of musical tragedy against the cultural background of an uncritically patriarchal culture of honor that could, on the one hand, atrociously treat foundlings and, on the other, mythologize them as "children of the Madonna" (chapter 2). He innovated his art of musical voice to give expression to the broken relationships that patriarchy inflicted here and elsewhere, and could not and would not acknowledge. As

---

[49] See, for a general defense of this position, Wayne Koestenbaum, *The Queen's Throat: Opera, Homosexuality, and the Mystery of Desire* (New York: Da Capo Press, 2001); see, in particular, pp. 176–97.

[50] For discussion of one recent expression of such a political movement in the United States, see Richards, *Women, Gays, and the Constitution*, pp. 362–457; on movements abroad, see note following.

[51] On Islamic fundamentalism as warring both on feminism and the separation of church and state, see Bernard Lewis, *What Went Wrong?: Western Impact and Middle Eastern Response* (Oxford: Oxford University Press, 2002); on the highly gendered sense of humiliation that motivates the terrorist violence of Islamic fundamentalists, see Mark Juergensmeyer, *Terror in the Mind of God*, at pp. 78, 154, 161–2, 182–97.

I have argued, his art enables us to hear the emotional desolation of broken relationship which patriarchy continues to inflict on men and women (for example, in American popular contempt for same-sex marriage), breaking the silence that a patriarchal mythology of gender in marriage still imposes on reasonable public discussion of such issues of fundamental injustice.[52] His musical art still speaks to us because it speaks truthfully to our divided consciousness of the alienated state of our psyches, how much we still mindlessly replay the tragedy of patriarchy, and the price we pay in desolating loss for our lack of self-knowledge. In their important study of the these issues in the development of young girls into adolescence, Lyn Brown and Carol Gilligan observed the impact of patriarchy on Judy, one of these young girls, in the following striking terms:

> "As Judy responds to the dangers of feeling her strong feelings by disconnecting from her bodily knowing, and as she associates knowing only with the intellect, with what goes on in her head, she loses the ground of felt experience and begins to talk *about*, rather than to speak, her feelings."[53]

If I am right about the personal and political psychology of patriarchy, as studied in Verdi's operas, such experiences of alienation are developmentally common in the experience of men and women, but have a particularly ferocious force in the development of men. The appeal of Verdi's art is that it enables us, as a mode of self-knowledge, to hear these feelings that we cannot speak, and thus to question how and why and whether such desolating loss can any longer reasonably be regarded as in the nature of things. We hear these feelings through music that haunts our consciousness, as Verdi's does – music that hums and dances through our quotidian lives, giving explanatory and normative structure to our most personal dreams and memories and hopes, holding us in its grasp with a sense that life can and must be lived from an embodied sense of life lived in relationship – open, vulnerable, loving, responsive, and humane.

Verdi gave me a way of knowing these things long before I could theorize about them. It was part of what was remarkable about my father that, of course, I heard Verdi's voice in my father's marvelously expressive operatic voice (which, as children, brought me and my sister to tears), one of the few times he could allow himself to voice in public the resistance to patriarchy I knew he believed in private life. Verdi's voice was one of my father's many gifts to me, a way in which we could understand as father and son

---

[52] See, on this point, Richards, *id.*, 438–53.
[53] See Lyn Mikel Brown and Carol Gilligan, *Meeting at the Crossroads: Women's Psychology and Girls' Development* (Cambridge, MA: Harvard University Press, 1992), p. 128.

things we could not otherwise discuss or even acknowledge. And my mother's name was Josephine, which, in Italian, is Giuseppina. My mother jauntily pointed out to me a number of times, with a proud lift of the head that always moved me, that she had the same name as Verdi's wife. She was nothing if not a rather relentlessly authentic moral teacher and critic, and her demanding moral point to her son was not a matter of similarity of name. It was a point about the nature and value of good relationships, like Verdi's to Strepponi and hers to my father and, as she came to see and even defend against her siblings, mine to my companion (after my father's death, she lived much of the time with us). My mother often would surprise me during those sad years, which were not easy for her after the loss of my father, by telling me with a penetrating smile that I reminded her of him. I certainly got my parents' point about relationships based on equal voice, which lie not only at the center of what I value in personal life but the compelling public value of dignity that I believe basic democratic justice requires us to respect, on terms of principle, in the lives of all persons.

My investigation of the power and appeal of Verdi's tragic art for me and others ends with a dream and memory that are always with me. The dream depicts a scene that could be from a Verdi opera, the memory is of such an opera.

The dream was on a night shortly after my mother died (my father had died ten years earlier). In the dream, I am inconsolably crying, a grief that no one can understand or touch. Two people embrace me, pleading and begging me in familiar voices not to grieve in this way they found terrifying and unendurable. I am solaced, consoled by a deep tenderness. As I wake, I realize the two people were my mother and father. I experience my first sense of relief from the burden of grief that had engulfed me, because the dream explained that I did not have to be, indeed was not alone with the loss. I later describe this experience to my companion and my sister as an experience of grace.

The memory is of taking my father and mother to see *Don Carlos* at the Metropolitan Opera from a side box when I was a young lawyer in New York. I watched my father closely during the great aria of patriarchal desolation of Philip II, "Ella giammai m'amo" ("She never loved me"). It had been very well sung, and my father, always a sharp critic of voices, made an O with his forefinger and thumb to signify artistic vocal excellence. He was radiant, thankful, and in tears; and my mother was also visibly moved. We all knew then through Verdi's musical voice why Philip's way was not our path. There was a way to live outside patriarchy.

# Bibliography

Abbate, Carolyn, *Unsung Voices: Opera and Musical Narrative in the Nineteenth Century* (Princeton: Princeton University Press, 1991).

Aeschylus, *The Oresteia*, trans. David R. Slavitt (Philadelphia: University of Pennsylvania Press, 1998).

Allen, Beverly and Mary Russo, eds., *Revisioning Italy: National Identity and Global Culture* (Minneapolis: University of Minnesota Press, 1997).

Apuleius, *The Golden Ass*, trans. E. J. Kenney (London: Penguin, 1998).

Ariosto, Ludovico, *Orlando Furioso*, Part One, trans. Barbara Reynolds (London: Penguin, 1975); *Orlando Furioso*, Part Two, trans. Barbara Reynolds (London: Penguin, 1977).

Armstrong, Vicki L., "Welcome to the 21st Century and the Legalization of Same-Sex Unions," *Thomas M. Cooley Law Reviews*, 18(1), 85–117 (2001).

Augustine, *Confessions*, trans. Henry Chadwick (Oxford: Oxford University Press, 1991).

Barnes, ed., Jonathan, *The Complete Works of Aristotle*, vol. 2 (Princeton: Princeton University Press, 1984).

Barton, H. Arnold, "Gustav III of Sweden and the Enlightenment," *Eighteenth-Century Studies*, vol. 6, issue 1 (autumn 1972), 1–34.

Beccaria, Cesare, *On Crimes and Punishments*, trans. Henry Paolucci (New York: Library of Liberal Arts, 1963 (originally published, 1764).

Bell, Millicent, *Shakespeare's Tragic Skepticism* (New Haven, CT: Yale University Press, 2002).

Bentley, Eric, *The Life of the Drama* (New York: Applause Theatre Books, 1991).

Blacking, John, *How Musical Is Man?* (Seattle: University of Washington Press, 1974).

Blondell, Ruby, Mary-Kay Gamel, Nancy Sorkin Rabinowitz, Bella Zweig, *Women on the Edge: Four Plays by Euripides* (New York: Routledge, 1999).

Bradley, A. C., *Shakespearean Tragedy* (Penguin: London, 1991).

Braude, Ann, *Radical Spirits: Spiritualism and Women's Rights in Nineteenth-Century America* (Boston: Beacon Press, 1989).

Braudel, Fernand, *Out of Italy: 1450–1650*, trans. Sian Reynolds (Tours: Flamarion, 1991).

Briggs, Jean L., *Never in Anger: Portrait of an Eskimo Family* (Cambridge, MA: Harvard University Press, 1970).

Brown, Lyn Mikel and Carol Gilligan, *Meeting at the Crossroads: Women's Psychology and Girls' Development* (Cambridge, MA: Harvard University Press, 1992).

Budd, Malcolm, *Music and the Emotions: The Philosophical Theories* (London: Routledge & Kegan Paul, 1992).

Budden, Julian, *The Operas of Verdi, vol. 1, From Oberto to Rigoletto* (New York: Oxford University Press, 1973).

——, *The Operas of Verdi, vol. 2, From Il Trovatore to La Forza Del Destino* (New York: Oxford University Press, 1978).

——, *The Opera of Verdi, vol. 3, From Don Carlos to Falstaff* (New York: Oxford University Press, 1981).

——, *Verdi* (London: J. M. Dent, 1985).

Buonomo, Leonardo, *Backward glances: Exploring Italy, Reinterpreting America (1831–1866)* (Madison: Fairleigh Dickinson University Press, 1996).

Calderon de la Barca, Pedro, *Life is a Dream*, trans. John Clifford (London: Nick Hern Books, 1998).

Campbell, J. K., *Honour, Family, and Patronage* (New York: Oxford University Press, 1964).

Clement, Catherine, *Opera or the Undoing of Women*, trans. Betsy Wing (Minneapolis: University of Minnesota Press, 1989).

Cooke, Deryck, *The Language of Music* (London: Oxford University Press, 1959).

Damasio, Antonio R., *Descartes' Error: Emotion, Reason, and the Human Brain* (New York: Avon Books, 1994).

——, *The Feeling of What Happens: Body and Emotion in the Making of Consciousness* (San Diego: A Harvest Book, 1999).

De Van, Gilles, *Verdi's Theater: Creating Drama through Music*, trans. Gilda Roberts (Chicago: University of Chicago Press, 1998).

Eagleton, Terry, *Sweet Violence: The Idea of the Tragic* (Oxford: Blackwell, 2003).

Ellmann, Richard, *Oscar Wilde* (London: Penguin, 1987).

El Saadawi, Nawal, *The Hidden Face of Eve: Women in the Arab World* translated and edited by Dr. Sherif Hetata (London and New York: Zed Books Ltd., 1980).

Euben, J. Peter, *The Tragedy of Political Theory: the Road Not Taken* (Princeton: Princeton University Press, 1990).

Evans, G. Blakemore et al., *The Riverside Shakespeare,* Second Edition (Boston: Houghton Mifflin Co., 1997).

Ferenczi, Sandor, *Final Contributions to the Problems and Methods of Psycho-Analysis* Michael Balint ed., Eric Mosbacher et al., trans. (London: The Hogarth Press, 1955).

Ferguson, Margaret W., Maureen Quilligan, and Nancy J. Vickers, *Rewriting the Renaissance: The Discourses of Sexual Difference in Early Modern Europe* (Chicago: University of Chicago Press, 1986).

Filmer, Robert, *Patriarcha and Other Writings* edited by Johann P. Sommerville (Cambridge: Cambridge University Press, 1991).

Foley, Helene P., *Female Acts in Greek Tragedy* (Princeton: Princeton University Press, 2001).

Forster, E. M., *Where Angels Fear to Tread* (New York: Vintage International, 1992).

Foxhall, Lin and John Salmon, eds., *When Men Were Men: Masculinity, Power and Identity in Classical Antiquity* (New York: Routledge, 1998).

Fraisse, Genevieve and Michelle Perrot, eds., *A History of Women in the West vol IV: Emerging Feminism from Revolution to World Was* (Cambridge, MA: Belknap Press of Harvard University Press, 1993).

Freeman, Joanne B., *Affairs of Honor: National Politics in the New Republic* (New Haven, CT: Yale University Press, 2001).

Gangulee, N., *Giuseppe Mazzini: Selected Writings* (Westport, CT: Greenwood Press, 1945).

Gardaphe, Fred L., *Italian Signs, American Streets: The Evolution of Italian American Narrative* (Durham: Duke University Press, 1996).

Gergen, Mary M. and Sara N. Davis, *Toward a New Psychology of Gender: A Reader* (New York: Routledge, 1997).

Gerhard, Anselm, *The Urbanization of Opera: Music Theater in Paris in the Nineteenth Century*, trans. Mary Whittall (Chicago: University of Chicago Press, 1998).

Gilligan, Carol, "Knowing and Not Knowing: Reflections on Manhood," p. 12 (Gender Lecture on Masculinities, University of Cambridge, UK, May 22, 2003).

——, *The Birth of Pleasure* (New York: Knopf, 2002).

Gilligan, James, *Preventing Violence* (New York: Thames & Hudson, 2001).

——, *Violence: Reflections on a National Epidemic* (New York: Vintage Books, 1997).

Gilmore, David D., ed., *Honour and Shame and the Unity of the Mediterranean* (Washington, D.C.: American Anthropological Association, 1987).

Lydia, Goehr, *The Quest for Voice: Music, Politics, and the Limits of Philosophy* (Berkeley: University of California Press, 1998).

Goldhill, Simon, *Reading Greek Tragedy* (Cambridge: Cambridge University Press, 1986).

Goldman, Albert and Evert Sprinchorn, eds., *Wagner on Music and Drama*, trans. H. Ashton Ellis (New York: Da Capo Press, 1964).

Goldstein, Joshua S., *War and Gender: How Gender Shapes the War System and Vice Versa* (Cambridge: Cambridge University Press, 2001).

Gossett, Philip, et al., *The New Grove Masters of Italian Opera* (New York: W. W. Norton, 1983).

Green, Richard, *The "Sissy Boy Syndrome" and the Development of Homosexuality* (New Haven: Yale University Press, 1987).

Greenberg, Kenneth S., *Honor and Slavery* (Princeton: Princeton University Press, 1996).

Grey, Thomas S., *Wagner's Musical Prose: Texts and Contexts* (Cambridge: Cambridge University Press, 1995).

Hallett, Judith P., *Fathers and Daughters in Roman Society: Women and the Elite Family* (Princeton, N J: Princeton University Press, 1984).

Halliwell, Leslie, *Halliwell's Film Guide*, 4th edition (New York: Charles Scribner's Sons, 1985).

Hallman, Diana R., *Opera, Liberalism, and Antisemitism in Nineteenth-Century France: The Politics of Haley's La Juive* (Cambridge: Cambridge University Press, 2002).

Hanslick, Eduard, *On the Musically Beautiful* translated by Geoffrey Payzant (Indianapolis, IN: Hackett Publishing Company, 1986).

Hedges, Chris, *War Is a Force That Gives Us Meaning* (New York: Public Affairs, 2002).

Hegel, *On Tragedy*, Anne and Henry Paolucci edition (New York: Harper & Row, 1962).

Herman, Judith, *Trauma and Recovery* (New York: Basic Books, 1997).

Hobsbawm, Eric, *Uncommon People: Resistance, Rebellion, and Jazz* (New York: The New Press, 1998).

Hugo, Victor, *The Dramas Complete and Unabridged of Victor Hugo, Volume X, Oliver Cromwell*, trans. I. G. Burnham (Philadelphia: George Barrie & Son, 1896).

Hunt, Robert, ed., *Personalities and Cultures: Readings in Psychological Anthropology* (Garden City, NY: The Natural History Press, 1967).

Ignatieff, Michael, *The Warrior's Honor: Ethnic War and the Modern Conscience* (New York: Henry Holt and Company, 1997).

Jacobs, James B., *Gotham Unbound: How New York City was Liberated from the Grip of Organized Crime* (New York: New York University Press, 1999).

James, Henry, *The Portrait of a Lady*, Robert D. Bamberg ed. (New York: W. W. Norton, 1995).

Juergensmeyer, Mark, *Terror in the Mind of God: The Global Rise of Religious Violence* (Berkeley: University of California Press, 2000).

Kamen, Henry, *Philip of Spain* (New Haven, CT: Yale University Press, 1997).

Kaufman, Walter, *Tragedy and Philosophy* (Garden City, NY: Doubleday, 1968).

Kerman, Joseph, *Opera as Drama* (New York: Vintage Books, 1956).

Kertzer, David I., *Sacrificed for Honor: Italian Infant Abandonment and the Politics of Reproductive Control* (Boston: Beacon Press, 1993).

Kertzer David I. and Richard P. Saller, *The Family in Italy from Antiquity to the Present* (New Haven, CT: Yale University Press, 1991).

Koestenbaum, Wayne, *The Queen's Throat: Opera, Homosexuality, and the Mystery of Desire* (New York: Da Capo Press, 2001).

LaCapra, Dominick, *Writing History, Writing Trauma* (Baltimore: The Johns Hopkins University Press, 2001).

Lacoue-Labarthe, Philippe, *Musica Ficta (Figures of Wagner)*, trans. Felicia McCarren (Stanford, CA: Stanford University Press, 1994).

Laqueur, Walter, *The Age of Terrorism* (Boston: Little, Brown, 1987).

Laurino, Maria, *Were You Always an Italian?: Ancestors and Other Icons of Italian America* (New York: W. W. Norton, 2000).

Leppert, Richard, *The Sight of Sound: Music, Representation, and the History of the Body* (Berkeley: University of California Press, 1993).

Levine, Lawrence W., *Black Culture and Black Consciousness: Afro-American Folk Thought from Slavery to Freedom* (Oxford: Oxford University Press, 1977).

Levinson, Jerrold, *Metaphysics, Art, and Metaphysics: Essays in Philosophical Aesthetics* (Ithaca: Cornell University Press, 1990).

——, "Music and Negative Emotion," *Pacific Philosophical Quarterly*, 63 (1982): 327–46.

Levith, Murray J., *Shakespeare's Italian Settings and Plays* (New York: St. Martin's Press, 1989).

Lewis, Bernard, *What Went Wrong?: Western Impact and Middle Eastern Response* (Oxford: Oxford University Press, 2002).

Leys, Ruth, *Trauma: A Genealogy* (Chicago: University of Chicago Press, 2000).

Locke, John, *Two Treatises of Government*, edited by Peter Laslett (Cambridge: Cambridge University Press, 1960).

Lodge, David, *Consciousness and the Novel: Connected Essays* (Cambridge, MA: Harvard University Press, 2002).

Maalouf, Amin, *In the Name of Identity: Violence and the Need to Belong*, trans. Barbara Bray (New York: Arcade Publishing, 2000).

Magee, Bryan, *Aspects of Wagner* (Oxford: Oxford University Press, 1988).

Magee, Bryan, *Wagner and Philosophy* (London: Allen Lane, The Penguin Press, 2000).

Marrapodi, Michele, A.J. Hoenselaars, Marcello Cappuzzo and L. Falzon Santucci, *Shakespeare's Italy: Functions of Italian Locations in Renaissance Drama* (Manchester: Manchester University Press, 1993).

Mendelsoln, Daniel, *Gender and the City in Euripides' Political Plays* (New York: Oxford University Press, 2002).

Merin, Yuval, *Equality for Same-Sex Couples: The Legal Recognition of Gay Partnerships in Europe and the United States* (Chicago: University of Chicago Press, 2002).

Meyer, Donald, *Sex and Power: The Rise of Women in America, Russia, Sweden, and Italy* (Middletown, CT: Wesleyan University Press, 1987).

Mill, John Stuart and Harriet Mill, *Essays on Sex Equality*, edited by Alice S. Ross (Chicago: University of Chicago Press, 1970).

Miller, William Ian, *Bloodtaking and Peacemaking: Feud, Law, and Society in Saga Iceland* (Chicago: University of Chicago Press, 1990).

——, *Humiliation and Other Essays on Honor, Social Discomfort, and Violence* (Ithaca: Cornell University Press, 1993).

Murnaghan, Sheila and Sandra R. Joshel, *Women and Slaves in Greco-Roman Culture* (London: Routledge, 1998).

Nattiez, Jean-Jacques, *Wagner Androgyne: A Study in Interpretation* (Princeton: Princeton University Press, 1993).

Nietzsche, Friedrich, *Beyond Good and Evil: Prelude to a Philosophy of the Future* trans. Helen Zimmern (Edinburgh: T.N. Foulis, 1907).

——, The *Birth of Tragedy and The Genealogy of Morals* trans. Francis Golffing (Garden City, NY: Doubleday & Co., 1956).

Nisbett, Richard E. and Dov Cohen, *Culture of Honor: The Psychology of Violence in the South* (Boulder, CO: Westview Press, 1996).

Nuland, Sherwin B., *Leonardo da Vinci* (New York: Lipper/Viking, 2000).

Nussbaum, Martha C., *The Fragility of Goodness: Luck and Ethics in Greek Tragedy and Philosophy* (Cambridge: Cambridge University Press, 1986).

——, *Upheavals of Thought: The Intelligence of Emotions* (Cambridge: Cambridge University Press, 2001).

Nuttall, A. D., *Why Does Tragedy Give Pleasure?* (Oxford: Clarendon Press, 1996).

O'Casey, Sean, *Three Dublin Plays* (London: Faber & Faber, 1998).

O'Connor, Maura, *The Romance of Italy and the English Political Imagination* (New York: St. Martin's Press, 1998).

Okin, Susan Moller, *Justice, Gender, and the Family* (New York: Basic Books, 1989).

Ortner, Sherry B., *The Politics and Erotics of Culture* (Boston: Beacon Press, 1996).

Osborne, Charles, *The Complete Operas of Verdi* (London: Indigo, 1997).

Paglia, Camille, "At Home With: Mario Puzo; It all Comes Back to Family", *New York Times*, May 8, 1997, section C, p. 1, col.

——, "Questions for: Mario Puzo", *New York Times Magazine*, Sunday, March 30, 1997, section 6, p. 15.

Parker, Geoffrey, *Philip II,* Third Edition (Peru, IL: Open Court Publishing, 1995).

Pateman, Carole, *The Sexual Contract* (Cambridge: Polity Press, 1988).

Peristiany, J. G., ed., *Honour and Shame: The Values of Mediterranean Society* (Chicago: University of Chicago Press).

Petrobelli, Pierluigi, *Music in the Theater: Essays on Verdi and Other Composers*, trans. Roger Parker (Princeton: Princeton University Press, 1994).

Phillips-Matz, Mary Jane, *Verdi: A Biography* (Oxford: Oxford University Press, 1993).

Plato, *The Symposium*, trans. Robin Waterfield (Oxford: Oxford University Press, 1994).

Pollack, William, *Real Boys: Rescuing Our Sons from the Myths of Boyhood* (New York; Henry Holt, 1998).

Potter, John, *Vocal Authority: Singing Style and Ideology* (Cambridge: Cambridge University Press, 1998).

Puzo, Mario, *The Fortunate Pilgrim* (London: Heinemann, 1964).

——, *The Godfather* (New York: Signet, 1978).

Rhode, Deborah L., *Justice and Gender* (Cambridge, MA: Harvard University Press, 1989).

Rhode, Deborah L., *Speaking of Sex: The Denial of Gender Inequality* (Cambridge, MA: Harvard University Press, 1997).

Rich, Adrienne, *Of Woman Born: Motherhood as Experience and Institution*, 10th anniversary ed. (New York: W. W. Norton, 1986).

Richards, David A. J., *A Theory of Reasons for Action* (Oxford: Clarendon Press, 1971).

——, *Conscience and the Constitution: History, Theory, and Law of the Reconstruction Amendments* (Princeton: Princeton University Press, 1993).

——, *Foundations of American Constitutionalism* (New York: Oxford University Press, 1998).

——, *Free Speech and the Politics of Identity* (Oxford: Oxford University Press, 1999).

——, *Identity and the Case for Gay Rights: Race, Gender, Religion as* Analogies (Chicago: University of Chicago Press, 1999).

——, *Italian American: The Racializing of an Ethnic Identity* (New York: New York University Press, 1999).

——, *Sex, Drugs, Death and the Law: An Essay on Decriminalization and Human Rights* (Totowa, N J: Rowman & Littlefield, 1982).

——, *The Moral Criticism of Law* (Encino, CA: Dickenson-Wadsworth, 1977).

——, *Toleration and the Constitution* (New York: Oxford University Press, 1986).

——, *Women, Gays, and the Constitution: The Grounds for Feminism and Gay Rights in Culture and Law* (Chicago: University of Chicago Press, 1998).

Ridley, Aaron, *Music, Value, and the Passions* (Ithaca: Cornell University Press, 1995).

Robinson, Paul, *Gay Lives: Homosexual Autobiography from John Addington Symonds to Paul Monette* (Chicago: University of Chicago Press, 1999).

——, *Opera and Ideas from Mozart to Strauss* (New York: Harper & Row, 1985).

——, *Opera, Sex, and Other Vital Matters* (Chicago: University of Chicago Press, 2002).

Rosselli, John, *The Life of Verdi* (Cambridge: Cambridge University Press, 2000).

Ruddick, Sara, *Maternal Thinking: Toward a Politics of Peace* (Boston: Beacon Press, 1989).

Said, Edward W., *Culture and Imperialism* (New York: Alfred A. Knopf, 1993).

Schneider, Jane and Peter Schneider, *Culture and Political Economy in Western Sicily* (New York: Academic Press, 1976).

Schneider, Jane, "Of Vigilance and Virgins: Honor, Shame and Access to Resources in Mediterranean Societies," *Ethnology*, 10:1–24 (1971).

Schiavone, Aldo, *The End of the Past: Ancient Rome and the Modern West*, trans. Margery J. Schneider (Cambridge, MA: Harvard University Press, 2000).

Schopenhauer, Arthur, *Essays and Aphorisms*, trans. R. J. Hollindale (Harmondsworth: Penguin, 1970).

——, *The World as Will and Representation*, 2 vols., trans. E. F. J. Payne (Indian Hills, CO: The Falcon's Wing Press, 1958).

Scott, Franklin D., *Sweden: The Nation's History* (Carbondale: Southern Illinois University Press, 1988), at pp. 268–86.

Scruton, Roger, *The Aesthetics of Music* (Oxford: Oxford University Press, 1999).

Sophocles, *Oedipus Tyrannus*, trans. Luci Berkowitz and Theodore F. Brunner (New York: W. W. Norton, 1970).

Sophocles, *The Theban Plays*, trans. E. F. Watling (Harmondsworth: Penguin, 1973).

Spierenburg, Peter, *Men and Violence: Gender, Honor, and Rituals in Modern Europe and America* (Columbus, Ohio: Ohio State University Press, 1998).

Steiner, George, *The Death of Tragedy* (New Haven: Yale University Press, 1996).

Stendhal, De (Marie-Henri Beyle), *On Love*, trans. H. B. V. (New York: Liveright, 1947).

——, *The Charterhouse of Parma*, trans. Margaret R. B. Shaw (London: Penguin, 1958).

——, *The Life of Rossini*, trans. Richard N. Coe (London: John Calder, 1985).

——, *The Red and the Black*, trans. Catherine Slater (New York: Oxford University Press, 1998).

Stern, Daniel N., *The Interpersonal World of the Infant: A View from Psychoanalysis and Developmental Psychology* (New York: Basic Books, 1985).

Storr, Anthony, *Music and the Mind* (New York: Ballantine Books, 1992).

Tanner, Michael, *Wagner* (London: Flamingo, 1997).

Tasso, Torquato, *Jerusalem Delivered*, trans. Anthony M. Esolen (Baltimore: The Johns Hopkins University Press, 2000).

*The Compact Edition of the Oxford English Dictionary*, vol. II (Oxford: Oxford University Press, 1971).

Tomasi, Lydia F., Piero Gastoldo and Thomas Row, *The Columbus People: Perspectives in Italian Immigration to the Americas and Australia* (New York: Center for Migration Studies, 1994).

Tomlinson, Gary, "Italian Romanticism and Italian Opera: An Essay in Their Affinities," *19th-Century Music*, X/1 (Summer 1986), at pp. 43–60.

van der Kolk, Bessel A., Alexander C. McFarlane, and Lares Weisaeth, editors, *Traumatic Stress: The Effects of Overwhelming Experience on Mind, Body, and Society* (New York: The Guilford Press, 1996).

Venturi, Franco, *Italy and the Enlightenment* (London: Longman, 1972).

Verdi, Giuseppe, *Aida*, libretto to CD recording conducted by Claudio Abbado, Coro e Orchestra del Teatro alla Scala, libretto by Antonio Ghislanzoni, translated by Richard Evidon/Adele Poindexter, Polydor International: Hamburg, 1982.

——, *Aroldo*, libretto to CD recording of Fabio Luisi, conducting Orchestra e coro del Maggio Musicale Fiorentino, libretto by Francesco Maria Piave, translated by Andrew Huth, Philips Classics: Germany, 2001.

——, *Don Carlos*, libretto to CD recording, Italian version, conducted by Carlo Maria Giulini, Orchestra of the Royal Opera House, Covent Garden, libretto by Josephy Mery and Camille du Locle, translated by Gwyn Morris, EMI Records, 2000.

——, *Don Carlos*, libretto to CD recording, French version, conducted by Claudio Abbado, Coro e Orchestra del Teatro alla Scala, libretto by Joseph Mery and Camille du Locle, translated by Andrew Porter, Polydor International: Hamburg, 1985.

——, *Falstaff*, libretto to CD recording, conducted by Leonard Bernstein, Vienna Philharmonic Orchestra, libretto by Arrigo Boito, CBS Records, 1966.

——, "Hymn of the Nation", libretto to CD recording, *Pavarotti plus*, Tibor Rudas production, conducted by James Levine, Philharmonia Orchestra and Philharmonia Chorus, libretto by Arrigo Boito, translated by Ken Chalmers, The Decca Record Company, 1995.

——, *Il Trovatore*, libretto to CD recording, James Levine, conductor, Metropolitan Opera Orchestra, libretto by Salvatore Cammarano and Leone Emanuele Bardare, translated by Lionel Salter, SONY Classical, 1994.

——, *I Vespri Siciliani*, libretto to CD recording, conducted by Riccardo Muti, conducting Orchestra e Coro del Teatro alla Scala, libretto by Eugene Scribe and Charles Duveyrier, translated into Italian by Arnaldo Fusinato, translated into English by Avril Bardoni, EMI Records: Hayes, Middlesex, England, 1990.

——, *Jerusalem*, libretto to CD recording, French version, conducted by Fabio Luisi, L'Orchestra de la Suisse Romande, libretto by Alphonse Royer and Gustave Vaez, translated into English by Andrew Huth, Phillips Classics: Germany, 2000.

——, *La Forza del Destino*, libretto to CD recording conducted by Riccardo Muti, Orchestra e Coro del Teatro Alla Scala, libretto by Francesco Maria Piave, EMI Records: Hayes, Middlesex, England, 1986.

——, *La Traviata*, libretto to CD recording, James Levine, conductor, The Metropolitan Opera Orchestra, libretto by Francesco Maria Piave, Deutsche Grammophon: Hamburg, 1982.

——, *Luisa Miller* libretto to CD recording conducted by Peter Maag, National Philharmonic Orchestra, libretto by Salvatore Cammarano, translated into English by Gwyn Morris, London: Decca Record Co., 1988.

——, *Macbeth*, libretto to CD recording conducted by Claudio Abbado, conductor, Coro e Orchestra del Teatro all Scala, libretto by Francesco Maria Piave, trasnlated into English by Peggie Cochrane, Deutsche Grammophon GmbH, Hamburg, 1996.

——, *Nabucco*, libretto to CD recording conducted by Riccardo Muti, Ambrosian Opera Chorus and Philharmonia Orchestra, libretto by Temistocle Solera, translated into English by Gwyn Morris, EMI Records: Hayes, Middlesex England, 1986.

——, *Pezzi Sacri*, libretto to CD recording conducted by Myung-Whun Chung, Coro e Orchestra dell'Accademia Nazionale di Santa Cecilia, Deutsche Gammophon: Hamburg, 2000.

——, *Requiem, Quattro Pezzi Sacri*, libretto to CD conducted by Carlo Maria Giulini, Philharmonia Chorus and Orchestra, EMI Records: Hayes, Middlesex England, 1991.

——, *Rigoletto*, libretto to CD recording, Riccardo Muti, conductor, Orchestra del Teatro alla Scala, libretto by Francesco Maria Piave, translated into English by Lionel Salter, SONY Classical, 1995.

——, *Otello*, libretto to CD recording conducted by Georg Solti, Chicago Symphony Orchestra, libretto by Arrigo Boito, translated into English by 1991, Decca Record Company: London, 1991.

——, *Un Ballo in Maschera*, libretto to CD recording by Georg Solti, National Philharmonic Orchestra, libretto by Antonio Somma, Decca Record Company: London, 1985.

Vernant, Jean-Pierre and Pierre Vidal-Naquet. *Myth and Tragedy in Ancient Greece*, trans. Janet Lloyd (New York: Zone Books, 1988).

Virgil, *The Aeneid*, trans. Robert Fitzgerald (New York: Vintage, 1990).

Viroli, Maurizio, *For Love of Country: An Essay on Patriotism and Nationalism* (Oxford: Clarendon Press, 1995).

Walker, Frank, *The Man Verdi* (London: J. M. Dent, 1962).

Weaver, William and Martin Chusid, eds., *The Verdi Companion* (New York: W. W. Norton, 1979).

Webster, John, *The Duchess of Malfi*, Elizabeth M. Brennan ed. (New York: W. W. Norton, 1993).

———, *The White Devil*, J. R. Mulryne ed. (Lincoln: University of Nebraska Press, 1969).

Werfel, Franz, and Paul Stefan, eds., *Verdi: The Man in His Letters*, trans. Edward Downes (New York: Vienna House, 1942).

Wiles, David, *Tragedy in Athens: Performance Space and Theatrical Meaning* (Cambridge: Cambridge University Press, 1997).

Williams, Craig A., Roman *Homosexuality: Ideologies of Masculinity in Classical Antiquity* (New York: Oxford University Press, 1999).

Williams, Raymond, *Modern Tragedy* (Stanford, CA: Stanford University Press, 1966).

Wollstonecraft, Mary, *A Vindication of the Rights of Women*, in *The Works of Mary Wollstonecraft*, ed. Janet Todd and Marilyn Butler (1790; New York: New York University Press, 1989), 5: 65–266.

Woolf, Virginia, *Three Guineas* (Harcourt Brace & Company: San Diego, 1938).

Wyatt-Brown, Bertram, *Southern Honor: Ethics and Behavior in the Old South* (New York: Oxford University Press, 1982).

Zeitlin, Froma I., *Playing the Other: Gender and Society in Classical Greek Literature* (Chicago: University of Chicago Press, 1996).

# Table of Cases

# Index